ISLAM AND CHRISTIANITY

Mutual Challenges and Understanding

ISLAM AND CHRISTIANITY

Mutual Challenges and Understanding

Christian W. Troll

Edited by
Akhtarul Wasey

SHIPRA

The book is a reproduction of the journal
Islam and the Modern Age, Vol. XLII Nos. 2-3, (2011).

Rs. 950; US$ 47.50

ISBN: 978-81-7541-809-7

First Published in India in 2015

Islam and Christianity: Mutual Challenges and Understanding

Published by:
SHIPRA PUBLICATIONS
LG 18-19, Pankaj Central Market, I.P. Ext.
Patparganj, Delhi-110092
Tel: 91-11-2223 5152, 2223 6152
E-mail: info@shiprapublication.com
www.shiprapublication.com

Editor's Note

History of Islam-Christianity relations has been conspicuous by confrontation and conflict much more than reconciliation and coexistence. The Christian world from the very beginning received the advent of Islam with an uneasy sense of disbelief and horrible shock. To Christians, Islam was an unnatural development in the sphere of religions and an unwanted interference in the unchallenged continuity of the Christian tradition. Islam's claim to being the manifestation of the latest and final divine revelation in the series of God-sent religions that preceded it, was unacceptable for the Christian world, partly because it was perceived as denting the Christian self-image of being the only source of deliverance and spiritual emancipation of mankind and partly because of the political and cultural domination the Christendom enjoyed in many parts of the contemporary world.

The Prophet of Islam held out a hand of reconciliation and coexistence to the Christians when he made them equal partners enjoying all the civil rights and religious freedom in the Islamic society at Madina. It was a great exercise in peaceful coexistence among religions and faiths, to serve as a model for the mankind of a pluralist society. But the grand experiment of forming a pluralist social organization based on human right could not go far in history as with the Muslim conquest of vast tracts of land covering the Eastern Roman Empire and Spain further intensified the rivalry between Islam and Christianity. This confrontation between the two faith structures came to a flash point with the onset of Crusades that continued for years together. These hostilities left permanent scars in the psyche of the followers of both the religions, with almost no organized effort on both the sides for initiating any form of dialogue, to come together and seek peace and reconciliation.

But individuals, in both the religions, who had insight and a yearning for peace and coexistence have always been trying in their private and public spheres to find ways to understand each other by removing misgivings and enlarging the shared spaces. It is the context in which the value and significance of Prof. Christian W. Troll's endeavours for the promotion of Islam-Christianity dialogue must be highlighted.

For Prof. Troll, going for a deeper understanding of Islam and Muslims and developing a bond of empathy with the Muslim world was a divine calling. As he says in one of his interviews, he was divinely ordained to take up the task of Christian-Muslim dialogue and this divine prompting came very early in his life. It was 1957 when he was preparing for priestly ordination that he felt an inner urge to pursue a deeper understanding of Muslims and Islam and their culture and religion. In 1959, Prof. Troll chanced to read an essay by Dutch Jesuit J.J. Houben, a professor of Islamology where the following lines caught his imagination.

> Not only the missionaries working in Muslim countries but every catholic throughout the world must realize that the fate of hundreds of millions of Muslims hands in the balance and that in order to help them to solve the diffculties along religious lines a deeper knowledge of their mentality and of Islam in general as a religion and as a polity is certainly one of the most pressing needs for the Catholics of our times.

These lines served as a green signal for Prof. Troll to step out on his way to Christian-Muslim dialogue. As he was making up his mind and preparing to go ahead with his plans, another divine consent came his way when archbishop, Josef Cardinal Frings of Cologne fully agreed with the idea of pursuing a closer study of Muslims and Islam. Consequently, Prof. Troll went to Lebanon to learn Arabic which he pursued with extraordinary interest and understanding.

Prof. Troll's engagement with Muslims and Islam found approval and also refreshed inspiration from the Second Vatican Council (1962–5) which stressed the need for interreligious dialogue and emphasized that 'reciprocal communication, mutual friendship and respect, as well as a joint effort for the sake of shared goals, all in the service of common search for the fuller realization of the truth'. In 1966 he went to work as a member of the Jesuit Community in Lahore, Pakistan in order to engage in the study of Muslim culture and interreligious dialogue. Later he went to the School of Oriental and African Studies in London to do a B.A. (Honours) course in Urdu language and literature. It is here that he wrote his Ph.D. thesis which was later published as a book *Sayyid Ahmad Khan: A Reinterpretation of Muslim Theology*.

In 1976, Prof. Troll came to Delhi to teach Islam and Christian-Muslim relations at the Vidyajyoti Institute of Religious Studies. During his work at the Institute, he formed Islamic Studies Association (ISA) and later founded a journal, *SALAAM*. ISA has done a great job in encouraging the Christians to get to know and reach out to Muslims better at different levels, with the hope that as a response Muslims too will gradually come closer to the Christians, to have a better understanding of Christianity.

Prof. Troll has since done thorough research and written extensively on many Islamic subjects including Shibli Nomani and Abul Kalam Azad, apart from intensely promoting the cause of Interfaith Dialogue the world over. This volume is our humble tribute to his enlightened soul and untiring endeavours to making this world a better place to live, through greater understanding among religions of the world.

Akhtarul Wasey

Contents

1

Christianity and Islam: Mutual Challenges Hans Zirker's Recent Work on Islam*

In a previous monograph, Christentum und Islam: Theologische Verwandschaft und Konkurrenz[2] Hans Zirker, Catholic professor of fundamental theology at the Gesamthochschule Essen, had explored the relationship between Christianity and Islam in so far as both religions claim to mediate God's revelation to humankind in its final shape.

In the present work he continues to reflect theologically on the mutual challenge that Islam and Christianity represent to each other within the culturally and religiously pluralistic, and increasingly secularized, societies of the contemporary world. He thus contributes to developing a theological hermeneutics that would enable the believers to understand the history of the religiously 'other' and to evaluate theologically the mutual relationship between the two religions.

Zirker wants to clarify for Christians how to encounter and view the faith of the Muslims in the Light of the presuppositions of their own faith. He stresses that dialogue and encounter need 'the distance of critical examination.' Without directly intending it, he contributes also to the Muslims' task of finding new Islamic answers to the theological challenge of Christianity to Islam.

Although the present volume has grown out of a variety of earlier essays, it offers consistent perspectives and approaches that mirror normative as well as empirical Islam in its plural nature. The work deals with 'Christian Perceptions of Islam and

* This essay was first published in *Orientalia Christiana Periodica*, vol. 61, Fasciculus I, 1995, pp. 571–80.

Theological Reactions' (I); 'Revelation-Guidance-Redemption' (II); 'God' (III); 'Religion and Society (I). Thus, although the work retains the character of a collection of essays, it does achieve a fair degree of coherence and comprehensiveness: it deals creatively with many of the key issues arising for Christian and also for Muslim religious thought from the encounter of the two faiths—in the context of the secular and plural society that has emerged since the eighteenth-century Enlightenment.

Here we can highlight only a limited number of questions and arguments from among the rich fare offered in this work which is marked by thorough and up-to-date information, analytical depth coupled with empathy for the Muslim vision of things and by a fair, non-partisan approach that, however, never cuts loose from its Christian moorings.

Christian-Muslim relations have to cope with a number of challenges that are specific, or at least of paramount importance, to the Christian-Muslim constellation. Hitherto in both theological traditions the tendency prevailed to consider the other faith simply as an insufficient earlier stage or an erroneous variant of one's own faith and hence to acknowledge the other faith only with reservation. Both, Christianity and Islam meet with the difficulty that they find their own teachings shared in parts by the other side and yet, at the same time, do not see fit to make these shared elements of faith a part of their own overall horizon of faith. Thus they have recourse to moral and intellectual defamation of key figures of the other faith, as for instance Christians do with regard to 'the Messenger' Muhammad, and Muslims with regard to 'the Apostle' Paul. Clearly, neither Christianity nor Islam have yet developed a hermeneutics fully apt for an understanding of the history of the origins of 'the opposite side', in other words, a hermeneutics that does justice to each religion's specific faith perspective and to the nature of their mutual relationship.

Specific and typical for the Christian-Muslim relationship is a certain 'awkwardness' or 'embarrassment': both religions demand universal assent to their respective proclamation of God's final revelation in and through them. And yet, in fact, none of them has been able to translate this proclaimed claim into reality nor is this likely to happen in the foreseeable future. In their fundamental opposition to one another—at least as far as the claim to universality and finality is concerned—Christianity and Islam are linked in a shared fate. Not surprisingly they have developed patterns of defamation 'enabling' them to discard those who don't accept their claim as 'stubborn of heart', 'un-repenting' or even 'depraved'. Yet, such a strategy loses power to convince in a historical context where sharp confrontation and powerful demonization of another religion are perceived by the public at large as undermining peaceful coexistence in an increasingly religio-culturally mixed, global society.

In such a context the criticism of religion and the proper concept of religious truth assume central importance. A mere exchange of theological arguments on the pattern of past apologetics does not seem to be conducive to communication and understanding. Besides the urgent, yet relatively modest, aim of promoting true understanding of the other religion and the utopian objective of reaching agreement with the other religion on the question of truth, a third goal becomes crucial: 'to identify the respective claims to universal validity in their "awkward", competitive character, and then to ask how far these claims can be responsibly defended' (cf. 24).

Since neither of the two religions, and in fact, none of the religions in general, can offer effectively—within the framework of our plural world—a truly comprehensive orientation, the effort of religious understanding must not restrict itself to dialogue about the respective dogmatic traditions of the faiths but has of necessity to include the wider discussion regarding the common social and political order, informed by the approaches and results of the social, economic and political sciences.

Islam challenges Christian theology to look at itself critically. Christians must perceive their faith and its expressions in the mirror of the other's experiences and reactions. Islam can and must be seen as an integral part of the impact Christianity has made and continues to make on history. Zirker asks the Christian theologian to face, above all, the question whether and how the claim to finality of the Christian faith can be genuinely reconciled with the fact of the continuing history of religions. It does not suffice to consider illegitimate a post-Christian religion as Islam, simply because it denies certain claims of the Christian faith. Christian theology will have to elaborate theological categories enabling it to account for Islam as a post-Christian religion that makes a credible claim to universality.

Zirker would like Christian theology to take more seriously the fact that Islam knew itself right from its beginning to be called to re-establish unity, clarity and balance in the context of what it perceived as extreme and exaggerated Christian positions regarding the teaching about God and the God-world relationship. Islam sees Christianity as having obscured the message of monotheism and of the unity of humankind by the way in which it developed and formulated the Christological and Trinitarian dogmas. He argues that Christian thought must not fail to perceive the relevance of Islam, precisely in so far as it is a post-Christian and theologically 'disturbing' reality which criticizes Christianity's understanding of the relationship between God and the world. Sincere Christian theological attention to Islam's critique of Christian theology would create the hermeneutical conditions for a more adequate Christian theological assessment of Islam and for a deepened and more differentiated view of its own tradition.

But for Muslim religious thought, too, the encounter with the living tradition of Christian faith and thought poses serious challenges. First of all, Muslims will have to learn to perceive and portray Christianity in such a way that the Christians know that they are understood and that their faith is taken serious. To what extent does what the Koran says about Christians express what mainstream Christianity past and present, in fact believes and proposes to live? Muslims will have to engage in a serious and comprehensive study of the biblical writings and of the Christians' understanding of their Scripture and their faith tradition as a whole. In doing so Muslims may well meet with a theological understanding of the two religions and their mutual relationship that clearly goes beyond the teaching of the Koran, at least as it has been interpreted up to now.

Eventually Islamic theology will have to face the even more difficult question of how to understand the interaction of divine revelation with the various factors of continuing history. Both, Christian and Islamic theology will have to state their respective understanding of revelation and history, taking fully account of the reality of the other as well as of those questions and objections that arise for them from the Enlightenment. Islamic religious thought here has much to catch up on.

Whoever shares the conviction that interreligious dialogue must go beyond a strategy of friendly encounter and that it involves more than mere learning about one another and inviting one another to one's own faith, cannot remain content with an attitude that clings to maintaining absolutely secure the pre-defined, ultimate 'frontiers' of 'the truth'. If we want to take seriously our partner, the author maintains, we cannot have dialogue without in some way or other 'relativizing our own position', in view of a possibly better insight into elements of our faith tradition that hitherto we may have considered an 'essential element' (p. 29).

Such 'relativizing' must not be confused with indifference to the truth. It rather constitutes a part of the experiment of a shared understanding where it would seem to be impossible for us to say in advance how far we will be able to hold our own. The alternative would be to withdraw from the risk of such openness by insisting that an *a priori*, clearly defined part of our convictions is to be kept 'reserved' as absolutely final, exempt from any revision.

However, the 'dialogue of life'—inescapable for any true coexistence in modern plural societies—carries its own conditions and consequences. The new context inevitably lead to 'displacements', 'faults' in the landscape of ideas and thought such as cannot be contained and regulated by pre-given, uniformly interpreted religious and magisterial directives.

On the other hand, a religion that from the outset relativizes itself and its values constitutes a contradiction in itself. It makes sense only, either as an element of an (illusory) universal syncretism or in an (ultimately) polytheistic context. 'A faith that claims to respect the other faith it encounters, has to give it a place within the whole of its own vision of faith, otherwise it cannot claim to take seriously the encounter. The dialogue between religions is not simply compliance and harmony but rather the clash of claims to absoluteness.'[3]

And yet, the claims to absoluteness in the different religions are not the same. They vary with the historical and geographical diversity of cultural climates. Hence one can speak justifiably of 'relative absoluteness'.

However, in addition to the fact of competition between the religions in general, another factor conditions the relationship between Christianity and Islam: the intensive consciousness each side has of its own *superiority*. This superiority normally concerns not so much the rivalry between the respective dogmatic convictions as the—often only subliminally and casually operative—valuation of the religious-cultural level of the other faith. On the Christian side, for example, such aspects of the religious teaching of Islam that are described as 'the radical, unmediated antithesis of God and man'; 'the understanding of revelation as instructions'; 'the centrality of the Book'; 'the insistence on unmediated and literal inspiration'; 'the high regard for the Law and the subordination of the person to the community and the Law which cements it': all these aspects are viewed by Christians as evidencing an inferior kind of religious consciousness and teaching—which contrast with their own evaluations of freedom and personality; of the human person as created as image and as child of God; of the value of human history and experience. Thus the Christian side is easily tempted to conclude that Islam, as proclaimed in the Koran and as instituted in and by the *umma*, did in fact fall behind the higher religio-cultural level that had already been reached in the history of religion by the appearance of Christianity. The fact that Christianity in confrontation with the modern age was forced to face the specific questions raised by the Enlightenment and by the process of social emancipation has further widened the gap between the two faiths and has reinforced the Christians' feeling of superiority vis-à-vis Islam.

However, in different but no less drastic ways, Muslims equally are conscious of their cultural-intellectual superiority. The reason for this are the Muslims' conviction of, for instance, 'the distance between the Church's doctrine and the teaching of Jesus'; 'the excessive linking in Christian doctrine of God's saving action with the person and work of Jesus Christ'; 'the mythological distortion of Jesus' person and work'; the unreliability of the biblical traditions as historical documents'; 'the speculative complications of the history of dogma and its ruinous consequences'; 'the theological incapacity of Christian thought to do justice to the phenomenon of Muhammad when contrasted with the Muslim recognition of Jesus as a prophet and, finally, the Christian faith's loss, during the modern age, of its moral vitality and its ability to effectively shape society' (p. 31).

Such an explosive contrast in the evaluation of one's own and the other side can be reduced only through patient, ongoing mutual attentiveness based on mutual respect and on a more realistic self-evaluation.

In the second and third section of the work Zirker takes up central elements of the Muslim faith as it finds normative expression in the theology of the Koran. His analyses—for instance, of such elements of Koranic teaching as creation, history, word of God, prophet, prophethood, guidance and revelation, of the Koranic data concerning 'Isa, Muhammad and the Koran itself—display familiarity with Koranic theology as well as precision and critical nuance.

However, of greatest interest are Zirker's comparative evaluations of these data with those of corresponding Christian theology. In this way he deals with the concept of 'history of salvation', the figure of Abraham as binding but also separating the three monotheistic religions, the political dimension of the profession of God in Islam and the role of political and military success in establishing and strengthening religion and, finally, the conception of Allah as a warrior God.

When comparing the biblical and Koranic notions of prophet and prophethood and the question of how Christians might legitimately qualify Muhammad as prophet it might have been useful to reflect on the person and career of Muhammad also in the light of such figures as Moses, Joshua and the major 'judges', all of them 'hero-liberators' who have in common one characteristic: they have been individually chosen by God for a mission of rescue, they were called by God not only to proclaim God's law but also translate it effectively into the life of their people, politically and militarily.

At times the author fails to maintain consistently the crucial distinction between the normative and the empirical levels of a given set of arguments. Whatever historical transformation the Church underwent in the course of its history, one of the radical differences between the Islamic and the Christian faith traditions would seem to consist precisely in the conspicuous difference between their respective foundational models. Whereas it is true that a clear distinction must be made between the expansion of Islam as sphere of political supremacy on the one hand and the question of forced conversion of individuals to the faith of Islam on the other, it remains important to keep clearly in mind the fact that whereas the Koran encourages and justifies the expansion of Islam as sphere of power and supremacy by military means, Jesus and the New Testament, to say the least, do not. This contrast on the normative level between the 'no' of Jesus to the use of military means in spreading and implementing the sphere of influence of his message, and the Koranic teaching of *jihad* is not sufficiently explained by the differences in the respective historical circumstances.

The option of Jesus for a non-military and even non-political exercise of messiahship contrasts with the option of the zealots of his time and environment. Jesus' disciples up to the time of the birth of the Easter faith, had the greater difficulty in understanding and appreciating Jesus' option to redeem and liberate by taking on the role of the 'suffering servant' (Isaiah 52:13ff). Equally, one can well imagine options the Prophet of Islam could have made other than that for statehood and military conquest, in and from Medina.

Zirker is right in pointing to the far-from-concluded task of Christian theology to clarify its view of the relationship between the Old and New Testament Scriptures. What ongoing authority and normativeness does Christianity assign to the Jewish Scriptures in its overall vision of faith and life? Recent catholic magisterial statements have made substantial contributions to answering this question.[4]

'Intercultural Learning' is the title of an outstanding chapter in the fourth section of the work. It precedes, and is intrinsically linked, with the final chapter that reflects on the implications of the notorious Rushdie Affair: 'Blasphemy or Freedom of Art?—Religious Outrage in Secular Society'. Whereas the author unambiguously rejects the Iranian *fatwa* concerning the novelist Salman Rushdie with is menace of death, he underlines the fact that even the artist cannot escape responsibility of respect for the ideological convictions and moral sensibilities of whole sections of society.

Zirker doesn't content himself with pointing out the rule stereotypes about Islam in non-religious and in Christian circles but also points to the factors on the Muslim side that to some extent at least explain them.

As no other religion Islam claims the right to shape the community of men and women according to its own standards—including the dimension of political order and international relations. Already before the Gulf War of 1991 everyone could learn via the mass media that in diverse regions of the world with reference to the principles of Islam even vehemently aggressive, political objectives are pursued (285).

Hence Islam *appears* to be essentially a menace to peaceful coexistence of ideologically and politically differentiated groups and peoples. Even where non-Muslims are ready to encounter the Muslims in their entourage open-mindedly, they easily will nurture a double mental reservation: one, that Islam is incompatible with plural coexistence—in this case Muslims are held to be fairly naïve, to say the least—or one assumes that in spite of different appearances, there persists an always virulent potential for aggression that can be activated at any point of time.

In the context of the increase of plural societies intercultural learning has become a crucial issue almost everywhere. How far can we motivate ourselves and others continuously to make the effort to understand the complicated issues involved and to correct incessantly our attitude, even when on the Muslim side we are confronted now and again with massive barriers?

Because for Zirker there exists between Muslims and Christians what he terms the 'didactic asymmetry', the Muslim side feels provoked more by secularization and the religio-ideological pluralism or even the indifference of the West than by the religion of Christianity as such. Hence any theological and didactical discussion of the relationship between Islam and Christianity has to take into account 'secularization' as the third pole of reference.

Besides the deeper reasons that form as it were a barrier for Christian thought, there exist among non-Muslims a number of prejudices rendering difficult a fair assessment of Muslim realities. In our day often they may appear in refined ways but they remain effective. They have to do mainly with the biographical image of Muhammad, the alleged expansion of Islam by means of fire and sword and the position of women in Islam.

Ultimately, Zirker argues, intercultural learning does not consist primarily in the effort to understand 'Islam' as a sum total of religious conceptions and doctrines but rather to understand the people that profess Islam and are shaped and influenced by it as to their outlook on life, their basic ethical orientation and social organization, the way they express their faiths, their specific sensitivities and fears. The complex reality of Islam cannot be grasped by a mere intellectual approach. Intercultural learning as far as possible has to be 'learning by participation'.

Within this perspective there emerge three objectives: first, the task to try again and again to understand the reasons for the conjunction of vicinity and distance between the two faiths, to recognize the reasons for this fact and to endure the continuing mutual 'otherness' with patience, second, to try to meet and get along with one another as communities in pragmatically limited situations; third, the task to reflect about the consequences of the fact that the contrast of the dogmatic position of both religions cannot be overcome by rational, theological arguments. Where we judge the external discussion to be little fruitful, there remains always the inescapable task of the *inner dialogue.*

In our age each religion is confronted with the dynamic task to remain true to itself within the changing conditions of society and, on the other hand, to prove itself capable to learn and willing to be corrected. In this process it is impossible to define clearly and *a priori* what must remain for all times and what must change in the service of the Absolute.

A quite comprehensive 'Literaturverzeichnis', 'Register der Bibel-und der Koranzitate' sowie 'Sach-und Personenregister' add to the value of this stimulating and original work. Although a number highly relevant French publications, especially some of the relevant works of R. Caspar, are listed in the bibliography, one misses the mention and critical acknowledgement of such authors as Claude Geffré and Henri Sanson who would seem to have contributed in recent years significantly to the discussion of some of the key questions Zirker raises in the present work.

NOTES

1. *Islam: Theologische und Gesellschaftliche Herausforderungen.* Dusseldorf: Patmos, 1993, 3678 S.
2. Dusseldorf, 1992; cf. review article by C.W. Troll in *Islam and Christian-Muslim Relations,* vol. 4, 1993, pp. 144–8 and the review by V. Poggi in *OCP*, vol. 60, 1994, pp. 677–8.
3. H. Ott, quoted on p. 30.
4. Cf. Jacques Dupuis, *Jesus-Christ a la rencontre des religions,* Paris: Desclee, 1989, pp. 151–60.

2

Can Christians and Muslims Pray Together?*

If any Event in Church History since the Second Vatican Council deserves the adjective 'epoch-making', it would be the interreligious encounter at Assisi on 27 October 1986, to which Pope John Paul II invited representatives of the most important Christian denominations and also of the world religions to pray for peace. Assisi was not about discussing prayer together; rather, all the participants were gathered in the same place, at St Francis' tomb, so that each religion or denomination might pray in its own way for peace. At the beginning of the meeting the Pope explained.

Religions are many and varied, and they refect the desire of men and women down through the ages to enter into a relationship with the Absolute Being. Prayer entails conversion of heart on our part. It means deepening our sense of the ultimate Reality. This is the very reason for our coming together in this place.[1]

Assisi and the Consequences

Not least through the creative commitment of the San Egidio community, the prayer-meeting in Assisi became the model for a world prayer movement for peace that includes believers of all faiths and embraces the whole earth across the boundaries of individual nations. In fact, since Assisi, awareness of a common dependence on God and a common responsibility for peace has grown among adherents of all religious—particularly among believers of the three monotheistic world religions. At the same

* This essay was first published in *The Way*, vol. 50, no. 1, January 2011, pp. 53–70.

time, admittedly, the voices and forces opposed to such a common religious consciousness and way of acting embracing the individual religions have also grown everywhere.

In 2003, the German bishops published *Leitlinien für multireligiöse Feiern von Christen, Juden und Muslimen* ('Guidelines for Multireligious Celebrations by Christians, Jews and Muslims').[2] After the example and model of prayer-meeting in Assisi, which, as the bishops write, avoided the danger of intermingling (syncretism) and respected the other's sincere search for God', multireligious celebrations between Christians and Jews, between Christians and Muslims, and between Christians, Jews and Muslims, are encouraged. The bishops make a distinction between 'multireligious celebrations', in which 'each religious group is responsible for its own contribution',[3] and what they all 'interreligious celebration. in which all turn to God together with words and signs carried out by all'.[4] They reject the latter form of celebration categorically, 'because here there is the danger of appropriating the other and blurring real difference'.[5] With respect to Christian-Muslim multi-religious celebrations the German bishops say:

> In shared celebrations Christians and Muslims can experience the fact that their lives are directed to the one God, despite different conceptions of God. So Christians and Muslims can discover that, as recipients of God's peace, they are called and obliged to mutual respect and, furthermore, to commitment to peace and respect for human rights in the world.[6]

In 2006, Cardinal Joachim Meisner published 'Archbishop's Guidelines on Multireligious Celebrations in Schools' for the archdiocese of Cologne. Such celebrations, he writes, are,

> ... not meaningful in the school context, because for children and young people it is diffcult to distinguish between multireligious celebrations and Catholic and ecumenical services, so that there is danger of confusion. Therefore in the archdiocese of Cologne no further celebrations should take place for pupils in schools.[7]

This decision by the cardinal is to be seen as the result of his considered religious pedagogy and pastoral judgement. The

Hamburg auxiliary bishop Hans-Jochen Jaschke, spokesman on interreligious dialogue for the German Bishops' Conference, said a few days later on German radio that, in his rejection of this form of celebration in schools, Cardinal Meisner was basically keeping to the 2003 guidelines of the German Bishops' Conference. The prohibition of such celebrations came from concern for children and respect for non-Christian religions' different conceptions of God. In His view multireligious celebrations in school should nevertheless be possible in individual cases.[8]

However, the Cologne guidelines add another statement to the sentence quoted:

The image of God in non-Christian religions is not identical with the God, who is Father of our Lord Jesus Christ. For that reason services together with members of non-Christian religions are not possible. And thus, every community can only pray alone to its God. If this happens in common, the other group must remain present in silence.

In the first sentence of this statement the image of God in non-Christian religions is compared 'with the God, who is Father of our Lord Jesus Christ'. There is a confusion of levels here. Correctly, an *image* of God should be compared with another image of God. If we start from the difference between image of God, even among the three so-called 'Abrahamic religions', does it necessarily follow from this difference that prayers said together by Christians and Muslims, and interreligious celebrations in this sense, must count as 'impossible' from the Christian point of view?

In my opinion, hardly certainly the image of God in the Islamic faith is not identical with the image of God in the Christian faith—to simplify, and not to take account the fact that, within both contemporary Islam and Christianity, there are extensive variations among images of God. And yet their respective images of God share such important elements that under certain circumstances Christians and Muslims can, and even should, pray to God together.

Against the background of these events, I would like to consider three questions. First, do Christians and Muslims believe in the same God? Second, can the prayer of Christians and the prayer of Muslims be considered a locus of their inner relatedness and closeness? Third, can Christians and Muslims encounter one another in prayer?

Do Christians and Muslims Believe in the Same God

The question of whether Muslims and Christians, in one way or another, can and should pray to God together, leads immediately to the question of whether they worship the same God. Before we go into this fundamental issue we ought first to take seriously the scarcely disputable fact that Islam and Christianity, together with Judaism, are monotheistic religions, that is, religions that confess the uniqueness and unity of God. In order words, Judaism, Christianity and Islam have a common root, as regards their respective confessions of God as one and unique, that distinguishes them from religions with mythical, impersonal or polytheistic concepts of God. Breaking away from myth characterizes monotheism as a particular path in the history of religions. This was first adopted by Israel and, following in Israel's footsteps, also by Christianity and Islam.

All the same, the considerable difference between the Christian and the Muslim confessions of God's unity should not thereby be relativized in any way, nor its significance undervalued. The Christian faith professes God's unity as a relationship of personal, triune love. The Muslim confession of God's unity dissociates itself explicitly, consciously and vehemently from this. If we want to live and promote honest, constructive relationships between Christians and Muslims, then we should on the one hand recognize the weight and importance of this difference between us, with all its consequences, but on the other hand keep in view the significance of the encounter between Christians and Muslims that is really possible, a meeting in the act of living faith, in the effective direction of the whole of life to the living God.

Islam is not simply a Christian heresy, as some theologians have presented it. Certainly the Koran, and thereby Islam, knows the person of Jesus and recognizes him as a prophet. Further, the Islamic faith is penetrated by many elements of biblical tradition. Nevertheless, deep differences in belief make Islam a religion distinct from Christianity. One of these is the Islamic denial of both the physical death of Jesus on the cross and the saving role and power of this non-violent act of self-giving love in the free acceptance the punishment of death through crucifixion; and another is the rejection of the mystery of God as Trinity.

Clear recognition of these differences, and others related to them, contributes on both the Christian and Muslim sides to living the mutual relationship in its reality. Recognition of these differences— with all their effects on the totality of the present faith-world and faith-view—is, as the Dutch-Egyptian expert on Islam Christian van Nispen tot Sevenaer rightly maintains, an expression of mutual respect.[9] But recognition of these serious differences does not mean that we should simply deny the depth and meaning of the encounter that Christians and Muslims can and should live in their faith in God.

Recognition of the Differences and of the Points in Common

The faith of Muslims—their witness to the unity and uniqueness of God, as well as their prayer, the whole of their worship, of which the alms tax, fasting and the pilgrimage to Mecca form part—is directed towards the living God, infinitely greater than all creation, who, as such, is at the same time infinitely close to His creatures. It is directed towards the Creator of heaven and earth, whose Being infinitely surpasses what we can imagine or name, and who is at the same time 'nearer to [us] than [our] jugular vein', as the Koran itself expresses it.[10]

This God of Islamic faith has raised many true worshippers and servants of God, women and men, in the community of Muslim believers, the *umma*, who have all, following Muhammad's call, been guided by Abraham, the father of obedience in faith. Abraham prays in Sura 26 (The Poets), 83: 'My Lord, grant me wisdom, join me with the rigtheous;' and in Sura 3 (The Family of 'Imran), 190-195, it says:

> There truly are signs in the creation of the heavens and earth, and in the alternation of night and day, for those with understanding, who remember God standing, sitting and lying down, who refect on the creation of the heavens and earth: 'Our Lord! You have not created all this without purpose—You are far above that!—so protect us from the torment of the Fire. Our Lord! You will truly humiliate those You commit to the Fire. The evildoers have no one to help them. Our Lord! We have heard someone calling us to faith—'Believe in your Lord'—and we have believed. Our Lord! Forgive us our sins, wipe out our bad deeds, and grant that we join the righteous when we die. Our

> Lord! Bestow upon us all that you have promised us through Your messengers—do not humiliate us on the Day of Resurrection—You never break Your promise.' Their Lord has answered them: 'I will not allow the deeds of any one of you to be lost, whether you are male or female.' (Tr. by M.A.S. Abdel Haleem).

Christians can and must recognize that the God in whom Muslims believe is not a creature, not an idol, not merely a lofty idea or pure representation, but the God in whom Christians also believe. That is true, despite the stated differences in views about God, with all their far-reaching consequences with respect to what both sides profess as crucial and central to their respective faiths, and what as a result should be accepted and followed as God's paramount and decisive main commandment.

In *Lumen Gentium*, the Constitution on the Church, Vatican II established that:

> ... the plan of salvation also includes those who acknowledge the Creator, in the frst place amongst whom are the Moslems: these profess to hold the faith of Abraham, and together with us they adore the one, merciful God, mankind's judge on the last day.[11]

This community in faith in the Creator, Preserver and Judge, and in prayer to the one God, according to the measure of Abraham's faith, allows Christians and Muslims an encounter in this faith, which enables us to stand 'together before God' in a real way. Indeed, then, it demands and implies that in this encounter we allow God absolute priority and thereby recognize that it is God Himself who binds us together and whose gift the encounter is. This is exactly what helps us also, Christians and Muslims, to live our profound differences in genuine respect for one another, while remaining true to our own consciences.

In so far as our faith is a real personal act and not simply a social inheritance taken on without thinking, and provided that, and in so far as, Christians and Muslims seek to live their relationship with God out of deepest conscience, we can also be together where we are different. We may say this because, and in so far as, we believe in one and the same God, and in this belief perceive the mystery presented by each person's journey with God. In this understanding, Christians and Muslims are brothers and sisters in God. Thus Pope John Paul II said to the Muslim representatives in Davao in the Philippines on 20 February 1981:

> I deliberately address you as brothers. we are especially brothers in God, who created us and whom we are trying to reach, in our own ways, through faith, prayer and worship, through the keeping of his law and through submission to his designs.[12]

In other words, real and profound differences in faith do not have to mean absolute separation as we stand together before God. Of course, if talking about God turns into a tournament or a battlefield, so to speak, very soon there is the danger of no longer talking about the living God who is, for all of us, first of all ineffable mystery. But what does 'mystery' really mean? In theological language, 'mystery' does not mean 'conundrum' but refers to something that grasps and encompasses us, rather than something we can grasp or encompass. The mystery invites us: not to eschew understanding, but to surpass what understanding can reach with its own power. Mystery is given through grace, through disinterested love. The mystery of divine love is in fact the real mystery, into which we enter by gift. It invites us to build a community of life with God Himself, which transcends every human idea about community and relationship.

Any physical unity, any unity which is not the unity of love, can be broken and divided. True unity is the unity experienced between persons, the unity of love. The more authentically persons are united through true love, the more unbreakable will their unity be. Experience of such unity in human love can allow us to accept the mystery of divine unity, the mystery of the greatest imaginable love.

Jesus Christ opens to us and shares with us the mystery of this love 'to the end'; better, 'to completion' (John 13:1). He received himself as total love of the Father; in a similar way he gives himself without reserve to God, his Father, in complete surrender to his disciples, indeed to all people. So he reveals himself as Son of God from all eternity. The mystery of God's triune life invites to share in the divine life—a life of connectedness and endless love—in which the unity itself is the absolute unity of absolute love.

Abraham as Model

Certainly the Koran and, following it, the whole tradition of Islamic religious thought, constantly emphasizes that it is not given to the human being to enter into the intimate life of God; the human being is not allowed to fathom the 'inner' life of the divine Being. But here too difference from the Christian belief does not mean total opposition; because it must not be forgotten how far the spiritual life of countless Muslim believers has been, and is, nourished by meditation on the 'Most Beautiful Names of God' (*asmā' Allāh al-husn"a*). Muslims have the task of imitating and living the 'attributes of God' (*sifāt Allāh*), as they await the appearance of the just and merciful Lord of Judgement.

The area in which Muslims come nearest to the mystery of God is undoubtedly, however, where they try to follow God's unsearchable will according to the model of Abraham. The Abraham of the Koran was ready at God's command to sacrifice his own son, without being able humanly to understand God's decision in any way. Through his submission and dedication (this is the meaning of the Arabic verbal noun '*islām*'), supported by believing trust, Abraham became the absolute model of the Muslim ('*muslim*': one who submits himself or herself to God).

In this unconditional and total submission Muslims can be granted a remarkable sense of the mystery of God: indeed in such a way that, according to Muslim faith, God's plan for a person can radically surpass what the believing Muslim is able to understand. This determination of the faithful Muslim to submit to the mystery of God's will reveals real greatness of faith, particularly in the face of the mystery of death.

Anyone who suggests that this attitude is simply a form of fatalism ignores its true meaning or misinterprets it. Christian van Nispen mentions in this connection the example of the notable Egyptian writer Tawfiq al-Hakim (1898–1987). In one of his novels al-Hakim describes how he experienced the trauma of his little son's early death. During the funeral he ran after his son's coffin and repeated, 'Your wisdom, Lord! Your wisdom, Lord!' (*hikmatuka, yā Rabb*).[13]

In Jesus Christ, the Christian faith discovers the unity of Communion and love as the ultimate meaning of God's unity and uniqueness. For in him we discover that God is first of all nonviolent, self-giving love, and that thereby divine love is the key to understanding the final meaning of all the qualities, or Names, of God. In Jesus we Christians also find the true meaning of the divine greatness—God's greatness makes itself known as the greatness of His self-sacrificing love, which surpasses all human imagination. God's true greatness reveals itself most radically when, in Jesus, He makes Himself the Messiah, the non-violent servant of each and every human being.

At the heart of Muslim faith is the resolute defence of divine greatness. One of the central expressions of the Islamic faith is '*Allāhu akbar*', God is ever greater, is great through and through, infinitely great. Alongside this it is sobering to note that again and again in the past there have been, and that there are also today worldwide, Muslim groups that strive for political ends in practice by using force, and in doing this do not consider themselves primarily as politicians, warriors or terrorists, but as consistent Muslims. These Muslims consider themselves to be, and behave as though they are, the only authentic, consistent Muslims. Groups of Muslims with these convictions sometimes develop an explicitly sectarian mentality. With that comes a radical fanaticism that can go as far as planning and carrying our suicide attacks in the name of Islam and can under some circumstances accept the killing of innocent civilians.

Christians may develop relations of dialogue with Muslims and thereby wish to make living and fruitful the religious and spiritual bonds between Islam and Christianity that have been mentioned. But, for the sake of the good cause, they should carefully consider what kind of Islam their dialogue partners advocate. Furthermore, how such persons or groups see their relationship to non-Muslim partners is important in the social and political realities of our time.

This prudence, which calls for a discerning knowledge, is also indispensable because there is scarcely a form of 'teaching office' in Islam that would correspond even approximately to the current evangelical or orthodox Christian form, and certainly not to the Catholic form of the teaching office. On the contrary, Muslims reject the idea of a teaching office decisively, and are on the whole proud of the fact that, as individuals or as group, they can work out and represent their own understanding of the Koranic message.

Islamic Fundamentalism

Today we are witnessing groups of Muslims, some of them very influential, who promote a decidedly 'Islamist' view of Islam in the name of the Koran, and seek to realize it by political, and sometimes militant and terrorist, means. Such groups consider to be infidels (*kuffār*)—who should be deprived of power, at least gradually, as it may be possible—not only non-Muslims, including Christians, but also Muslims who do not adhere to their own radical Islamist views, or even oppose them. These groups acknowledge and support democratic structures only to the extent that they serve the development of Islamic political power-structures, the final establishment of which throughout remains their objective.

It seems to me that there is no point in religious-spiritual dialogue with Muslims and Muslim groups who are attached to such a view of Islam, because the indispensable basic presuppositions for it to succeed are lacking. Genuine religious and spiritual dialogue in the context of our modern societies seems to me meaningful only with Muslims and Christians who share our fundamental secular, democratic values and, logically, therefore ultimately recognize the separation of politics and religion, and are not working towards an Islamic, or for that matter a Christian, state. An alleged religious and spiritual dialogue with proven Islamists does not serve the truth. It represents a deception and bafflement of genuine servants of God, whether of the Christian or Islamic faith.

In accordance with Jesus Christ's teaching, topically embodied in the documents of Vatican II, the Church calls its members to live in conformity with Christ and to make the final revelation of the true divine greatness in Jesus visible and tangible, by authentic and creative exercise of service to one's neighbour especially where that neighbour is marginalized and forgotten. Then the greatness of God will become a place of fruitful spiritual contest, instead of being an object of quarrel and dispute, pride and unkindness between Christians and Muslims.

From all this it emerges that Christians and Muslims are invited, first of all by God, but then through the silent expectation of so many people, to be 'witnesses to the One and Unique', in the difference of their views of faith, in sometimes painful respect for this difference, and in encounter. Understood in this way encounter can create genuine solidarity, a certain unity—deep and mysterious also in the difference between the Christian and Muslim views of faith. This will to unity in difference honours God, to whom both Christians and Muslims pray, and honours human beings, 'created in God's image' as the Bible says (Genesis 1: 26–9), and placed as 'God's vicegerent on earth' (*khalīfa*) as the Koran (2: 30) and the Bible (Psalm 8: 6–9) teach.

Prayer as Space for Inner Relatedness and Closeness?

If Christians and Muslims are fundamentally brothers and sisters before the one God, and if Muslims, in the words of *Lumen Gentium*, 'along with us adore the one and merciful God, who on the last day will judge mankind',[14] then the spiritual efforts of the Muslim faithful cannot leave believing Christians unmoved. Pope John Paul II said on 22 December 1986, looking back on the meeting for prayer in Assisi already mentioned:

> Every authentic prayer is under the infuence of the Spirit 'who intercedes insistently for us. because we do not even know how to pray as we ought', but he prays in us 'with unutterable groaning' and 'the one who searches hearts knows what are the desires of the Spirit' (Romans 8:26-27). We can indeed maintain that every authentic prayer is called forth by the Holy Spirit, who is mysteriously present in the heart of every person. This too was seen at Assisi: the unity that comes from the fact that every man and women is capable of praying, that is of submitting oneself totally to God and of recognizing oneself to be poor in front of him. Prayer is one of the means to realize the plan of god among men.[15]

In all religions prayer is the place, **par excellence**, where the faithful live and express their relationship with God. While the specific behaviour of the believer, in word and action, is the most radical realization of his or her faith, prayer represents the very spirit of his faith. Often prayer is marked by the same paradox as everything that we say about God. If God is really at the same time 'the absolute', 'the whole', 'the wholly other' and 'the absolute mystery' which surpasses all understanding and speech, then prayer as relationship with this God is both fullness and richness, and yet emptiness and powerlessness.

Without starting to discuss other religions here, I think that what has been said applies both to Islam and to Christianity. In this I am thoroughly aware of the danger and the reality of various forms of distortion in contemporary belief and prayer as practiced in any specified religion. At all events we can speak fittingly about prayer only with respect and a certain restraint, because in doing so we touch on what is quite simple and at the same time ineffable, most sublime and most precious in the life of people of faith.

The religious differ with regard both to attitudes in prayer and to the content of prayer. From this it is understandable that Christian and Muslim prayer are not the same or interchangeable. This difference is to be respected. It is certainly also true that along with the possibility of an encounter in faith in the one living God there is also the possibility of such an encounter in prayer. Further, the obligation of Muslims and Christians to recognize one another before the one Creator and Judge, to share with one another and, in short, to encounter one another in dialogue is likely constantly to evoke desire and perhaps to arouse awareness of the obligation— precisely in a world which largely forgets God—to witness to this common task, glorifying together before God, and constantly to ask God together for help to know our common responsibility and to carry it out better.

Obligation to Dialogue-Obligation to Prayer

It is no easy matter to hold the two ends of this paradox together somehow—the difference in views of faith and attitudes to prayer, on the one hand, and the commitment to encounter one another in prayer, on the other. But simply to make a contradiction out of this tension and paradox is inadmissible and highly damaging. This is the more true as today the tendency is predominant to present Islam and Christianity as fundamentally opposed to one another, even as completely and essentially in conflict with one another.

There exist in Christianity, with its numerous denominations, an endless number of types and forms of prayer. There is liturgical prayer, the high point of which is the Eucharist or Holy Communion. There are the prayers that belong to the celebration of the various sacraments, and also the official communal prayer of the Church, the Divine Office. Finally there are all the forms of devout and free prayer carried on individually or congregationally.

Christians know that in all their prayer they are taken up through God's Spirit into the movement of the risen Jesus to the Father, in which he receives everything from the Father and hands everything over to the Father. So prayer is life, and life is prayer.

In Islam—Sunni with its four schools or rites, and Shia in its various forms—the ritual prayer (*salāt*) is first of all, according to the creed, the prime duty of religious observance. It forms the second Pillar of Islam. It is to be made five times a day, at fixed times and according to an established ritual. So its rhythm is stamped on daily life. At midday on Friday, this prayer has a still stronger obligation and a specifically communal character. It follows immediately after the Friday sermon. On the two great feasts, the breaking of the fast at the end of Ramadan and the sacrificial feast in Dhu'l-Hijja, the pilgrimage month, the morning prayer has a special significance, as do the prayers on particular occasions such as funerals.

Alongside official and ritually prescribed prayer, there is in Islam the 'Prayer of Invocation' (*duā*), a free prayer consisting chiefly of insistent requests and enquiries, but which may also contain praise, thanksgiving and petitions for forgiveness. It is free, which however does not mean that known texts cannot be found in it. Such prayer exists for all occasions and with all possible intentions. However, there is no complete separation between the prayer of invocation and the official ritual prayer, since within the ritual prayer there are moments when prayers of invocation can be inserted silently.

The nature of the prayer of invocation makes it possible to allow interreligious encounter a regular and recognized place in it. We can pray for one another before God, the Living and the One, Christians for Muslims and Muslims for Christians. Muslims have constantly said to me, 'Father, pray for me, pray for my children.' And when in return I ask the Muslims to pray for me, they are pleasantly surprised.

Can Christians and Muslims Encounter One Another in Prayer?

In the light of these facts a further question occurs: whether we, Christians and Muslims, can encounter one another in prayer. What seems to me to be of primary importance regarding such encounters is precisely what does not seem important, but is very close to everyday experience. Becoming self-aware and interiorly recognizing the fact that we are standing 'together before God' are already a first step, initially invisible but effective all the same, towards living together in peace. This step signifies an inner approach to one another and at the same time an opening to God. It can be strengthened through occasions of being together before God in silence. Further, each in his or her own prayer can, so to speak, 'carry the other before God', precisely during regular ritual or liturgical prayer. During or after such prayer there is the opportunity to pray specifically for one another before God.

An encounter in prayer can also take place through silent participation in the other's liturgical prayer, admittedly without full accompaniment in speech and symbolic gestures. Here it is a matter of discreet participation in liturgical prayer by the Muslim or Christian as guest, in an attitude of respect and prayerful presence.

Then, in personal contacts and especially in significant life events—important decisions, occasions of great joy or of pain and suffering—it is certainly meaningful and appropriate for Christians and Muslims who already know and value each other as spouses, relatives, neighbours, colleagues and fellow combatants in the struggle against dishonesty and injustices in society, to know that they stand together before God. It is meaningful and appropriate for them to put their feelings of gratitude, joy or apprehension and their requests into words together—words to the common Lord of our hearts and our fate.

Lastly there is the possibility at certain group meetings of opening an inner space of prayer together. How such prayers, spoken in common by Christians and Muslims as a group, can proceed will depend strongly on the type and nature of those taking part, and they will certainly always remain exceptional. For the practice of common prayer remains constantly marked by the element of simplification and reduction on both sides, and by the risk, one to be taken extremely seriously, of reducing prayer to the lowest common denominator of both faith-worlds. Here it is important to ensure that the common prayer of Christians and Muslims does not eventually replace all other practices of prayer within the religions, as can happen particularly quickly in schools and religiously mixed youth-groups.

We must maintain one thing above all. If prayer is to remain genuine, believers need constantly to remain bonded with their own faith-community's practice of prayer, with the 'sacred space' from which they come and with which they are familiar. Children and young people, particularly, must first of all grow in this space and put down deep roots in it. Those officially concerned with interreligious dialogue have said useful things about this; collections of prayers from Christianity, Islam and other religions have been published. Above all, the genuineness of the encounter is important. It is not the spectacular that counts; what is decisive is whether what is done symbolically and expressed in words represents the reality and quality of the participants' meeting.

A particularly beautiful prayer is that of the 'Religious Brotherhood' in Cairo, which has met monthly for decades. At the beginning of a meeting all the participants, Muslims, Jews and Christians, say the following words together:

> God, to You we turn,
> In You we place our trust,
> It's You for whose help we ask.
> Urgently we ask:
> Give us the power of faith in You
> And the power to act rightly through the guidance of Your Prophets and messengers.
> And we ask You, O God, to make every one of us
> Loyal to his faith and his religion,
> Without narrow-mindedness which harms us ourselves,
> Without fanaticism that does injustice to our fellow citizens.
> We beseech You, our Lord,
> Bless our religious brotherhood.
> Grant that sincerity determines us here,
> Justice be the goal pursued here.
> Peace be the good we fnd here.
> O Thou Living, Thou Eternal
> To Thee be praise and honour.
> Amen

Together Before God

To the question of common prayer with Muslims there is no single and also no unambiguous answer. The possible times and places, the forms and particular situations of prayer are really too various.

Moreover, the question of common prayer throws up countless fundamental questions of theology and of Christian-Islamic dialogue as such. With this question we are moving on to sensitive ground.

However, this fact will and should in no way prevent Christians from desiring encounter with Muslims before God and in prayer, from knowing themselves to be responsible before God jointly and mutually with Muslims. Nor should it prevent them from finding themselves together—wherever there are meaningful opportunities— for common supplication of God, for praise of the one whom both faith-communities confess as their Creator, Preserver and Judge, by whom they know themselves to be called in common responsibility.

In 1964, in his ground-breaking encyclical *Ecclesian suam*, Pope Paul VI named four virtues that should characterize dialogue. These virtues can also be related to common prayer between Muslims and Christians. Paul VI wrote that there is need of clarity, meekness, confidence and prudence.[16] Guided by these virtues, the common prayer of Christians and Muslims, in its various forms and on different occasions, can bring forth something lasting. It will advance the quality of living together on the part of Christians and Muslims as neighbours and also of many others marked (or even no longer marked) by religion in the increasingly pluralized societies of our one world. Thus it will offer worthy honour and praise to the Father of all.

NOTES

1. John Paul II, address to the representatives of the Christian Churches and ecclesial communities gathered in Assisi for the World Day of Prayer (17 October 1986), n.4, available at http://www.vatican.va/ holy_father/ John_paul_ii/speeches/1986/october/documents/hf_ip-ii_spe_19861027_ prayer-peace-assisi_en.html.
2. (Bonn: DBK Sekretariat, 2003), Second revised edition under the title *Leitlinien für das Gebet bei Treffen von Christen, Juden und Muslimen* is available at http:/liturgie.de/liturgie/pub/op/download/170.pdf
3. *Leitlinien für das Gebet bei Treffen von Christen, Juden und Muslimen*, p. 20.
4. *Ibid.*
5. *Ibid.*

6. *Ibid.*
7. Available at www.koeln.de/artikel/INC/koelns-Kardinal-Meisner.
8. See *Katholische Nachrichten Agentur Pressebild* (11 December 2006) and *Frankfurter Rundschau* (9 December 2006).
9. Christian van Nispen tot Sevenaer, *Chrétiens et musulmans frères devant Dieu*? Paris: l'Atelier, 2004, pp. 106-9.
10. Koran 50:16. The English translation used here is Abdullah Yusuf Ali, *The Holy Koran, Text, Translation and Commentary*, Lahore: Sh. Muhammad Ashraf, 1934.
11. *Lumen gentium*, 16.
12. *Interreligious Dialogue: The Official Teaching of the Catholic Church from the Second Vatican Council to John Paul II* (1963-95), ed. F. Gioia, Boston: Pauline Books and Media, 1997, n. 363.
13. Van Nispen tot Sevenaer, *Chrétiens et musulmans*, 144.
14. *Lumen gentium*, 16.
15. *Interreligious Dialogue*, n. 572, *see Ad gentes*, 3.
16. Christian W. Troll SJ was professor of Islamic Studies at New Delhi and then taught at Birmingham and at the Pontifical Oriental Institute in Rome. He now works as an honourary professor at the Graduate School of Philosophy and Theology, Sankt Georgen, Frankfurt, Germany.

3

Muhammad—Prophet for Christians Also?*

'We Muslims recognize Jesus as a prophet and revere him. Why do you Christians not accept Muhammad as a prophet in the same way?' Among Christians with Muslim friends and acquaintances who talk about religious issues, there are unlikely to be many who have not encountered this question before. Often it will have been pointed out that the West even to this day insolently and hurtfully denigrates Muhammad in images and words, libelling his character and his name in an unspeakable manner.

In reply to these accusations of injury and libel Christians will express with deep regret the enormous extent of ignorance of past generations in terms of other cultures and religions. This ignorance was often linked with fear and deep discontent about 'the Muslims': that is, the Saracens, the Turks, etc. The renewed flaring up of such vilification is, at least in part, connected to the subliminal fears of large groups of society in Europe about Islamist terrorist attacks. It is also connected with the rapidly increasing visibility of Muslim groups and movements as a consequence of specifically Islamic dress and the construction of widely visible mosques in the centres of Western European cities.

However, this first question of Muslims with its implied request for the mutual recognition of Jesus and Muhammad as prophets goes even deeper. At first it ostensibly appears to have some degree of plausibility. After careful analysis, however, it becomes apparent that the stated parallel between the Muslim's reverence of Jesus and the Christian rejection of Muhammad is

* This essay was first pubished in *The Legacy of John Paul II*, ed. Michael A. Hayes, Gerald O'Collins, SJ, pp. 252–68.

deceptive. Because where Muslims revere Jesus as a prophet in the sense of their Koran based faith, they simply follow their creed. The Jesus depicted in Islam identifies with the Koran's message and lives in accordance with the rules laid down in the Koran. To recognize this Jesus does not cost Muslims anything, because the role of the Jesus of the Koran is precisely that: to support the belief in Muhammed as the final true prophet, and therefore the veracity of the Koran. If, on the other hand, Christians seriously accept Muhammad's claim they turn away from everything laid down in Christianity's most important creedal documents.

What is it, therefore, that Muslim partners are asking of Christians? The faithful Muslim is convinced that Islam is the true religion, 'the religion of the truth' *(dīn al-haqq)* (sura 9, 33). On the basis of this conviction Muslims know themselves to be instructed to invite Christians to recognize the truth of Islam, and to enter by conversion into the community of Muslims.

The Term 'Prophet' in Islam

For believing Muslims a true prophet is someone who brings a message from God and who works with absolute determination towards the effective implementation of this message. The Islamic belief in the unchanging message of true prophets has at its core the doctrine of God's uniqueness and unity and of the responsibility each individual has before God, the creator and judge. It is the message that has been proclaimed by all true prophets since Adam. It is written into the nature of each human being (see also sura 30, 30), and each person is now obliged to recognize and accept this message. It is contained in its final, complete and utterly clear form in the text of the Koran as it was faithfully delivered by Muhammad. Today this message reaches everyone through the faithful witness of the *umma* as a whole, as well as of its single members. Each person is asked to become a Muslim, to publicly become a member of the Islamic community and therefore to walk the 'straight path' of the revealed law. That path is laid down in great detail in the text of the Koran, the reliable statements of Muhammad ('sound' Hadiths), and in the *sharīā* (i.e. Islamic Law), derived from these two sources. In following this path the Muslim witnesses to the truth and struggles for the 'clear victory' *(al-fath al-mubīn,* for example, sura 48, 1) of Islam in this world.

Christians find the request to reorganize Muhammad as a prophet difficult, when Mohammed and his teachings are presented as the final and universal norm. Muslims never tire of assuring Christians that Muhammad is the last messenger from God and the seal of the prophets, whose coming was predicted by Moses and Jesus. Furthermore, they state that it is one of the central teachings of Islam that Muhammad is the prophet God sent to *all* nations. The Koran, they say, is the unchanged, verbatim message which Muhammad over a period of 21-232 years received bit by bit through the Angel Gabriel from God, and which he wrote down faithful to each letter. The Koran is thus said to be binding for all nations of all times. All other messages proclaimed by any other authentic prophet are *only valid for a certain nation for a certain period in time.* According to Islamic faith the prophets before Muhammad, including Jesus (*Īsa ibn Maryam*) are Muhammad's harbingers or representatives. Practically all forms of Islam teach that these prophets accepted Muhammed's prophetic leadership and his superiority quasi in advance.

Christians don't find even a hint of a prediction about the coming of the prophet Mohammed in their sacred writings, although some Muslims are convinced that the verses from St. John's Gospel (14,16-17) in which Jesus promises the coming of a comforter, the paraclete, are to be interpreted as the prediction of the future coming of Muhammad.[1]

Furthermore, Christians do not share the Muslim belief that Jesus, like Muhammad, had received revelatory scripture, the *injīl*, from God through the angel *Jibril* (Gabriel). On the contrary, Christians believe that the person of Jesus himself is the final revelation from God, which cannot be superseded.

If one wants to carry out such a structural comparison at all, one could say: 'The position Jesus occupies in Christian faith as the timeless and uncreated Word co-existent with God, can be compared to the position the Koran occupies in the Muslim faith, in as far as it is believed to be the uncreated Word of God. It would be possible to say that, according to Muslim faith, in the Koran the Word of God as it were has become book ('inliberation' as against incarnation).

Because of their faith Christians are therefore unable to agree to the Koran's claim, and thus the Muslim claim, that Jesus is a representative of Muhammad, and that he had been commissioned to bring a message to one specific nation at one specific time in history. Rather, in the Christian faith Jesus is the decisive revelation of God for all people at all times and in all places. In him God, in sovereign freedom, has created solidarity with mankind. This shows that the above-mentioned Muslim beliefs about Muhammad and the Koran are not acceptable to Christians, and they cannot be a mutual playing field between Christians and Muslims.

Is There a Middle Ground in This Question?

From the beginning of the last century some Catholic theologians have been developing certain new perspectives and attempting to uncover principles which might make it possible to recognize Muhammad as a prophet. In terms of the powerful *prophetic experience* that marks the beginning of this major movement of Islam, it was argued that it is possible to call Muhammad a prophet.

From this perspective, however, the term prophet assumes a new meaning, which I believe to be different from the biblical as well as the Koran's meaning of the word. The question to be asked is: do those who understand the word of the prophet as explained above, also support the Koran's summon to absolute obedience to the prophet and his teachings? Or do they leave it to the individual to select at will from the prophet's teachings and leave the rest alone?

Much depends on how we deal with the undeniable fact that, from the Christian point of view, the message of the Prophet of Islam contains obvious theological errors. Certainly there exists the opinion that ultimately the message of the Koran would not contain anything that contradicts the Christian message. In other words, the rejections and condemnations of the Koran would refer only to distorted depictions of Christianity, which Christians also reject. Also, there are those who don't mind that a prophetic message contains doctrinally dubious statements. Furthermore, some occasionally ask: do doctrinal statements still matter in this day and age?

One point must be made without a doubt: Muslims react in a very emotional and negative way when the term prophet is devalued in whatever shape or form. Let me give an example. At the second congress in Cordoba (21–7 March 1977) a Christian speaker, Prof. Gregorio Ruiz, presented an overview of the meanings of the word prophet. He explained that today the term has a rather broad meaning. It describes a person with extraordinary insight and intuition, who is sensitive to specific situations in society and who has left a lasting impression in history. In this sense, for example, Karl Marx (1818–83) could be called a prophet. He added that he personally had no problem with calling Muhammad a prophet in this sociological sense. It is not surprising that the majority of Muslims present at this large conference could not agree with this view and the parallels depicted. On the contrary, they were rather offended.[2]

Would it then be preferable to speak of Muhammad as a prophet more or less akin to the great prophets of the Old Covenant? It is hardly likely that Muslims would be happy with this option. Many of them say: If a Christian says that Muhammad is a prophet, without subsequently becoming a Muslim, then he either does not understand his own (Christian) faith or he is a hypocrite.

Critical Openness to Muhammad's Life and Teachings

Our question does not simply concern a word or the title 'prophet', but the confession and the acceptance of the truth the title 'prophet' describes and which is the second part of the Muslim creed. For Christians Muhammad cannot be a 'prophet' in the sense this title has in the Koran and therefore in the Muslim faith. To accept Muhammad in the sense of the Koran and of Islam as a prophet means simply: to accept the teachings of the Koran about Muhammad and about Muhammad's claim to be a prophet, and therefore also to consider the life of Muhammad to be a 'beautiful and good model' (*uswa hasana*, 33, 21) for ones own life and the life of all people.

At the same time, and as already indicated, Christians will distance themselves decisively from any libel and condemnation of Muhammad, but will attempt to recognize and honour his exceptional historic persona, his role as the founder of Islam and his place in the faith, the piety and the religious thinking of Muslims. They will then explain whether, as faithful Christians, they can only reject Muhammad's teachings and his life, or whether these may, after all, powerfully bring to light major aspects of God's truth— that truth which Christians for their part see reflected in the light of human reason, made visible through faith in the person and the teachings of Jesus Christ.

Ultimately, this essay therefore follows the Koran's own request (5, 47) to the 'people of the gospel' to 'discern what God has sent down in him *(liyahkum ahl al-injīl bimā anzala Allāhu fīhi)*'; in other words, to discern which aspects of Muhammad's life and teachings are acceptable for believing Christians, maybe even exemplary and worthy of admiration, and which aspects from the point of view of the Christian faith, appear questionable, unacceptable and requiring salvation.

The Option of the Koran and of Muhammad for Political Power

Our statements about the life and the teachings of Mohammed are based on the text of the Koran, which we read in the context of fundamental information provided in the classical biography of Muhammad (i.e. the *sīrat al-nabī*, especially the book: *Sýārat Rasūl Allāh* by Ibn Ishāq [*c.*704-67], ed. Ibn Hisham [d. 833],[3] and the earliest Koran commentaries discussing 'the occasions of revelation', the *asbāb al-nuzūl*). No evaluation of the phenomenon of the messenger *(rasūl)* can avoid engagement with his message *(risāla)* as it is given to us in the text of the Koran. We take the Koran to be the text which Muhammad believed to be revealed by God, the statements of which wholly reflect his beliefs. In other words, whatever the Koran says we take to be Muhammad's message and teaching.

Everything in the Koran is to be understood as revelation in the name of the Lord (see sura *96*). From the first sura revealed in ad 609 and 610 to the last ones revealed in 632 the Koran represents claims and challenges for those it addresses. It requires of them to believe in Muhammad's appointed mission from God against any possible question and doubt.

The Christian observer and student must primarily consider the quality of the confrontation, even the enmity, between the prophet and his audience. It is important to comprehend the breadth of the truth that defines the battleground, as well as the factors which cause the hostile argument. It is not about the 'whether' but the 'how' of the confrontation. The question is: to what extent does the Koran's message as given by Mohammed correspond with the means Mohammed chose to achieve the supremacy of his message in his times and in his sphere of influence. The *hijra* in 622 is the linchpin in the prophet's history, the corner stone of the Koran and of the prophetic career: the *hijra* initiates Muhammad's prophetic leadership.

What is the core of the message, which caused the antagonism, even the open enmity, between the prophet and the people in Mecca? The basic tenets of this message are easily named. First, the request for unconditional recognition of the one and only God and, implied in this, the condemnation of polytheism and idolatry as foolishness; second, the proclamation of the reality that all people without exception will be subject to God's judgement, and thus their call away from comfortable forgetfulness and away from any other form of irresponsible living. His audience accused Mohammed of being 'crazy' (81, 22), no longer a mere 'soothsayer' (52, 29), a simple 'poet' (37, 52, 30), a copier of 'tales from the past' (68, 15), of using 'magic' (cf. 43, 30). If God had appointed someone, then surely he would have appointed a powerful personality, a 'man who is prominent' (43, 31). Someone like that would have had more credibility than this Mohammed. Furthermore, Mohammed was accused of destroying the old tradition and of denigrating the forefathers (43, 21–3).

For over 10 years Mohammed suffered derision, defamation, conspiracy and accusation. The stories of the patriarchs in the Koran therefore strongly reflect the virtue of faithful suffering and perseverance for God's sake. However, they also reflect the final triumph of the career and message of the patriarchs. The texts of these early Mecca years are also influenced by the sharp dichotomy between those led into truth on the one hand, and those who err (*muslimūn* and *kāfirūn*), those who accept the message and those who turn away from it, the winners and the losers. The writings clearly condemn the hardening of the hearts of those who listen to the prophet and their resistance to the truth of his message, and threaten them with the coming final judgement and its punishments.

Emigration from Mecca Hijra

In view of the hardening opposition during the late Mecca years, the Koran and his trusted prophet Muhammad moved towards *hijra* (emigration, not flight!), away from the restrictive confrontation with the rigid rejection of his own tribe, the Quraysh, and away from mere preaching, towards fighting by means of physical force. After 13 years of patient witness by word alone, and in the light of the rejection of Muhammad and his claim by the society of Mecca, who resisted him proudly and proved to be incorrigible, Muhammad opted for emigration. The failure of God's word and frustration of the 'manifest victory *(al-fath al-mubīn)*' of the 'religion of truth' were inconceivable and were not allowed to happen under any circumstances. In other words, failure had to be averted by any possible means.

To understand the emigration from Mecca *(hijra)* as failure, as though Muhammad had cast aside his calling and his responsibility, is a misunderstanding. Rather, looked at from the whole of the Koran's message, *hijra* is the obedient consequence of this calling. With the invitation to Yathrib/Medina and the promise to defend him and his prophetic claims, Muhammad and his followers received a unique opportunity to go united into self-imposed exile to create a solid foundation, an instrument with which the still neutral tribes and people in Yathrib could be converted to Islam by means of diplomatic skill and political pressure. It began to look possible that Mecca, which had refused to turn to Islam and its messenger, but which had not been able to prevent the messenger's emigration, would eventually be vulnerable to the returning exiles.

With his battles, the battle of Badr (624), Uhud (625) and the battle of the trench (627) Muhammad simply followed the basic logic of questioning the power of the tribe governing Mecca, the Quraysh, and attacking this tribe who protected pagan faith and its structures. From the beginning this radical questioning of the power of the pagan rulers of Mecca had been one of the aims and signs of Muhammad's mission. After the victory of Badr, which is described in the Koran as *yawm al-furqān* (the Day of Distinction, also Day of Decision, 8, 41), it became important to strengthen Medina's resources in steady, partly politically religious and partly military consolidation, to increase Muhammad's reputation, to conquer the surrounding tribes and finally, to return victoriously to Mecca. For the non-Muslims of Medina the conflict resulted in suspicions or accusations of secretly agreeing with the opponents, or even of cooperating with them. Even neutrality became suspicious. The Jewish tribes of Medina were under particular suspicion, because the prophet's initial assumption that they would accept him turned out to have been erroneous. The forced banishment, the confiscation of property and the dispersion of the tribes are the saddest chapters of the *sira* and the Koran. The most memorable victims were the Jewish tribes Banu Nādir, the Qaynuqā' and the Qurayza, whereby the latter suffered the execution of all their male members and the sale of all their women and children into slavery, with Muhammad's specific approval.[4]

Yes, one can and should see beyond individual episodes, even if they are as tragic as those mentioned here, and include in the assessment the whole complex of tribal, ritual, cultural psychology and legal regulations, as well as the collective strategy of war situations. The harshness of the punishment could thus be legitimated and the accusation could be qualified. However, the more strongly these circumstances are used as explanations and even excuses, the more pressing the deep theological problem: How can the believer combine the Koran's endorsement and the use of political and military force by the prophet with the claim of Koran and *sira* to final religious validity?

The armed *jihād* against Mecca led to victory and at the same time to *islām*, the act of subjugation of the conquered to the reign of Allah, as well as his prophet and his *umma*. The bloody battles of the first of the caliphs immediately after Muhammad's death showed the extent of fragility of tribe's *isl"am*, which was often no more than external subjugation to the power of the messenger, but lacking true faith (cf. sura 49, 4).

The ancient inscription on Muhammad's grave in Medina: 'Peace be upon thee, O Apostle. We witness that thou hast truly delivered the message, that thou hast striven in the way of God until God glorified His religion and perfected it.'[5] Expresses poignantly the vital unity of the witness of the Word and the political and military efforts in the life and teaching of Muhammad and therefore in our understanding of the Koran.

The Political and Military Dimension of Muhammad's Life and Teaching

When Muslims seek Christian acceptance of Muhammad they cannot avoid serious engagement with the historical information in the *sīra* and the corresponding texts in the Koran, and their normative meaning in the overall Islamic vision of faith. Islamic mystic and modern Muslim idealists use different methods for abstracting from the political and the military dimensions: that is, the *jihād*-dimension of the *sīra and* the corresponding texts in the

Koran. But no picture of Muhammad can ultimately set aside or negate historic facts and their claim to be normative, and a Christian assessment of Mohammed must take account of this dimension in his life and his message. The fundamental problem Christians have with regard to Muhammad's own understanding of his mission is the use of violence because of holy indignation over the rejection of the authority of God and his prophet. From a biblical-prophetic and Christian point of view, the prophetic mission, in so far as it is implemented by using political and military force, loses those qualities of truth and justice it tried to justify.

The important contemporary thinker Fazlur Rahman (1919-88) does not share this view:

> Muhammad never lost his hope for success, nor the truly terrible and brutal recognition that the requirement to be successful had been *his God given duty.* It is a component of the Koran's teaching that the mere bringing of the message, the experience of disappointment and the suffering of failure represent an immature spirituality.[6]

The question here is what, precisely, we are to understand by the terms 'immature' and 'spirituality'. In this context it is important to note that the Koran, and therefore Mohammed, simply turns the politically active patriarchs and judges of the Old Testament into true representatives of prophetic action: Moses, David, Abraham, the iconoclast. They are all of them heroes of success, examples for the prophet of Islam, while the turn away from power for the sake of the integrity of the Word, and who passionately believe that it is better to fail honourably than to obtain dishonourable success.[7]

This silence is not an accident; it corresponds with the norms and the spirit of the Koran. If the Koran and Muhammad's prophesies had included Jeremiah and all the suffering servants of biblical tradition, it would have resulted in an intolerable questioning of firm Muslim basic convictions, as they are expressed so clearly in Fazlur Rahman's statement. To put this in another way: Muhammad does not stand in the tradition of the prophets who have become decisive for our picture of biblical prophets and the character of their message.

According to our conviction, the faithful 'mere' delivering of the message *(balāgh),* which Rahman so categorically condemns as an indication of immature spirituality, does not expose someone to the temptation to claim that which is God's alone (see sura 3, 79-80) in the same way as the implementation of the message by the determined use of force and violent means. The temptation to claim that which is God's alone threatens especially the messenger and the message, when they apply political and military force. Such political and military might requires and justifies self-interest as well as enmity, which in turn spoil and darken the message. In order to retain his freedom as witness of God's Word, Jeremiah had to ensure his own freedom of thought and to fight strongly against any possible political instrumentalization of his person and his message. Ultimately he paid the price for this.

Also to be taken into account is that prophetic refusal to use force and violence is correlative to God's wish to receive a genuine answer to his invitation and his will from mankind. This answer must be based solely on love, not on the fear of punishment and the consequences people would have to fear from the prophet's hand if they rejected the call. The prophet's suffering in the service of the Word is no more and no less than his partnership with godly grace in its inherent abstinence from any force *(lā ikrāha fi 'l-dīn,* sura 2, 256) in the face of violent rejection of God's will by mankind.

The explains why Muslim thinkers interpret the fact that Jesus' prophetic path does not include a political and military dimension as a 'privation' forced on him by the Romans, and not the perfect and final form of prophetic existence and prophetic fate.[8] Kenneth Cragg, to whom we are indebted greatly with regard to the basic ideas of this essay, fittingly comments on this question by alluding to Paul's famous statement in 1 Cor 1.24: 'according to the description of the Koran God's power and wisdom are not seen in the crucifixion of His servant Jesus, but in his rescue from the same.'[9]

Christian thinking, which has been shaped by the teachings of the Gospel, will always consider it to be a burden and a tragedy, that violence and the resulting force are so firmly and unquestioningly anchored in the normative sources, in the exemplary biography of the prophet of Islam. The pattern of Muhammad's *sīra,* from the *hijra* as conscious emigration to the final glorious conquering of Mecca, are in conflict with the way of Jesus the Messiah: via the humiliation of the cross to the resurrection, whose visible power and glory will break out and shine fully only in the coming world. From the living origins onwards there remains a disparity between Jesus and Muhammad.

Koran and Muhammad Measured Against the Gospels

We will not engage here in the traditional controversial critique of the central topic of this centuries old controversy, such as corruption *(tahrīf)* or the reliability of biblical writing, displacement *(naskh)* of Jesus' authority through Muhammad, the way to the resurrection via the cross, and finally the question of the definitiveness of the prophet and the message—although these topics will require continued discussion. Instead we begin with the central doctrine of the Koran and Muhammad himself: the truth of God and humankind. Discussion of Christology and the doctrine of salvation has to take as its starting point the place where the deepest convictions of Islam and Christianity meet. There is a greater hope of being heard by our honestly enquiring Muslim discussion partners, if we place our questions regarding Muhammad's and therefore the Koran's message in a context that is their own. Maybe then Christian beliefs can be understood at the level that is so vital for understanding the deepest basic convictions of Islam from the point of view of the Christian faith.

The central concern of Islam is primarily to lead humankind on the right path before and to God. When we consider and describe the central concerns of the Gospel based on Islamic affirmations, we are not primarily defending Christianity. Rather, based on the relevant teachings of the Koran, we are concerned with the representation of God's sovereignty and 'justification' of humankind as described in Gospels.

With this approach we are closer to Paul's own thinking and method: 'for we do not preach ourselves but Jesus Christ the Lord, and ourselves as your slaves for the sake of Jesus' (2 Cor. 4.5). From the perspective of the Christian faith we therefore ask: Is the depiction of God's sovereignty in the Koran sufficiently complete, deep and consistent? Can the Koran's understanding of the definitiveness of a message that does not go beyond the law truly convince us? Does the person, who according to the Koran is on the right path, completely and truly experience salvation?

Beginning and ending our conversation about Muhammad and the Koran with God, we cannot go wrong. It will help if we begin with the Koran's belief in Muhammad as the 'seal of the prophets' and the Koran as the 'seal of prophecy'. According to the Koran prophecy reaches its pinnacle in guidance, teaching, directive, warning and exhortation. Understood in this way the relevance of the creator is largely limited to the educational. The Koran sees prophets as the tutors of humankind. God's tuition illuminates, informs, guides, encourages and warns. It disciplines, prevents and binds. The whole world is a school. God's guidance through the prophet, who is God's 'representative' (*khalīfa,* sura 2, 30; 38, 26), instructs people to live a righteous life. In this consists the duty and the dignity of the person correctly guided.

Creation, Revelation and Lawgiving in the Koran

However laudable and magnificent the Koran's statements about God, creation and the law may be, compared with the revelation in Jesus Christ they are incomplete and fragmentary. Is guidance from God truly all that humankind requires? Is there not to be a 'more'? Does the teaching of the law through prohibition and commandment fulfil the deepest intentions of the law and the law maker? Do the biblical prophets and Jesus not help us to discover dimensions in God's sovereignty, which go far beyond the categories of 'education' and 'commandment'?

Matthew 11, 9 speaks of 'more than a prophet'. This 'more' determines the whole of the New Testament. It is the 'more' of the messianic actions towards salvation. It is the 'more' of God's loving engagement, beyond the educational and disciplinary measures of the law, that has always been rejected by humankind and will always be rejected. It is the 'more' of the coming of God himself in flesh and in person, in suffering and in salvation—far beyond the spoken word.

Guidance (*hudā*) and the Law (*sharī'a*) do have their dignity and their benefit. However, the question is whether they provide a final and ultimately effective answer to mankind's continued half-heartedness, rebellion against the law, the questioning of the claims made by the law and the law maker, and, finally, pseudo-worship and a life altogether without God (*min dūni'llah* 2, 107). Despite God's guidance, threats and punishments the core sins continue: hardness of heart, hypocrisy, pride, the admiration of oneself. What can guidance achieve in the face of the depths of evil in humankind, and of those people who ignore the guidance and make themselves immune against it? Is prophecy the only, unique and final means to heal these wounds of humanity? Only those who underestimate the seriousness of mankind's situation and the extent of God's authority will simply answer this with yes. The Gospels teach us to understand that the creed *Allāhu Akbar* (cf. *Deus semper major; God is always greater*!) has to be understood more broadly and deeply. Such a deep understanding of the true greatness of God should therefore be the main and most stimulating topic of theological conversion between Christians and Muslims. The issue is nothing less than the core belief about God in our respective faiths!

In sura 6, 91 it is said of the Jews of Medina: 'They have never valued God as He should be valued'. The Gospel of Christ says that pointing to God's transcendence alone is insufficient to value God. The emphasis on God's transcendence must be balanced and extended by another: the emphasis on God's involvement visible in God's uniting of His own self with humankind, beings of endless yearning and magnanimity, but also of weakness and addiction to the power of sin.

Through Muhammad, the Koran also speaks strongly of God's closeness to humankind: 'We are closer to him than his jugular vein' (50:16). The Koran thinks about this closeness in conjunction with distance and aloofness, which are matched by the submission and compliance of creation. The Gospels, however, speak of yet another dimension of God's transcendence: of a dimension that is realized in God's love, of the connection of God with humankind solely because of grace. As a consequence of vigorously rejecting any idol worship as well as any connection of people with idols, is it possible that Islam has suffered a tragic loss as regard God's association with humankind through grace? May be this loss resulted precisely from the prophet's urgent and uncompromising call to denounce God's association with idols. Christians will ask whether God's transcendence is most truly retained and valued when we defend it not only against pagan idols, but also against all human sin. According to Christian understanding, *Allāhu Akbar* ('God is the greatest') is a cry of joy about God's gift of salvation from sin, the ultimate healing of sin's deadly sting. The cry is more than a mere triumph over polytheism.

There can be no doubt that Muslims and Christians are united in their faith in the one God. The Christian faith, however, says:

'there is an immediate and unlimited concern of God for the well being of humankind.' For God, creation also means risk, obligation, even God's free entering into a kind of liability.

Creation includes a plan from God: it is aimed at cooperation, at *islām*, at a submission of the created to God's call which is the creature's appropriate response. This intended free response of people in submission and devotion cannot be automatic, nor is it guaranteed. Puppets do not need prophets. That which God the creator has given through his guidance as His will for humankind must in turn also be wanted by humankind. But if that is how creation is enacted, does it then go hand in hand with a kind of 'immunity', with a kind of invulnerability and in this sense of 'exaltedness' of God vis-à-vis humanity caught up deeply in error and in sin, as the Koran does not tire to point out?

The same logic applies to God, the God of revelation and giver of the law, because guidance and law are at one with creation and express its goals. It can be said that there is, in principle, no divergence between Muhammad's and Jesus' teachings regarding God's involvement with human affairs. The debate centres only around its expression and extent. Do transcendence and God's greatness on the one hand and God's radical involvement with humankind on the other truly have to be seen as contrary and competing with each other? In other words, does God's way of looking after humankind have to be limited to the law, legal exhortation and judgement?

Christ's standard goes further, right up to the grace of self-giving in the incarnation and in suffering love. While the Koran does not entirely reject salvation as in consistent with God's sovereignty, for the Gospels life depends on God's free gift in Jesus Christ. Christians believe that our faith in the always greater God makes it impossible to reject this gift as too improbable. The Christian faith ascribes to God's greatness an ultimate freedom that has only one dimension—self-giving love. In the face of the Koran's claim that God was not allowed to and could not do more than send a prophet, the Christian belief proclaims God as the One who comes and gives himself in logos-love.

The image of God in the Koran and revealed by Muhammad leaves no room for a suffering God. Suffering is something put onto God externally, which would limit and disgrace him. God therefore has to be seen as free from suffering and incapable of pain. God's freedom from suffering understood in this way is something Christians can agree with. However, in the Christian proclamation of God as the Father of the Crucified One, a love is shown which is, completely sovereign and free and suffers purely for love. Seen in this way, in the light of the core meaning of creation and prophesy which has been shown to us by the core revelation of Jesus, God's sovereignty is questioned much more deeply shown by a faith, that however pious, denies God the use of all his sovereignty against evil through the all-conquering majesty of his descending love, right up to Gethsemane and Golgotha. From the Christian point of view the concern about God's immunity from risk, relationship and sharing in suffering is, paradoxically, the 'infidel' proclamation of a misunderstood divine unity.

In conclusion we should say: Muhammad is an outstanding religious and political founder-figure, who has led many people to God, but who has not recognized the love of God and the greatness of his call to humankind, which has been shown in the life, suffering, crucifixion and resurrection of Jesus Christ.

NOTES

1. See for example the notes of Abdullah Yusuf Ali in the widely accepted *The Holy Koran. Text, Translation and Commentary* (Lahore, 1934; countless reprints) on sura 61,6.
2. See also: Emilio Galiundo Aguilar, 'The Second International Muslim-Christian Congress of Cordoba (21–7 March 1977); in *Islamochristiana,* vol. 3, 1977, pp. 207–28. As to the reactions to the lecture of Prof. Ruiz, see *ibid.*, p. 214.
3. *Sirat Rasul Allah by Ibn Ishaq* [c.704–67] ed. Ibn Hisham [*d.* 833]. Trans. into English by A. Guillaume, Oxford: Oxford University Press, 1955.
4. Johan Bouman, *Dewr Koran und die Juden*, Darmstadt: Wissenschaftliche Buchgesellschaft, 1990, pp. 69–92, esp. pp. 85–6.
5. Quoted in K. Cragg, *Muhammad and the Christian: A Question of Response*, Maryknoll, NY: Orbis Books, 1984, p. 26.
6. Fazlur Rahman, *Islam*, Chicago and London University of Chicago Press, 1979, p. 16, also p. 21
7. Kenneth Cragg, *Muhammad*, p. 43.
8. *Vgl. Ahmad Schawqi, Al-Schawqiyyīt* (Cairo 1948), quoted in Cragg, *Muhammad*, p. 46
9. Cragg, *Muhammad*, p. 46.

4

The Ethical and Political Dimensions of Dialogue*

The Situation After 11 September 2001

There is an extensive body of writing on interreligious dialogue. Works in this field tend to consider two or more religions, such as Islam and Christianity, understanding them as more or less developed systems and coherent organisms. They tend also to assert the need for adherents of the various faiths to relate to one another on an individual or group basis. Without such dialogue, it is categorically stated, there can be no peace. There are also detailed discussions of themes such as 'characteristics of dialogue,' 'anxieties over dialogue,' 'developing a capacity for dialogue,' and 'dialogue and global ethics.' Such dialogue is then presented as firmly based in the authoritative texts of the different religions.

Here, however, we shall consciously be taking a different approach. By explaining certain basic concepts we shall first attempt to achieve some understanding of the multilayered realities that are today denoted by the terms 'Muslims' and 'Islam.' Then we shall describe certain underlying tendencies in the attitudes of non-Muslims to Muslims in Europe today. We shall consider what our responses should be in view of our religious and ethical responsibilities as Christians and citizens. These discussions are offered as a contribution toward the goal of the respectful and just coexistence of peoples and groups of different cultures and religions. Such coexistence assumes an active

---

* This essay was first published in *al-Ma'arif*, Lahore, ed. Kazi Javed, January-June 2012, pp. 21–41.

recognition of human rights and also requires a process of honest exchange over the religious experience and teachings of the specific groups involved. It is naturally also necessary to identify the criteria underlying our assessments and to consider openly the conditions without which it appears impossible to achieve coexistence with respect for difference. A 'political' dialogue of this kind—in the widest and best sense of the world—can also enable and inspire us, as believers committed to different religious traditions, to pursue a more focused religious and spiritual dialogue within which we can consider our common search for truth and meaning.

It is possible to define five broad types of response to the question of the connection between Islam and the epoch-making events of 11 September 2001, along with the countless other terrorist acts carried out in the name of Islam before and after this date:

1. Islam is to blame for everything. It is a global threat. The Muslims of Europe are a Trojan horse for worldwide Islamic power.
2. These events have really very little to do with Islam. The terrorists are essentially anti-American, anti-global and anti-Zionist; they are only secondarily Muslims. The role played by Islam is therefore at most only accidental and complementary.
3. Religious commitment is in itself a form of madness, disposing people to extremist ideologies and activities and so endangering the wider human race.
4. These terrorist acts are a perversion of Islam and the consequence of colonialism and continuing neo-colonialism. In contrast, true Islam is essentially a religion of peace.
5. Terrorist acts represent a massive exploitation of 'Islam' for political goals.

Islam is thus constantly mentioned as a central factor in these discussions. To be able to assess these arguments accurately, however, we must first clarify certain frequently used concepts. It is also worth identifying within these discussions levels and spheres that need to be considered separately. It seems essential to make such distinctions if we wish to speak adequately of the complex reality of 'Islam' and to avoid simplistic and misleading accounts of it.

Facets of the Reality of Islam Today

Islam and Islām

The Arabic verbal noun *islām* indicates the act of submission or surrender to the sovereignty of the one God and his will. A good illustration of this primary, underlying meaning of *islām* occurs at Q 2:130-32: 'Who but a fool would forsake the religion of Abraham? We have chosen him in this world and he will rank among the righteousness in the Hereafter. His Lord said to him, 'Submit yourself *[aslim]* to Me.' Abraham replied, 'I submit myself *[aslamtu]* to the Lord of the Universe,' and commanded his sons to do the same, as did Jacob: 'My sons, God has chosen your religion for you, so make sure you submit yourselves *[muslimīn]* to Him, to your dying moment.'

In response to these words of the Koran, Christians will ultimately want to ask: Who has lived out such *islām* more perfectly than the nonviolent, crucified Jesus of Nazareth?

The English word Islam, written with a capital I, however, normally indicates the religion of which the Koran is the foundational text and of which Muhammad is the prophet. If, for understandable reasons, public discussion is currently dominated by the political and militant aspects of Islam, we should on no account lose sight of the bigger picture of Islam, including its spiritual and cultural dimensions. We must not succumb to the temptation to see Muslims and Islam exclusively in the light of terrorist acts carried out in the name of Islam, or in the light of the segregated communities formed by some groups of Muslim immigrants and their mosques in many parts of Europe today. Especially in present circumstances we must constantly remind ourselves that Islam in its totality is a religious, cultural, and political phenomenon. Islam is one of the great religions of the world. For more than fourteen hundred years, the Islamic faith and the values anchored in it have enabled many millions of people to lead a life that is rich in human and religious terms and to find meaningful answers to life's deepest questions. The Islamic vision has had a formative cultural impact on whole historical eras and regions of the world; we are indebted to it for its decisive contributions to the history of human civilization.

Nearly all of us have probably already encountered these aspects of Islam, whether by visiting a museum of Islamic culture and art, by sightseeing in cities such as Istanbul, Cairo, Damascus, Isfahan, and Agra, or perhaps by experiencing a major Islamic festival in a society shaped by a Muslim majority population. At the normative level there are two constant factors: on the one hand, the teaching and life of Muhammad, condensed in the *sūra* (biography) of the Prophet, and, on the other hand, the foundational scripture of Islam, the Koran, which is regarded as the very Word of God. From the beginning onward, over the centuries, both Koran and *sūra* have been interpreted in a countless variety of ways and in a great range of historical and regional contexts, and both have been deeply imprinted on the faith and life of Muslims. Two periods are commonly distinguished within both the life of the prophet and the evolution of the 114 suras of the Koran: the Meccan (610-22) and the Medinan (622-32). These are both linked and at the same time separated by the *hijra,* or migration from Mecca to Medina, in 622. In Mecca the message is proclaimed, demanding that God alone should be worshipped and his righteous ways observed in Medina the revealed truth about the unity of God and humanity is put into practical effect by the Messenger of God, making use of all the diplomatic, political, and military means available to him. God's commandments are no longer merely to be proclaimed; rather, it is right to apply them and thus extend as far as possible the sphere of God's sovereignty, in the form of the Islamic order. However, a key question here is naturally: In what ways and by what means is this to take place? In actual historical practice, Islam has repeatedly formed compromises with (or, more neutrally, one might say has accommodated itself to) a great variety of local and regional cultures and their customs, legal traditions, sensitivities, and whole ways of life. So in the course of history there has developed a huge range of local and regional forms of Muslim life, and thus also constant accommodations regarding both the extent and the details of the application of. In the medieval sultanates of Asia and Africa whole areas of public law and politics were governed not by the *sharīā* but by local traditions. In other words, alongside the corpus of laws regarded as derived from divinely revealed commandments, the validity of local customary law was also recognized.

Surveying the contemporary Islamic world, we can, broadly speaking, identify three main streams: (1) a cultural, moderate Islam of the middle way; (2) an Islamist (or fundamentalist) Islam focused on the text; and (3) an Islam undergoing radical reinterpretation according to the spirit of the text.

Here we should also mention, albeit in passing and very selectively, some of further relevant distinctions within the total reality of Islam. The primary division is that between Sunnis and Shiites, but each of these two major traditions is further subdivided into many other groups. Within Shiite Islam, there are, for example, the Isma'ilis (who include the Khojas, led by the Aga Khan, and the Bohras), the Alawites of Syria, and the Alevites of Turkey. The four traditional Schools of Law within Sunni Islam have extensive territorial domains and attract strong group loyalty, but they do not in any way constitute religious sects. Indeed, in the very diversity of their legal rulings they demonstrate the capacity of Islamic law to adapt to diverse circumstances. Sufism, multiple and idiosyncratic as its forms are, is also not properly classified as a sect or sects.

Islamists and Islamism[1]

This is not the place to go into the similarities between Jewish, Christian, and Islamic fundamentalisms, all based on an ideology of scripture as all-sufficient guide in every situation of life, regardless of the historical context and original aims of the scripture in question. Nor is it possible here to consider other fundamentalisms derived from non-monotheistic traditions. The following features can, however, be identified as distinguishing features of contemporary Islamic fundamentalism.

First, the turn against secularism and the pursuit of human autonomy, which of course has been a feature of all religious societies in response to the impact of the modern, takes in this case the specific form of a longing to reestablish the Islamic state and to reintroduce the *shar'īa*—in other words, a longing to recreate 'Medina' today.

Second, as modern civilization has not emerged from of its own Islamic cultural tradition, the fundamentalist rejection of essential aspects of modern civilization as the character of an anti-

Western reaction (naturally varying in intensity). The fullest expression of this reaction is the conviction (programmatically spelt out by Hizb ut-Tahir, for example) that the whole 'West' should be considered by Muslims as *dār al-harb* (the sphere or house of war).

Third, it is of course the case that Islamism exists in a great variety of forms.

An important criterion for distinguishing between them lies in the different answers that would be given to the question of what are the legitimate, or indeed prescribed, methods to be adopted in seeking to establish the Islamic state, the rule of Sharia, and the Islamic order defined by it.

The long history and the recent, dramatic growth of Islamist movements and tendencies have been comprehensively treated elsewhere. Drawing on the pioneering work of Rotraud Wielandt, however, one fact should be particularly emphasized. Contemporary Islamist groups have no unified, organizational centre and often diverge significantly in the details of their respective visions. Equally, they are linked by a multiplicity of shared convictions and attitudes, at the core of which is an impulse toward a comprehensive ordering of political, social, and individual life based on the text of the Koran and the canonical traditions about the sayings and exemplary actions of the Prophet (Hadith). Within this vision:

- Islam = religion and state
- The Koran = the constitution of the Islamic state
- *sharī'a* = the perfect legal system, guaranteeing justice

Islamism's understanding of history involves both a utopianism oriented to the past and also a powerful overleaping of much within the gathered traditions of Islam. The ideals projected by Islamism thus in fact present a mixture of pre-modern values together with certain key concepts derived from Western modernity

What is the main cause of the popular appeal of Islamism? In the first instance one should certainly recognize the affinity between traditional Islam and fundamentalist perspectives (which of course does not imply that Islamism will necessarily determine the future of Islam as a whole). So what, then, are the links between traditional Islam and Islamist thought? Chief among them is a literalist approach to interpretation of the text of the Koran and the Hadith. To these foundational texts is ascribed a comprehensive, universal authority to legislate on all spheres of life. Furthermore, in its understanding of history, Islamist thought is focused on the past, with the Koran and the biography of the Prophet Muhammad holding a normative significance that scarcely can be overstated. This all means that at key points it is a relatively small step from medieval tradition to the central concepts of contemporary Islamism.

In seeking to explain the rise and the nature of Islamism we should also note the influence of wider developments running parallel to it. The rapid advance of urbanization and the associated weakening of rural patterns of life, together with increasing Westernization, have led to an identity crisis in Muslim societies. Local governments appear helpless in the face of mass poverty in slums and suburbs. There is also the impact of the policies of Western states which despise the principles of international law and pursue only extreme self-interest, leading to humiliation for Muslims, for example, in Palestine, Iraq, Afghanistan, and Saudi Arabia. Finally one should mention the phenomenal growth in the influence of the mass media—especially films, television, and Internet—on the thoughts, feelings, and imaginative world of the younger generations.

The remedy for all these ills, in the eyes of the Islamists, is Islam, conceived of as a perfect, sovereign system. They are convinced that Islam offers effective social justice as well as the opening up of a way out of the present uncertainty brought about by social and cultural change. Through the authority of the Koran and the Hadith, interpreted literally, and through the establishment of the Islamic state and the comprehensive introduction of the, Islam can also lead from individual confusion to collective clarity. Islamists are furthermore convinced that Muslims will once more have the power and authority that the divine plan for history has always intended for them. Islamist thinking thus looks forward to a much simpler moral reality, expressed internally by *sharī'a* punishments and externally by a clear picture of the enemy: non-Islam is the sphere of ignorance and lack of civilization, the realm of Satan himself. There thus results a new group identity coming to expression in a worldwide revival of *umma*-consciousness, as distinct from the definition of Muslim identity on the basis of race or nation.

Violence and Terrorism in the Name of Islam

The majority of Islamists follow the strategy of avoiding direct confrontation with the authorities within their own state or, at the international level, with the community of nations and its organizations and structures. Rather, they welcome the opportunities offered by democratic societies to reach their Islamist goals gradually. Their strategies look very different in the varying contexts around the countries and regions of the world.

Only relatively small groups have adopted violent tactics but, making skilful use of global networks and modern media, their actions have enabled them to make a disproportionate impact. The coverage that they receive in the media enables them easily to deflect public attention away from moderate Islam. They declare the political order maintained by their own state to be illegitimate and dictatorial and thus justify their use of terror as defensive *jihād,* which they argue that the Koran fully permits and indeed requires. For radical Islamists, the world of non-Islamist Islam belongs to the world of unbelief, which it is also right to seek to weaken and to overcome by means of military jihād so that, ultimately, true Islam and its *sharī'a* can be universally established.

The foregoing discussion demands that we ask what exactly is meant by the much discussed term *jihād*, especially as it is treated in the Koran.[2] While *jihād* certainly does not constitute a 'sixth pillar' of Islam (except in the view of Shiites and some Islamist movements), it is certainly a theme that cannot be overlooked in the Koran or in the life of the Prophet. According to the clear evidence of the text of the Koran, in more than 80 per cent of its occurrences the term *jihād* refers to engaging in warfare for the sake of the faith. Particular significance attaches to verses 5 and 29 of the ninth sura, traditionally considered the last sura to have been revealed and so also the sura in the light of which all earlier suras are to be interpreted. These verses call on the believers proactively to fight against polytheists and unbelieving Jews and Christians. If the polytheists do not surrender and become Muslims they are to be killed (9, 5), while Jews and Christians conquered by the Muslims are to be humbled and pay the *jizya* tax (9, 29).[3] The idea is present already in the Koran that those who die fighting for the faith—martyrs, in Islamic terminology—enter paradise directly (3, 195; 47, 4–6).

Islam is today widely presented by Muslims as having been a religion of peace from the very beginning. In support of this view, Muslims often claim that from earliest times the struggle against unbelievers was described as the 'lesser' *jihād*, while the struggle of every believer against the lower impulses of his or her own soul was known as the 'greater' *jihād*. Although it should be noted that this argument is based on a hadith that does not belong to the category of reliably transmitted traditions, one can nevertheless only welcome the fact that most contemporary Muslim authors insist that *jihād* must be understood in a purely defensive sense. This of course leaves us with the problem of how exactly to define what constitutes legitimate military 'defence,' a concept that can be very widely applied, as, for example, in the argument that the battles that led to the rapid expansion of the early Islamic empire in the Near East were defensive warfare necessary for the survival of the Muslim community. It is anyway necessary for Muslims to be able to give an explanation (which would need to be plausible in terms of Islamic scholarship) as to why they would not defend the idea of religious warfare, despite the fact that, as we have seen, many Koranic verses appear to speak a different language. It should certainly not be assumed that contemporary Muslims cannot engage critically with the problematic inheritance of traditional Islamic thought about *jihād*, in a broadly analogous manner to modern Christian reflection on religion and warfare. This, however, is scarcely likely to succeed without the development and dissemination of approaches to Koranic interpretation suited to the modern world.

There are Muslim groups today, scattered throughout the world, that do in fact pursue political goals by violent means. Their members do not see themselves primarily as politicians, soldiers, or terrorists, but as committed Muslims indeed they consider themselves the only true believers and they behave accordingly. Such groups sometimes develop a markedly sectarian and fanatical mentality, which can inspire members to sacrifice their very lives in pursuit of their goals.

Western Perspectives on Islam

The West's Share in Responsibility for the Present Situation

The cause of the hatred motivating members of such extreme

groups as were just now mentioned are as much political and social as religious. Many Islamic countries have to struggle with the fact that their development of new economic resources cannot keep up with the pace of population growth. They are plagued by mass poverty and other grave social ills, caused by repressive styles of government, poor economic management, and corrupt political leaders. It must, however, be acknowledged that such leaders are often supported and exploited by Western governments in pursuit of their own political and economic interests and that the world economic order is (to put it mildly) skewed in the interests of the Western industrial nations. Furthermore, the long-term effects of European colonialism can still be felt in many of these countries. Johannes Reissner comments:

> It is essentially European-Western policies which have made 'Islam' into a factor in international politics. The argument that these policies are responsible for the conditions throughout the Islamic world which promote political violence is not intended to promote the kinds of post-colonial self-laceration or 'Europe-bashing' which can serve to diminish the responsibility of the Muslim actors involved. It remains questionable whether. we are suffciently conscious of the fact that European-Western policies constitute an essential factor (if not necessarily the decisive factor) in the Islamic world over the last 200 years.[4]

A growth in such consciousness would certainly help Western societies and states to approach the problems of the Muslim world as problems for which we must all share responsibility.

The Complex Variety of Attitudes Toward Muslims and Islam

Here we limit our discussion to European societies which recognize that the new presence of Muslims and of Islam poses challenges to which they must respond. Two very different attitudes on the part of non-Muslims stand out.

1. There is, first, the attitude that in England has been strikingly described with the new expression 'Islamophobia' (by analogy with 'xenophobia'). Its constituent elements include ignorance, anxiety, and hatred, in various mixtures and to varying degrees of

intensity. People are anxious about Muslims, anxious about the rapid demographic growth of the Muslim population in their own country and throughout Europe, anxious above all because of the flood of violent images from Muslim societies. People ask themselves questions such as whether the Muslims among us have truly turned away from the ideal of political and military struggle against non-Muslims aimed at the establishment or expansion of Islamic rule; whether it is really true, as the representatives of some Muslim organizations claim, that Islam is fundamentally a religion of peace; or whether it is really true, as many scholars of religious studies constantly observe, that a theology of peace has been or is being developed by Muslims to replace the theory of 'holy war.' Such people also feel anxious when they hear of successful attempts to take over states of formerly secular constitution (such as Nigeria) through the gradual application of the *shariā*, so that the non-Muslims there ultimately become second-class citizens or are threatened with this prospect. They also feel anxious when certain groups that had previously appeared to be outsiders within our societies (in Berlin, Toronto, and parts of Great Britain, for example) make demands for the establishment and official recognition of the *shari'a* for Muslims in spheres such as family and inheritance law, or even speak of the ideal that in the foreseeable future there will be a geographical area (in Berlin, say) that will be entirely governed by Islam and its laws. And as people constantly hear reports of Islamic punishments or terrorist acts, and of things done in the name of Islam that seem unnecessarily harsh.

2. It is of course recognized that most Muslims and Muslim organizations in Europe are loyal to their respective states and will speak out on behalf of the existing social order. For example, the Islamic Charter, published in Germany in February 2002, among the other significant points which it makes, unambiguously recognizes the right of Muslims to change their religion. There are, however, understandable questions and anxieties, not least because of the lack of clarity and the many ambiguous passages in documents such as this Charter.[5]

There is a widespread anxiety that through the new presence of Islam in its midst, Europe will be overwhelmed by alien influences. It seems clear that certain Muslim groups and organizations constantly refuse to engage with any conviction in a process of integration with the societies in which they find themselves. This is a process in which it is hoped that both sides, Muslim and non-Muslim, should be prepared for change and reciprocal accommodation as a new pattern of social relationships emerges, and we see the development of both a Europe marked by a new religious and cultural diversity and also an Islam that has adapted to its Europe context.[6]

There are many people within the majority society of Germany, particularly sociologists, anthropologists, theologians, and those working in the media, who are strongly committed to the ideal of a multicultural society and passionately promote as generous an interpretation as possible of laws and regulations in the direction of the acceptance of multiculturalism; they would, for example, tend to sup[port the idea that Muslims should have their own legal structures, at least in the sphere of personal law. It is somewhat peculiar that many of those who advocate this approach also argue for a revision of current German legislation about state-Church relations in the direction of a clear separation between religion and state, in the style of French *laicité*.

In contrast, the main German churches argue for the secular, democratic constitution, which is upheld by the Basic Law (*Grundgesetz*) of the German Federal Republic, as providing both a basis and guidelines for a dialogue directed toward integration within a flourishing civil society. Civil society provides a place where trust and cooperation in daily life can grow. Policies concerned with integration must provide carefully for the possibility of an open dialogue.

In his Berlin Speech delivered on 12 May 2000, the president of the Federal Republic of Germany, Johannes Rau (1931-2006), made the following comments:

> Integration: this does not mean the loss of roots and identity through assimilation. It is the alternative to cultures living alongside each other without any relationship or possibility of unity. Integration: this is about the common values linking all people together with bonds which must constantly be renewed. Those who wish

> to live long-term in Germany have no need to deny their origins, but they must be prepared to work together with others to create an open society, in the spirit of the Fundamental Law [*Grundgesetz*]. Only then can we be and remain an open society, in which there are no islands detached from the mainland of social consensus.[7]

In a document published in September 2003, the Catholic bishops of Germany explicitly commit themselves to the secular legal order, which 'guarantees the fundamental legal equality of citizens of different religions,' in contrast to both the ordo of medieval Christendom and the classical *dhimma* system, which to varying degrees is still effective in virtually all parts of the Islamic world. The bishops add: 'As the legal foundation for the religious freedom of Christians, Muslims, other believers and non-believers, the Fundamental Law can only promote and protect religious harmony in the long term if the claims which it makes are universally recognized as valid.'[8] It therefore seems to me important that our Muslim partners should not interpret the emergence of the concept of secularism out of the Western Christian tradition as a development specific to 'the West,' in the sense that the significance of secularism is ultimately limited to the region in which it arose. Rather, it is valid to argue that the development of secularism had to take place once individual human rights began to be taken seriously and once, at the same time, there was in the religiously plural societies and states a desire for coexistence in justice and solidarity that are necessary for the protection of these rights and liberties.

It is in the end essential for all Muslims to grasp that the secular-democratic legal order is an absolute requirement if coexistence in diversity, solidarity, and justice is to be possible. For non-Muslims it is a further concern that their Muslim fellow citizens should be able both to recognize the framework of a secular, pluralist, democratic system and also to reconcile this position with the sources of their faith, the Koran and Sunna. They will thus be able to promote this kind of political order and its underlying values on the basis of their faith, in the context of modern patterns of society, which all around the world are marked by religious pluralism. A task for Christians in this context is to make it clear, through their involvement in state and society, as well as in their personal encounters with Muslims, that secularism does not mean at all godlessness or non-religion.

One could at this point consider further how far, within religiously and ethically motivated dialogue between Muslims and non-Muslims, a focus on the specific question of politics can serve the causes of peace and prosperity in our societies. In this regard, a modern, critical approach to the training of Muslims in theology and religious studies should give an important place to the further development of political dialogue, along with discussion of the vocational goals of journalists, teachers of religious education in schools, and those in academic careers.

As regards areas for dialogue, beyond the directly political themes it is also worth addressing the question of values and perhaps especially the urgent topic of human dignity. Dialogue on this subject can prompt Christians and Muslims to look into what constitutes this dignity; their resulting insights can motivate them to ask questions about the moral norms of their societies, or even the need for legal reform. The values that should be put into effect universally are referred to as 'human rights.' Here it would be possible, drawing on Muslim sources and Christian texts such as the documents of Vatican II, to produce a detailed map of the necessary fields for cooperation between Christians and Muslims, together with all people of good will. There is, for example, a particularly urgent need for dialogue in the sphere of bioethics.

The Need for Policies Informed by Intercultural and Interreligious Dialogue

A Worldwide Alliance Against Terrorism

In response to the unending succession of terrorist acts carried out by groups claiming to be motivated by Islam and the interests of Muslims, it is necessary to construct a worldwide alliance against terrorism. This alliance would need to transcend cultural differences, to be united around clear goals, and to be supported by the United Nations. Insofar as terrorism kills indiscriminately in order to achieve its goals, any Koranically informed Muslim really ought in principle to reject it. And indeed all Islamic scholars do reject such terrorism as disobedient to God's commandments.

But the question remains: What about the use and justification of terrorist methods in contexts of wars of liberation, whether fought by Muslims or by others (in, for example, Chechnya, the southern Philippines, Palestine, Kosovo, Norhern Ireland, the Basque Country)? At a summit held in Casablanca on 13 and 14 November 1994, the Islamic Conference (then consisting of fifty-one states and the PLO) made a clear distinction between Islamic freedom fighters *(mujāhidīn) and* extremist Islamic terrorists. But what if one is convinced that at present the whole Islamic world is enslaved and exploited and that it is therefore, in its entirely, involved in a war of liberation?

The rejection of terrorism by Muslim legal scholars mentioned above does not, however, in any sense imply that the same scholars would publicly argue in favour of the idea that Muslims should enter into a worldwide, Western led alliance to combat (Muslim) terrorism. The majority of Muslim believers and many, if not most, preachers still think in the dualist categories which divide the world into *dār al-harb* (the sphere of war) and *dār al-islam* (the sphere of Islam). Muslims in minority situations see their relationship to the existing majority in terms of a treaty. As long as they are not directly threatened by the majority and are able to carry out their essential religious duties, they are bound as if by a treaty to observe the laws of the land.

It should, however, be noted here that there is a reformist school of contemporary Islamic thought (notably exemplified by the Swiss Islamic scholar Tariq Ramadan (b.1962) which rejects the old division of the world into 'the sphere of Islam' and 'the sphere of war' and instead describes the whole world as 'the sphere of witness *(dār al-shahāda).*'[9] It remains to be seen whether the influence of this new discourse leads to the decisive and permanent supplanting of the classical patterns of thought and action with regard to the use and justification of force in pursuit of Islamic interests.

The Need for Radical Change on the Part of Non-Muslims Also

Terrorism will not be overcome until the powerful and wealthy nations and alliances start to demonstrate greater consistency in terms of political and socio-economic justice. We must recognize unconditionally that all people have the same dignity and the same fundamental rights. Through global networking, people living everywhere on the earth have become very close to one another, nations and regions of the world can therefore no longer seek to cut themselves off or hide from one another without causing tensions, grievances, and disasters. We must aim to live in a genuine spirit of global neighbourliness, thinking and acting in the consciousness that in the present world all people in reality are our neighbours. There is thus an urgent need for effective policies to achieve greater global justice, working on the basis of human rights principles. Consequently, the following steps must be taken. First, at the level of dealing with symptoms, punishment of acts of terrorist violence should be strictly limited to those who are genuinely guilty of them and not meted out in a wider and indiscriminate fashion. Second, the political duplicity of Western leaders who speak of democracy and human rights but at the same time support and even install undemocratic rulers in Islamic countries must come to an end. Double standards must be replaced by policies that genuinely seek justice for the countries of the Islamic world, most of whose governments and populations are today deeply disoriented. Sincere efforts must be made to convert attitudes (hearts) and ways of thought (minds) through dialogue between well-informed, thorough scholars on both sides. Such dialogues should not simply exclude Islamists; rather, there is a need here for careful discernment, in view of the particular circumstances. Christian dialogue partners who are theologically educated and who bring attitudes of critical openness should assist the Muslim scholars in their task of accomplishing the reform of Muslim societies in their own way; in other words, Muslims would be encouraged and enabled to engage constructively with the modern world which has been shaped by Europe and which has also so significantly impacted life in the Islamic world. The possibility should also be opened up to wider circles of Muslims, as has already begun at some German universities in collaboration with various Muslim institutions, to train as preachers, teachers of religion, and workers in the media.

To summarize, the debate over the possibility of Islam as a whole coming to a modified self-understanding seems to me out of date. For in historical reality there never has been an Islam as such—and there never will be—but rather the Islam of Muslims who themselves decide, according to their own convictions, what is and is not possible in their religion. The essential question for us all is therefore whether, in the future, Muslims as a faith community will adjust themselves to the wider world with its commitment to human rights as defined by the United Nations, or whether they will try to subordinate the world to Islam and the *umma*. Will they interpret their scripture and the story of their founder in a new way that enables them to adjust to the modern world with a sense of Islamic integrity? And then we also must ask whether we non-Muslim fellow citizens are ready to contribute what we can to help this happen.

It seems to me that Islam will be able to play its own distinctive part in the global concert of religions and cultures when and insofar as Muslims succeed in developing the will and the necessary structures. They will also need to reach among themselves widely held religious and ethical positions that (supported by the will of the majority) make it possible to enter fully into the structures of the world community even in societies and states where the majority of the citizens are Muslims. In other words, what is required is an effective renewal of *ijmā'* (consensus over religious and ethical questions). At an international Christian-Muslim seminar in the wake of 9/11, convened by the archbishop of Canterbury at Lambeth Palace in January 2002, Prince Hassan of Jordan (1947–) argued that unless Muslim leaders and religious scholars could succeed in speaking with one voice on significant religious and ethical questions, the Muslim community would not be able to survive as a genuinely religious and ethical body on the international stage.[10] In this regard non-Muslims can also make a contribution through good will, critical openness, and specific initiatives in dialogue.

As Muslims and Christians engage with one another in genuine dialogue, even if it is entirely focused on social or political themes, an underlying question keeps emerging. Bearing in mind their universal truth-claims, is it possible for Christianity and Islam to understand themselves in such a way that they can accept pluralist societies and the tolerance that these demand, and do so not reluctantly but with conviction and good conscience?

However, the discussion of this important issue would seem to the outside the scope of this essay.

NOTES

1. This section draws extensively on Rotraud Wielandt's essay: 'Zeitgenös-sisicher islamischer Fundamentalismus—Hintergründe

und Perspektiven,' in *Der neue Fundamentalismus: Rettung oder Gefahr für Gesellschaft und Religion?*, ed. K. Kienzler, Düsseldorf: Patmos Verlag, 1990, pp. 46–66.

2. Here we follow closely the discussion in Sekretariat der Deutschen Bischofskonferenz, ed., *Christen und Muslime in Deutschland* (Arbeitshilfen 172) (Bonn: Sekretariat der Deutschen Bischofskonferenz, 2003), sections 142–53.
3. A collection if the most significant interpretations of the complex verses by a variety of Muslim exegetes can be found in *Der Koran: Arabisch/Deutsch*, translation and commentary by Adel Theodor Khoury (Gutersloh:_ Chr. Kaiser/Gütersloher Verlagshaus, 2004 ff.). It should be noted that modernist Muslims interpret these verses differently from the classical tradition.
4. Johannes Reissner, 'Der Islam als Faktor der Weltpolitik,' in U. Anderson, ed., Der Islam in der Politik, Schwalbach: Wochenschau Verlag, 2004, pp. 49–50.
5. See Christian W. Troll, 'Germany's Islamic Charter, with a commentary by Christian Troll', *Encounter* (Rome) 290, December 2002.
6. By this we mean, without insisting on the term 'Euro-Islam', an Islam that participates in civil society and shares its values, a form of Islamic life and thought which 'is in harmony with the essential concepts of the culture of modernity (democracy, individual human rights, civil society and pluralism) and accepts the value system of pluralism' (Bassam Tibi, 'Der Euro-Islam als Brücke zwischen Islam und Europa,' http://print perlentaucher.de/artikel/3764.html).
7. Evangelischer Pressedienst (Hannover), Dokumentation 22a (22 May 2000).
8. Sekretariat der Deutschen Bischofskonferenz, ed., *Christen und Muslime in Deutschland*, sections 162–5.
9. Tariq Ramadan, *Western Muslims and the Future of Islam*, Oxford: Oxford University Press, 2004, pp. 63–5.
10. From notes taken by the author who was present at the seminar.

5

Dialogue and Religious Truth Claims in Christianity and Islam*

The Fundamental Question

There really is no such thing as a relationship of religions as such with each other, and therefore we also cannot speak of a relationship between religions, 'shaped by the spirit of dialogue'. It is living persons and human societies that meet and in more or less respectful ways interact with each other, speak with and about each other, and decide to come to terms with each other or not. Therein many factors play a decisive role, such as established cultural phenomena, customs, the legacy of historical circumstances, possible fear of the loss or diminishing of one's identity and similar concerns.

Have the specific characteristics of a given religion—including its doctrines—therefore nothing to do with how people as individuals and as groups interact with each other? This cannot be the case because many people—if not even most—in their ethos are stamped in different ways and to different degrees by the teaching and rituals of their religion, as well as by their respective holy texts and religious institutions. Accordingly the religious factor does play a role, even if only as one factor among the many others (such as economic, psychological or political factors) influencing one's thinking, feelings, dealings and behaviour towards others.

---

* This essay was first publsihed in *World Christianity in Muslim Encounter: Essays in Memory of David A. Kerr*, vol. 2, ed. Stephen R. Goodwin, pp. 43–53.

Thus it can be said that a certain tension exists between the truth claim of a religion on the one hand and tolerance, which generally today one implicitly must regard as a virtue, on the other. Here, in what is necessary brevity, we investigate the strands of tradition of Christianity and Islam and ask how in the light of their respective truth claim today they understand themselves and relate to each other. Do they know themselves to be called to respect one another and even to learn from one another?

One should address next the area of tension between the poles of truth claim and claim to tolerance in Christianity (and here especially in its contemporary Catholic variety, which, without any hubris, may be considered the most important worldwide and, in its self-understanding, the most tangible group among the Christians). Therefore, I attempt to present how this looks analogously in the realm of contemporary Islamic culture. Finally, I formulate some basic points of reference for a type of Christian-Muslim thinking and acting that would be marked by a spirit of dialogue.

The central question, then, is this: Can the religious worlds of Christianity and Islam, given their respective truth claim, come to an understanding whereby they not just hesitantly and reluctantly accept, as it were, a socio-political pluralism and its required tolerance, but also feel compelled both to recognize the Other in her/his Otherness, and to step in and act as effectively as possible for socially just treatment on their behalf? In other words, on the basis of their specific religious views and their religious conscience, can Christians and Muslims work together in partnership for the well-being of all? And further, can Christian and Islamic doctrines and ethics together develop or provide a value system, along with a corresponding moral conviction and motivation that in essence emerges for the purposes of thriving in pluralistic societies and for pluralistic co-operation at the global level?

Here the theme is being taken up on the normative level alone. However, from there we also want to anticipate discussion about concrete chances and difficulties, as well as the possibilities and barriers, of Christian-Muslim co-existence and co-operation in our pluralistic societies.

Truth Claims and Requirements for Tolerance from the Christian Perspective

The Church's Claim to Religious Truth and the Right of Each Person and Community to Social and Civic Freedom

Revealed Truth

According to the witness of the New Testament and established in the consciousness of the Church, the truth claim of the Church is to be sent (*gesandt zu sein*) in the completeness and power of Jesus Christ. The Church knows in faith that it is appointed to be a working sign, an instrument and bearer of the message of Truth, of a message that brings a saving reality to light that until then had remained hidden. This Truth wants to be understood as an event that seeks to press into the public forum and become accepted.

This leads to the following question: Can this Church, which believes itself to be a sign and instrument of the revealed Truth entrusted to her, in the view of competing truth claims in pluralistic societies, earnestly claim to tolerate non-Christian individuals and groups—that is, individuals and groups that (at least insofar as Islam is concerned) in similar ways lay claim to be a witness of Truth, which they hold to be universal and final? Beyond this, can this Church credibly call upon its members to respect these others as believing persons, to potentially learn from them, and even in certain ways, to need them?

Pluralism. Legal and Ethical-Religious Levels

Pluralist composition in different constellations is probably a defining feature of contemporary society/ies. The word 'pluralism' refers generally to a situation in which—in a person's thinking, their outlook and their explanation of reality—a great heterogeneous variety of systems co-exist, without one of these systems monopolizing or seeking to monopolize the others.

In what follows, we ask first how does the Church envisage co-existence in a pluralistic society on the level of justice, and how does it evaluate this? Is it acceptable for the Church to coexist with social groups that represent and promote beliefs about humanity and societal living that are contrary to its own truth claim? Correspondingly, in the context of a pluralistic society, is it essentially a matter of how the Church sees its relationship to the other religions on an ethical-religious level, especially her relationship to Islam, a religion whose conception of religious and ethical truth differs substantially from that of the Church, and which considers its own view of individual and community life to not only be final and conclusive, but also to be God-revealed Truth?

The traditional, normative Roman Catholic standpoint on the question of civic co-existence in situations of religious or ideological difference was characterized by persistent rejection of civic tolerance. The Church had always refused to accept tolerance as a *de-iure* principle. Wherever and in whatever measure she had practiced tolerance in the past, the Church had only expressed the readiness to accept tolerance as an objective evil—in the sense of a concession to the facts on the ground

The background of the earlier position of the Church was, according to the expression of Ernst-Wolfgang Böckenförde, 'the principle of the primacy of Truth over freedom, and with that the associated thesis, that no privilege for error over Truth can be permitted; or otherwise conceived, that belief constitutes a legal fiduciary relationship (*ein rechtsartiges Treueverhältnis*) whose violation is punishable as a 'breach of law'.[1] Crucial to the Church's teaching in this matter before the Second Vatican Council was that the issue was not about people as persons, but rather about 'Truth,' that is to say, about an abstract concept. In this view the human Person was in fact reduced to be an object of Truth. Justice was not afforded the human Person *per se*, that is to say, as an outflow of a Person as being, or for the protection of a Person's human freedom, but rather only in the capacity and insofar as the human Person is situated within the religious and moral Truth. So it was that in concrete life, where Truth does not exist as an essence by itself, but rather as the conviction of truth of real people, everything just lay in the hands of one authority that determined what Truth was. In practice only the Church and those who belonged to her were in possession of justice. In order to secure religious freedom for all citizens, the modern state had no other alternative but to oppose this theory of the Church and to prevent her from putting it into practice. In this way the modern state paved the way for religious freedom against the incipient resistance of the Church.

From 'Right of the Truth' to 'Right of the Person'

With the Declaration '*Dignitatis Humanae*' of the Second Vatican

Council the universal Church took the step from insisting on the 'Right of the Truth' to insisting on the 'Right of the Person'. It understood '*ius ad libertatem religiosam*' (right to religious freedom) as an unconditional and publicly acknowledged right of the human Person—whether alone or in relation to others, or, in other words, as freedom of private and public practice of religion corresponding to the requirements of one's personal conscience. This right stands independent of whether the religious conviction of a particular individual is objectively true or not, and is also independent of the way in which a truth of a particular individual is practiced.

So, for example, the Church no longer raised any claim to a privileged place in the state. Further, the Catholic State would no longer be seen as the most worthwhile ideal form of a political system. Certainly the Church did not intend that the disintegration of its privileged place should also mean the abandonment of its responsibility to the truth claim of the Catholic faith. She continues to teach the necessity of all persons to search for, recognize and preserve the Truth, especially in those matters that involve God and His Church. The Church does not contradict itself in this matter insofar as she distinguishes between the legal order on the one hand and the ethical obligations on the other. She speaks about the responsibility to seek and hold to the Truth, always in the sense of a moral duty, and leaves untouched the right to the freedom of religion that turns against every form of interference from either the side of individual persons or from the side of the political courts.

Clearly religious freedom in the context of the legal framework had to face up to the problem of its limits—limits that arose out of necessity to protect order and freedom in civil society. In practice, it is not easy to determine these restrains. The Declaration of the Second Vatican Council's '*Dignitatis Humanae*' refers here to the term 'public order': 'Individual men and social groups are bound by the moral law to have respect both for the rights of others and for their own duties toward others and for the common welfare of all' (Article 7). Accordingly this religious freedom in no way represents a general character for socially inhospitable and intolerant behaviour. It must be controlled through the principle of 'social compatibility', which fundamentally stands for legal freedom for all. Personal freedom finds its limits in the freedom of others.

Precisely at this point a wide field opens for dialogue between all groups that make up modern society at national and global levels and, not least, between Muslims and Christians. The goal of such dialogue should be the following: On the one side, to continually define the parameters of public order that emerge as inalienable for its implementation and sustainability, and which are supported and defended by all participants of the polity. On the other side, the concern is to motivate the various religious and ideological groupings that make up today's pluralistic society to actively support the 'common welfare' (understood in the comprehensive sense) of pluralistic civil society on the basis of their respective confessions

The catalogue of responsibilities for Christian-Muslim dialogue also includes the question, To what extent Christians and Muslims as citizens of a particular state—and as fellow-citizens worldwide— can reach an ethical consensus, the component of which is an undivided and binding ethos—ultimately for the whole of humanity.[2] Conversely, efforts in this regard should never overlook that a dialogue of this kind must necessarily stand in profound agreement with the religious truth that becomes known, is witnessed and is nourished through faith.

The Witness of the Church for the Truth: Her Proclamation Mandate and Inter-Religious Dialogue

We have already asked whether the Church as an instrument of one such Truth—as confessed in the faith, and as is revealed in Jesus Christ—can raise the honest claim to be open to other religions and their truth claim and message. How can the mission (*Sendung*) of the Church be understood in a way that goes hand in hand with that which we understand as dialogue, a dialogue that includes as its essential element candid openness to the faith convictions of the interlocutor? Now, it is the conviction of the Christian faith that the fulfillment of revelation is offered by the Church in Christ. However that conviction does not release her from the duty to listen and to learn. The Church as one whole must come to terms with the evident notion that He/she does not have a monopoly of possessing as it were the Truth; Rather He/she must be aware of the fact that it is rather the Truth that wants to take ever more possession of the believer, and this holds true for the community of believers, the Church, as well. Even if the dialogue partner may not yet have heard of this revelation, in which God disclosed himself through Jesus Christ, it is nevertheless possible, that she/he—through the power of the Spirit of Christ, which through the rays of Truth enlightens the hearts of all humanity[3]—is already captured by this Truth, which she/he still seeks. In reality Christians and others aspire to Truth through dialogue.[4]

Dialogue and proclamation thus represent *inter alia* two different measures to articulate and implement the sending of the Church in living. Other measures for instance, are the service of *Caritas* or engagement for justice. In these instances proclamation and dialogue have two different objectives. Although inter-religious dialogue should not be understood as a means to proclaim the Gospel, it nevertheless remains open to this possibility.[5]

Contemporary Islam, Societal Pluralism, Tolerance and Dialogue

The Umma and 'Others' in Classical Islamic Teaching

Islam's self-understanding as it finds expression in the Koran is not that of a new religion but rather as a cleansing and restoration of the unique monotheistic religion, which the Creator had foreseen for humanity from the beginning. The Muslim *umma* bears witness to this 'Islam' through its faith and through the Muslims' 'practice of good and the forbidding of evil' (*al amr bi 'l ma'rūf wa al-nahy min al-munkar,* cf. sura 3,110). In obedience to God and in brotherly equity the *umma* understands itself as the chosen carrier of all God's blessings, strengthened through His spirit. It will grow and have success (Cf. sura 8, 72.74; 23, 1; 33, 71; 49, 9–19; 58, 22).

Unbelievers constitute the counterpart to the *umma*. They are accused of the sin of equating other gods or things with Allah (*shirk*). These sins God can never forgive (sura 4, 48.116; 31, 13). Because the unbelievers have abjured the unity and oneness of God, they are threatened with damnation at the Last Judgement (39, 60.71–2). God will punish them both in this life and the next (33, 73; 48, 6). However, with an eye towards the possibility of conversion and salvation, the *umma* also can tolerate unbelievers (sura 9, 6). But fundamentally the relationship between the *umma* and the *mushrikūn* (polytheists that 'associate a partner with God') is once and for all decided: These are not only the enemy of God but also the worst opponents of believers (sura 5, 82; here the Jews are named apart from Christians).

In Islamic perspective, human history stretches from the creation to the end of time. At the beginning the whole human race lived in unbroken unity. Their *fitra* (or nature) enables human beings to acknowledge and serve the one God. Thus, the intention and goal of the prophetic proclamation is to preserve this unbroken unity.

But precisely this proclamation of one belief and of one cult of worship also provides the cause for the division of humanity into believers and unbelievers. The justice of God, which takes place in history, determines a double fate that corresponds to this division: Believers are saved and rewarded, and unbelievers are punished with humiliation and destruction. This division of humanity into two halves runs throughout history and is based both on the free decisions made by people and at the same time on divine righteousness. On the one hand men and women can, by means of their natural gifts, understand and accept the word of revelation and on the other hand. God's power preserves their works from the invasion of chaos that would result from idol worship. What begins in unity ends in the division of belief and unbelief, salvation and damnation, reward and punishment, Paradise and Hell.

Contemporary Interpretations of the Koran-Determined Relationship of the Ummah to 'Others'

The Integralist, Monolithic Version

To this point our discussion has movec forward on this basis: The message of the Koran as it unfolded in the world of the Prophet of Islam in the seventh century, delivered a divine judgement and also demanded that first the tribes of Arabia and then the whole world should recognize radical monotheism and Muhammad as its last prophet, 'the seal of the prophets.' As long as it remains true to itself, Islam, in the shape of the *umma*, gives testimony to the unity of God and the mission of Muhammad, and puts all humanity before God's judgement. This implies the divine command effectively to render and position God's judgement and challenge into today's context. But what does 'effectively render' mean? One possible answer is to hold to hold firmly to the classical

Islamic sociopolitical infrastructure, as this was realized in Mecca and Medina, and to strive after this ideal, at least as a goal to aim for, in every new situation over the centuries.

An answer of this sort denies any positive value to historical change. Developments and new insights do not really exist, according to this view. In this view 'progress' is reached only through revision of the deviations and errors of the last centuries. Foundation and criterion for all subsequent times is the unadulterated law-giving phase of Islam, shaped by the Koran, and which according to Sunni understanding, also includes the epoch of the four Caliphs (*al-rāshidūn*) that correctly led Islam. This worldview implies a literalist and unhistorical or timeless 'reading' of the Koran. In regard to the revelation of the Koran and the foundational model of the Meccan and Medinan periods, this reading rejects, on the one side, any distinction of a metaphysical and ethical-moral level and, on the other side, a legislative or judicial level.

Consequently, those religious and political thinkers that privilege this fundamentalist approach to Islam and its foundational period call for a ceaseless effort towards the realization of a universal Islamic state that should be organized according to the model of Medina.[6] According to Hasan al-Banna (1906–49), founder of the Muslim Brotherhood (*al-ikhwān al-muslimūn*) and representative of the fundamentalist understanding of the Koran and Islam, such a conviction will set everything into motion in order to establish Islamic sovereignty in the whole world. As he would have it, this goal will be reached through the conquest of both political and military mobilization of the whole *umma*.[7] With disarming openness al-Banna defended *jihād* (holy war), the goal of which is, according to his interpretation of the law, 'to slay unbelievers' and 'to destroy their Temple and to shatter their gods'[8] Al-Banna understands this to mean even 'the duty to fight against the People of the Book', which in reality means to take action against everyone who does not accept Islam.[9] Al-Banna wrote in Egypt in the 1920s and 1930s and in a predominantly Muslim society that suffered under colonial bondage. Even to this day his ideas have great powers of attraction. But also many non-Islamist, traditional theologians and legal experts, appear not to accept any real alternative to the ideal of an Islamic, theocratic regime. This would be accomplished through Muslims 'who have the power in the lands in which they live'.[10] As for Muslims that live in non-Muslim lands, 'they can only make a sincere and earnest attempt, within the limits of possibility, to stir the ruling class or influential groups to absorb into their political system as much Islamic teaching as possible.'[11]

Interpretation in Light of the Different Levels of the Koran

However, other Muslim scholars, such as for instance Fazlur Rahman (1919-88) from Pakistan, Mohamed Talbi (1921-) from Tunis and Syed Vahiduddin (1909-98) from India, appeal with various accents for a fully other kind of approach.

Their views can generally be summarized as follows: Many injunctions of the Koran refer to a specific historical situation that is not repeatable. Thus political means, which in that situation were demanded, today may no longer be so, or at least not in the same way. Rather, one has 'to distinguish their [i.e. the Statements of the Koran's] moral value/content and their purely legal aspect. The moral content has a permanent feature whereas the legislative infrastructure must not fail to adapt itself to circumstances which were not foreseen'.[12] Cases in point would be what the Koran prescribes with regard to dealing with military opposition and slavery, with the idolaters, Bedouins and Jews, then, in their specific historical conditioning.[13] Thus according to Syed Vahiduddin, 'moral and spiritual values and principles claim universal validity and demand compliance without any compromise, social practices with their implicit norms and mores are relative and time-bound.'[14] Islamic teaching concerning the relationship of Muslims with non-Muslims in the opinion of Vahiduddin, does not have to be read narrowly from the limited context of the life of the Prophet in Mecca and Medina, but should be developed from the framework of the message of the Koran and from its general moral principles.[15]

The *umma* will always remain entrusted (*amāna*) with the precious word of God, that makes its appeal on all people and on the whole creation (cf. sura 7, 158). The *umma* is commissioned to invite (*da'wa*[16]) everyone to the building of a single community of brothers that 'loves God with one's whole heart, and each other in God'.[17] It is an invitation to the purity of monotheism and to practical brotherhood in justice, an invitation to true humility under the divine law. The catholicity of this consummate community is still a utopia. For its realization it needs the credible witness of Muslims, an exemplary belief, and a contagious practice of faith. Doesn't the Koran itself say, '. Had Allah willed He could have made you one community. But that he may try you by that which he hath given you (He has made you as you are). So vice one with another in good works.' (sura 5, 48, cf. 11, 118; 16, 93; also 2, 104; 2, 143). The challenging invitation, which goes out from the *umma muslima* to humanity, presupposes the freedom of the individual to accept or refuse the invitation.

But Vahiduddin continues still further: Besides the possibility to join the Islamic *umma* in its extant, concretely institutional form, there are other ways to positively respond to the encounter with Islam, because Islam can be reached in different dimensions. For Islam in its original and universal dimension, *islām* as an attitude of devotion to the absolute God in a spirit of brotherhood, can be recognized in the most diverse symbols and patterns of faith and practice, in all religions and ideologies, past and present. Conversely, the original and universal Islam may be recognized in all religions and ideologies of the past and present as the profile of commitment in brotherhood to the absolute God, and in the various symbols and models of belief and action. Ultimately every response to the call of the 'hidden mystery', the source of all existence, is a personal outworking of Islam. When so viewed, the religious harmony of Islam (which is supported by the Islamic spirit) and the understanding of Islam (in all its observable and hidden dimensions) would become operant as an all-penetrating process that since the very beginning was and now is called upon to bestow the expression and definitive imprint to the reality of Islam

Vahiduddin appeals here for a 'Koranic humanism', which 'is sustained from the vision of man as *khalīfa* on earth, the vicegerent who has to carry out the will of God and yet who is given freedom enough to deviate from His injunctions'.[18] God could have prevented any free decision against the original unity by an individual or group. But he created women and men free so that differences in belief and behaviour could arise. Hence it ultimately does not depend on conformity to a given system of forms and symbols, but rather on competing in doing good (cf. sura 5, 48). In other words, all depends on whatever measure a person contributes to that which the Koran calls *ma'ma'rūf* (right conduct), and avoids that which is signified as *munkar* (reprehensible; cf. sura 3, 110.114 and parallels).[19]

Concluding Remarks: the Imperative of the Koran Today

It would be a fundamental misunderstanding of Islamic thinking, were one to adopt the commonly given assumptions of the tendency to withdraw from the legislative and political world into a purely private and non-political/religious sphere. Contemporary Muslims like Mohamed Talbi, Syed Vahiduddin and many others[20] represent the completely opposite conception, that, if the Muslim *umma* wants to enter the constantly changing *arena* of social legislation and political influence, it cannot be interested in developing its own special world. Rather, together with others, it should participate in fostering the common welfare with the aim to reach maximum justice worldwide. In our pluralistic societies it is essential to work together with others on the basis of mutual respect and real equality. The spiritual mindset that is necessary from Muslim believers as witness of God in a pluralistic world may be seen as this: to listen to God, who is near to every person. It is a mindset of respect in regard to the deepest obligations of the other—and it is a manner of agreeing with all who seek and strive sincerely for what is true, good and beautiful.

It should thus be clear from Christian and Muslim belief that there are established theological grounds for fruitful and invigorating coexistence and cooperation between Christians and Muslims in secular (in both the sense of pluralistically established as well as maintaining the separation of state and religion) democratic societies. However, the urgent question is this: Will such a way of thinking as we have here presented prevail on a broad basis in the majority of Muslim societies in the foreseeable future? In our reciprocally interdependent, inter-connected world, there hardly would seem to be a genuinely acceptable alternative.

NOTES

1. In *Second Ecumenical Vatican Council, Declaration Regarding Religious Freedom*. With by Ernst-Wolfgang Böckenförde (Munster 1968), p. 6. (Cf. also Christian W. Troll, 'Remarks to the contents and meaning of the Declaration of the Second Vatican Council about religious freedom *'Dignitatis Humanae'*, in *Islam und Europa als Thema der Deutsch-Türkischen Zusammenarbeit, III. Religion und Tradition:*

Determinanten moderner Zivilgesellschaften? (Ankara: German Embassy in Ankara, 2004), pp. 36–42.

2. Cf. Hans Küng, *Global Responsibility: In Search of a New World Ethic*, London, 1991, pp. 27ff.
3. Second Vatican Council, *Declaration of the Relationship of the Church to Non-Christian Readings* (*Nostra Aetate*), Article 2.
4. Secretariatus Pro Non-Christianis, 'Dialogue and mission. Thoughts and instructions over the position of the Church to the adherents of other religions', in *L'Osservatore Romano* (A weekly in the German language), vol. 14, nos. 34–5, 1984, 10f., here p. 10. See also: *Päpstlicher Rat für den Interreligösen Dialog/Kongregation für die Evangelisierung der Völker; Dialog und Verkündigung*, 19 May 1991. Published by the Secretariat of the German Bishops' Conference, nos. 49–50, 80.
5. Secretariatus Pro Non-Christianis, *Dialogue and Mission*, no. 77.
6. 'Model (paradigm) from Medina': The specific religious-political form that Islam took on in the first centuries after the emigration (622) in Medina.
7. Syed Vahiduddin, ed. Christian W. Troll, *Islam in India. Studies and Commentaries*, vol. 3: *Islamic Experience in Contemporary Thought*, Delhi: Chanakya Publications, 1986, p. 236
8. Cited by Syed Vahiduddin p. 237, n. 4. Cf. *Five Tracts of Hasan al-Banna (1906–1949). A Selection from the Madshmu'a Rasa'il al-Imam al Shahid Hasan al-Banna*, tr. Charles Wendell, Berkeley, 1978, pp. 80–4, 134–5.
9. *Five Tracts*, pp. 80–4, 134–5.
10. Mohammad Manzoor Nomani, *Islamic Faith and Practice*, trans. Md. Asif Kidwai, Lucknow, 1973, p. 140.
11. Nomani, p. 140.
12. Quoted in the Editor's Introduction to Syed Vahiduddin, ed. Christian W. Troll, *Islam in India: Studies and Commentaries*, vol. 3: *Islamic Experience in Contemporary Thought*, Delhi: Chanakya Publications, 1986, p. 15.
13. *Ibid.*, (paraphrased).
14. *Ibid.*
15. *Ibid.*, 10ff. (paraphrased).
16. Literarally, 'invitation'. Today: *terminus technicus* for 'Islamic mission'.
17. Ibn Hisham, *Sirat an-nabī*, Cairo, no date, 348; Cf. Koran 3:104.
18. Vahiduddin, pp. 141–2.
19. Sure 3:17; Cf. Z.H. Faruqi (note 4), passim.
20. For more information about contemporary thinkers of this direction, see in Christian W. Troll, 'Progressive Thinking in Contemporary

Islam', in *Encounter: Documents for Christian-Muslim Understanding* (PISAI, Roma, N. 317-18), January-February 2007), pp. 27ff. Reprint in: *SALAAM*, Quarterly to Promote Understanding, vol. 28, no. 3, New Delhi, July 2007, pp. 97–121. Arabic rendering of this text by Dr. Hamid Fadlalla: 'Al-fikr al-taqaddumi fī'l-Islām al-mu'Êsir: nadara Naqdiyya', in *Al-Mustaqbal al-Arabi*, Beirut, 340, June 2007, pp. 6–23.

6

Catholic Teachings on Interreligious Dialogue: Analysis of Some Recent Official Documents, with Special Reference to Christian-Muslim Relations

Introductory Remarks

The Contribution has a precise and restricted scope. It wants to introduce *official Roman Catholic teachings on interreligious dialogue and its development,* with special reference to Christian-Muslim dialogue.[1]

We shall first of all analyse some relevant documents of the Holy See, edited by Francesco Gioia: *Interreligious Dialogue. The Official Teaching of the Catholic Church (1963-1995).*[2] Secondly, we shall look, by way of example, at the relevant official teaching in the Arab Near East and in the Maghreb.[3] Thus we hope to show how, on the level of patriarchal and Episcopal teaching, the Catholic vision promoted by the Second Vatican Council and the Holy See has been applied, modified and developed in regions, marked by different geographical, socio-political and cultural contexts. The magisterium of the Church comprises besides the teaching of the bishops of Rome that of other bishops and their regional and national conferences.[4]

Throughout this discussion it will be important to remember that the official documents of the Church are always, in one way

---

* This essay was first published in *Muslim-Christian Perceptions of Dialogue Today: Experience and Expectations*, ed. Jacques Waardenburg, Leuven, Paris: Sterling; Virginia: Peeters, 2000, pp. 233–75.

or the other, the fruit of a process of consultation among fellow bishops or/and of relevant commissions of experts and single specialists in the field. In this way, the official teaching mirrors, albeit in varying degrees, the thinking of wider circles in the Catholic Church. At the same time the official teaching stimulates and directs the Church's thought and action, not least that of those specifically concerned with interreligious relations and dialogue.

The present essay presents some significant and distinctive teachings of these documents on the theme of Christian-Muslim encounter and dialogue and in each case pays attention to significant developments. However, before focusing on the specific nature of Christian-Muslim relations, it would seem to be useful and even necessary to introduce succinctly to the theological foundations of interreligious dialogue as such.[5] Chronologically, statements on interreligious dialogue in general and its theological foundations preceded those on Christian-Muslim relations. Furthermore, in the body of teaching on Christian-Muslim relations the underlying theological vision of dialogue is present throughout

We shall first ask then, in which way the overall faith vision of the Church impels her to dialogue, what are the meaning and intentions of dialogue and what its requirements, forms and modes.

1. Dialogue According to Vatican II and the Holy See

1.1. Intrerreligious Dialogue in General

1.1.1. The Encyclical Letter Ecclesiam Suam (ES)

Ecclesiam Suam, Pope Paul VI's (1897–1978), Pope from 1963) programmatic Encyclical Letter, was published on 6 August 1964, between the second and third sessions of the Second Vatican Council. At that point in time those Vatican II documents that were to deal with interreligious dialogue (NA; GS) were still being discussed. The Secretariat for Non-Christians had been created by the Pope on 17 May 1964, that is less than three months before the date of the publication of the Encyclical.

Ecclesian Suam clearly marked the 'entry of dialogue in general into the new perspective inherent in the Church's programme of renewal and the opening up to the world that the Council desired.

The term 'dialogue' itself appeared here for the first time in an official Church document'.[6]

In the Pope's own words, the encyclical is concerned with the 'problem of dialogue [colloquium] between the Church and the modern world' (ES 14). Dialogue, as the Pope sees it, is to be conceived as 'a method of accomplishing the apostolic mission. It is an example of the art of spiritual communication' (ES 81). The Church, says the Pope, must be 'ever ready to carry on the dialogue with all men of good will, within and without her own sphere' (ES 93).

The encyclical continues with an outline of a number of concentric circles 'around the central point in which God has placed us (the Church]' (ES *96).* Paul VI makes a distinction between four concentric circles, beginning with the most remote (all humanity and the universe), then proceeding through a second (the faithful of other religions) and a third (other Christians), and ending with the innermost circle (dialogue within the Catholic Church itself).

The second circle 'is made up of those who above all adore the one, Supreme God whom we too adore', including not only the Jews and Muslims but also 'the followers of the great Afro-Asian religions. indeed, honesty compels us to declare openly our conviction', the pope continues, 'that there is but one true religion, the religion of Christianity. It is our hope that all who seek God and adore Him may come to acknowledge its truth' (ES 107=G 133).[7]

Nevertheless, 'we do. recognize and respect the moral and spiritual values of the various non-Christian religions and we desire to join with them in promoting and defending common ideals of religious liberty, human brotherhood, good culture, social welfare and civil order' (ES 108).

Clearly, the theological evaluation of other religions as well as the area open to dialogue, in *Ecclesiam Suam* are real though quite restricted. The role and place of dialogue in the Church's overall mission are not otherwise developed or specified.

1.1.2. The Documents of Vatican II

The Second Vatican Council (1962-5) built upon the breakthrough made by Paul VI in this encyclical. It was indeed the first one in the Church's long conciliar history to speak positively of other religions of humankind.[8] In the first place, the documents of Vatican II exhibit a will to recognize 'those elements of truth and grace which are found among peoples' (AG 9; see also AG 3). These elements are seen as 'a ray of that truth which enlightens all men' (NA 2).

Second, the Council showed increasing awareness of the universal influence of the Holy Spirit well beyond the frontiers of Christianity, affecting indeed the whole universe. The Spirit of God—who is also the Spirit of Christ—fills the universe (GS 11). *Ad Gentes,* the 'Decree of the Church's Missionary Activity' and *Gaudium et Spes,* the 'Pastoral Constitution on the Church in the Modern World'— both products of the last session of the Council (1965)—refer explicitly to this universal presence of the Spirit in space and time: 'Without doubt, the Holy Spirit was at work in the world before Christ was glorified' (AG 4). He is also there in the present-day world in the aspirations of all men and women for a better quality of life (GS 38), for a social order more worthy of humanity (GS 24) and for universal fellowship (GS 39).

The Holy Spirit's enduring influence keeps alive in humanity the question of people's religious destiny (GS 41), offering men and women the light and strength to confront it (GS 10). They have been bought by Christ and have become new creatures in the Holy Spirit (GS 37). 'For since Christ died for all, and since all human beings are in fact called to one and the same destiny, which is divine, we must hold that the Holy Spirit offers to all the possibility of being made partners, in a way known to God, in the paschal mystery' (GS 22). Thus revitalized and brought together in the Spirit of the risen Christ, humanity advances toward the consummation of human history (GS 45)—with a living hope that is the gift of the Spirit (GS 93).

What has been stated here is the basis of any interreligious dialogue in the documents of Vatican II. The Council asks the members of the Church to initiate this dialogue. We already find an exhortation of this kind in *Nostra Aetate* (1965). The Church urges her children 'to enter with prudence and charity into discussion and collaboration with members of other religions' and exhorts them 'while witnessing to their own faith and way of life' to 'acknowledge, preserve and encourage the spiritual and moral truths found among non-Christians, also their social life and culture' (NA 2).

Ad Gentes sees this approach exemplified in the life of Jesus as described in the Gospels:

> Just as Christ penetrated to the hearts of men and by a truly human dialogue led them to the divine light, so too his disciples, profoundly pervaded by the Spirit of Christ, should know and converse with those among whom they live, that through sincere and patient dialogue they themselves might learn of the riches which a generous God has distributed among the nations. They must at the same time endeavour to illuminate these riches with the light of the Gospel, set them free, and bring them once more under the dominion of God the Saviour. (AG 11; see also DM 15 and DP 85)

The 'Magna Charta' of dialogue according to Vatican II is to be found in GS 92 where the Council recalls, but in a reverse order, the four concentric circles already described in the Encyclical *Ecclesiam Suam*. In regard to the believers of other religious traditions, the text expresses the 'hope that sincere dialogue will spur us all on to receive the impulses of the Spirit with fidelity and to act upon them with alacrity.'

> For our part, our eagerness for such dialogue, conducted with appropriate discretion and leading to truth by way of love alone, excludes nobody; we would like to include those who respect outstanding human values without realizing who the author of those values is, as well as those who oppose the Church and persecute it in various ways. Since God the Father is the beginning and the end of all things, we are all called to be brothers; we ought to work together without violence and without deceit to build up the world in a spirit of genuine peace. (GS 92)

Never had any Catholic ecumenical council declared so unambiguously the belief that the Spirit (i.e. Holy Spirit) is at work in all religious traditions and that therefore all, equally, are called to be attentive and obedient to Him and His inspirations.

1.1.3. Emphases After Vatican II

The magisterium of John Paul II (1920–; Pope from 1978) has significantly developed the theme of the universal presence of the

Holy Spirit, a faith vision that underlies, as well as imperiously demands, dialogical openness, respect, a learning attitude and also critical discernment.[9]

In *Redemptoris Missio* (1990) (Encyclical Letter on the Permanent Validity of the Church's Missionary Mandate)—John Paul II provides a key to understanding the present-day magisterium's vision of interreligious dialogue:

> I have repeatedly called this fact to mind, and it has guided me in my meetings with a wide variety of peoples. The Church's relationship with other religions is dictated by a two-fold respect: 'Respect for man in his quest for answers to the deepest questions of his life, and respect for the action of the Spirit in man.'
>
> ... the universal activity of the Spirit is not to be separated from his particular activity within the Body of Christ, which is the Church. Indeed, it is always the Spirit who is at work, both when He gives life to the Church and impels her to proclaim Christ, and when he implants and develops the gifts in all individuals and peoples, guiding the Church to discover these gifts, to foster them and to receive them through dialogue. Every form of the Spirit's presence is to be welcomed with respect and gratitude, but the discernment of His presence is the responsibility of the Church, to which Christ gave his Spirit in order to guide her to the truth (cf. John 16:13). (RM 29 = G 177)

One important element of this vision of the active presence of Holy Spirit outside the visible Church is the teaching that interreligious dialogue consists of giving and receiving. The Christian has something to gain from dialogue and will in fact derive a dual advantage from it. On the one hand, there will be an enrichment of the Christian's own faith; through the experience and the witness of the other person the Christian will be able to discern more profoundly certain dimensions of the divine mystery that he or she might not see so clearly and that perhaps do not stand out so clearly in the Christian tradition. On the other hand, he or she will receive a purification of faith. The shock of encounter will often force the Christian to question something, whether it is a matter of revising certain gratuitous assumptions or of destroying deeprooted prejudices or even of revising too narrow notions or viewpoints. The benefits of dialogue also constitute a challenge for the Christian.

1.1.4. Meaning and Goals of Dialogue

Vatican II failed to indicate the place of interreligious dialogue in the Church's mission *(Sendung)*. In 1984 the document *The Attitude of the Catholic Church to Believers of Other religions: Reflections and Guidelines for Dialogue and Mission* was published by the then Secretariat for Non-Christians, in 1990 renamed 'Pontifical Council for Interreligious Dialogue'. It showed that the question of how to view the relationship between mission—and more specifically of one of the mission's essential elements, proclamation of the Gospel—on the one hand and of dialogue on the other, was much discussed and received a quite different answer in the post-Vatican II Church. This document was the result of a long process of worldwide consultation among bishops, theologians and practitioners of interreligious dialogue.

The mission of the Church 'is one but it is carried out in different ways depending on the conditions in which the mission is undertaken' (DM 11). Interreligious dialogue is one of the principal forms making up the complex reality that is the Church's mission of evangelization: presence and witness of life, involvement in service to humanity, liturgical life, prayer and contemplation, interreligious dialogue, preaching or proclamation, catechesis.

Whereas dialogue stands for communication, for an attitude of respect and friendship and can have many forms and expressions, proclamation in contrast, is an invitation to faith in Jesus Christ and to entry into the community of the believers which is the Church. Accordingly, dialogue and proclamation represent different approaches in the one evangelizing mission of the Church. They have distinct aims. Dialogue does not serve as a mere means to an ulterior goal, and were it to advance the 'conversion' of one partner to the other's religious tradition: 'Dialogue is the integrating element of mission in the sense that all missionary activity is brought about in respect for the person and culture and it can be a specific activity both where proclamation is possible and necessary, and where it is impossible'.[10] By its very nature dialogue tends to a more profound conversion of the one and the other to God. In the last analysis, its proper end is the common conversion of Christians and of members of other religious traditions to the same God. Interreligious dialogue viewed in this perspective is part of a process of reciprocal challenge and mutual transformation.

In the light of this teaching John Paul II interpreted the Day of interreligious Prayer and Fasting for Peace at Assisi on 27 October 1986 'as an anticipation of what God would like the developing history of humanity to be: a fraternal journey in which we accompany one another towards the transcendent goal which he sets for us. an awareness of the fact that by ourselves alone we will fail' (G 546).[11]

1.1.5. Requirements of Dialogue

If dialogue for the Catholic believer essentially is listening to the Holy Spirit, the attitude of a person engaging in dialogue must be consistent with this. With a clear consciousness of past failures in dialogue each partner must enter into the religious experience and overall vision of the other party, trying to understand it from within. This effort represents an arduous but necessary preparation for a sincere meeting and true exchange between individuals or communities. The Document *Dialogue and Proclamation: Reflections and Orientations on Interreligious Dialogue and the Proclamation of the Gospel of Jesus Christ* of 1991 (DP 47-54) enumerates the dispositions for interreligious dialogue (e.g., 'balance', 'religious conviction', 'openness to truth') and the obstacles to it (e.g. 'insufficient grounding in one's own faith', 'cultural differences and socio-political factors', 'self-sufficiency', 'suspicions about the other's motives', 'polemical spirit', 'intolerance, religious indifference') They would seem to refer to individuals and communities.[12]

1.2. Pope John Paul II: Aspects of Christian-Muslim Dialogue

1.2.1. Theological Foundations

Nostra Aetate (1965) in section 3 had highlighted some important aspects of the Muslim's response to God that strike a chord in the heart of the Christian. John Paul II has significantly deepened and developed the Council's statements on Christian-Muslim relations. Thomas Michel, for many years in charge of the Christian-Muslim Relations desk in the Pontifical Council for interreligious Dialogue, does not exaggerate when he states:

> ... no pope has devoted so much attention to the relations between Christians and Muslims as has Pope John Paul II. Both in his addresses to Christians living in the midst of Muslims in Asia, Africa and the Middle East, and Europe, as well as in his speeches to Muslims in the context of his travels to various Islamic countries the present pope has attempted to lay the bases for Christian-Muslim dialogue and the principles for living together among the followers of these two monotheistic faith.[13]

The following statements of John Paul Ii would seem to be of particular importance in this context:

1979 To the Catholic Community at Ankara (G 337-340)
1981 To Representatives of Muslims in the Philippines (G 363-367)
1985 To the Young Muslims of Morocco at Casablanca (G 465-475)
1989 To the Latin Bishops of the Arab Region (G 618-621)
1990 To the Representatives of Various Religions in Tanzania (G 686-691)
1991 Ramadan Message (G 706-709)
1991 To the Bishops of North Africa (G 725-736)
1992 To the Leaders of Senegal (G 742-750)
1993 To Representatives of the European Islamic Community (G 786)

These statements single out two areas of truth, affirmed by both faiths, as constituting the foundation for the link between Christians and Muslims. One such area concerns the human person. In both faiths God is perceived as the source of human dignity—expressed by titles like those given in the Koran to the human person—vice-regent of God and steward of creation. John Paul II is aware of the true humanism that is taught by both religions. Both faiths envision the human person as the masterpiece of God's creative activity, gifted with an immeasurable innate dignity and purpose.[14] The source of human rights, values and duties is God who enables women and men to love and who desires that we express our fidelity by good works.

The area of truth is the faith of Abraham which unites Muslims and Christians with their Jewish brethren (e.g. G 743 [Senegal 1992]). Jews, Christians and Muslims belong to what can be called 'the tradition of Abraham'. Outstanding elements in this 'Abrahamic' faith relationship are intimate friendship with God (Abraham, al-Khalil); flawless faith in God when he is ready to leave his native land in obedience to go where God was leading him; pure monotheism since God alone is to be worshipped and adored (cf. *ibid.*).[15]

1.2.2. Christians and Muslims Share a Special Responsibility

Given these important, special links—links that justify speaking of Muslims and Christians as 'brothers in God' (G 363 [Davao 1981])—Christians and Muslims share a special responsibility within the wider human family. They should witness together, each in his or her own distinct tradition, 'to the spiritual values of which the world has need' (G 468 [Casablanca 1985]).

From the speech at Casablanca in 1985 onwards we detect an emphasis on the need to dialogue about and witness together to certain values which the Christian side frequently perceives as being neglected or misunderstood by the Muslim side. We could mention, for instance, respect for the other religious traditions in their otherness (G 468); full religious freedom, including the permission to change one's religious allegiance as well as protection of each person's own religious decisions (*ibid.*); reciprocity in all spheres, especially as to granting the full exercise of the religious freedoms (G 469); recognition and respect of our differences (G 474; cf. 689 [Tanzania 1990] and 620 [Gulf 1989]).

At Casablanca in 1985 John Paul II, in tune with the Koranic theme of God-willed pluralism, states his belief, 'that today, God invites us [Christians and Muslims] to change our old practices. We must respect each other, and we must also stimulate each other in good works on the path of God' (G 474).

In Tanzania (in 1990) he recognizes the deep commitment of both traditions to spreading their faith and inviting to it (G 689); in putting this commitment into practice Christians and Muslims must respect fully the freedom of religious choice and practice of other individuals and communities (Cf. G 696 [1990, to the bishops of the Philippines]). If this is done, then the religious differences of themselves will not disrupt life. True belief in God and the desire to serve Him are prescribed as paths not of domination but of peace. Already in 1984 *Dialogue and Mission* spelled out in detail the teaching (based on the Second Vatican Council's 'Declaration on Religious Liberty', *Dignitatis Humanae*), that in preaching the faith any hint of coercion must be absent (DM 18-19).

Addressing the Islamic leaders of Senegal at Dakar in 1992 he quotes the final paragraph of section 3 of *Nostra Aetate* and adds: 'I repeat that appeal to you today. Let us together make a sincere effort to come to a deeper mutual understanding. Let our collaboration for humanity, in the name of God, be a blessing and benefit for all people!' (G 749).

1.2.3. Characteristics of Christian-Muslim Dialogue[16]

Dialogue between Christian and Muslims must be build upon existing bonds and begin with mutual recognition. Since the two faith communities have so many common elements, it is natural that they have much to discuss.

By means of dialogue they come to see the many values, practices and teachings which both religions embrace. By dialogue, the existing spiritual bond between them can and must be developed. In dialogue, each community invites the other to come to know better its heritage and to understand and accept the differences between them. The Pope salutes the efforts in dialogue that have been made until today, and he urges both communities to expand their scope.

The term dialogue indicates a variety of relationships. There is dialogue at the level of scholars and there is that dialogue which occurs in the encounters of daily life, in families, neighbourhoods, schools, and places of work. It is the latter form of dialogue, for which the term 'dialogue of life' has become common during these past years.[17]

Christians and Muslims, states the Pope, must face together the problems of society today, must search together for solutions to the great common human concerns. They must give an active response to the crises facing the human family. Thus, in his Senegal address of 1992 John Paul II singled out collaborations for a more just society and acting for peace as two central tasks to be confronted together by Muslims and Christians:

> But our commitment to do God's will lead us beyond the task of living together in harmony. Modern life has many problems. In dialogue, we who believe in the goodness of God have a special duty to address the problems of our people and search together for solutions which can make

> modern society more just more humane, more respectful of the rights, dignity and human freedom for each individual. Christians and Muslims have a special duty to work for peace, to collaborate in building the social structures, national and international, for reducing tensions and to prevent them from escalating into violent conficts. (G 745-46)

However, in order that joint action be taken by Christians and Muslims to confront the actual problems of life, both communities must move beyond the past and 'change old practices'. Both as individuals and as communities, all must examine their consciences and reject arrogance, the thirst for power, fanaticism, defeatism, and fear. Christians and Muslims must realize that they have a need for each another and that a world which is longing for peace, brotherhood, and harmony, needs to see fraternal coexistence between these two communities.[18]

2. Dialogue in the Arab World

2.1. The Middle East

2.1.1. Three Pastoral Letters of the Catholic Patriarchs of the East

During the early 1990's the Council of the Catholic Patriarchs of the East[19] have held three consecutive working sessions, at the end of each of which they published a letter to the members of their Churches, in two official versions: Arabic and French. (see Patriarches, 1991; 1992; 1994) The first, relatively shorter letter, entitled: *Un temps décisive pour les Églises du Moyen-Orient,* mentions the key issues the Council is concerned with. The subsequent two: *Letters Pastorales* deal with these issues in some detail.

There is first of all the question of the identity of the 'Middle East Catholics'. If they want to thrive, they will have to move away from trying merely to survive, from looking back nostalgically and being preoccupied with themselves. They have to free themselves from a confessionalistic[20] outlook, become interested in 'the others', wanting to relate to them, assuming their life and concerns.

The patriarchs state that it is high time to pass from being 'entités confessionelles' to being 'des Églises vivantes' who live in a creative interaction with the surrounding milieu 'which God has willed for us and which we have assumed as ours.' (Patriarches,

1991, P. 939) Only in this way will the Christians make an effective contribution in the various areas of public life. There are and will be great difficulties, but these should be seen as a stimulus to rediscover and deepen their Christian identity, in coexistence with others. (cf. *ibid.*, p. 939)

The message makes a specially painful—'la mort dans l'?me'—mention of 'the catastrophic flux of emigration. This flux eats away at the organism of our Church, hinders our march and deprives our Churches and our countries of the generous service which we owe to them.' (*ibid.*) Urging even greater intra-Christian ecumenical efforts they state: 'In the Orient we will be Christians together we will be Christians together or we shall not be Christians at all.' (*ibid.*)

As to Christian-Muslim relations the patriarchs first of all emphasise the elementary fact of the century-old cultural kinship of Arab Christians and Muslims:

> Our *convivialité* throughout the centuries constitutes, despite all diffculties, the solid ground on which we have to base our common action in the service of an egalitarian and harmonious society where no one whosoever feels himself a stranger or rejected. Our kinship of civilization is our historical patrimony (*Nôtre parente de civilization est nôtre patrimoine historique*). We are decided to preserve it, to develop it, to go anew to its roots (*réenraciner*) and to reactivate it. (*ibid.*, p. 940)

But it is not enough to understand co-existence as mere absence of violence and war. The aim must be to arrive at the kind of 'creative and fruitful relationship with guarantees to each believer in God in our countries stability and tranquility, shielded from the mechanisms of hate, fanaticism, discrimination and the refusal of other.' (*ibid.*) A condition for reaching this goal is the effort to live 'our authentic spiritual and religious values on the level of a healthy and sincere citizenship in such a way that there will be place for all, whatever the diversity of their allegiances may be (quelle que soit la diversité de leurs appartenances)' [*sic!*] (*ibid.*).

The second, much longer letter of the patriarchs: *La présence chrétienne en Orient: témoignage et mission* (The Christian Presence in the Orient: Witness and Mission) (Patriarches, 1992), starts with an analysis of the changes and the new facts that mark the world in which the Catholic Oriental Christians live and with which they have to engage themselves: the world at large, the Arab world and the other Christian Churches. A substantial part of the letter reflects on faith and prayer, on the will to become 'incarnate' in Arab civilization, on the spirit of service and ecumenical, openness, all presented as 'modes of an effective *présence chrétienne*'. This *présence,* the patriarchs insist, must be genuinely dialogical, in the spirit of the Vatican II documents which defined the Church with regard to its identity and mission, as a 'Church of dialogue'. (Patriarchs, 1992, p. 606)

The same imperative follows from the fact that the Middle East from time immemorial has been the place of origin and encounter of great civilizations—with all the tensions and contacts, conflicts and affinities this entailed. This region is deeply marked by pluralism. Thus history and geography have made 'dialogue' their 'fundamental vocation and the greatest challenge it is facing.' (*ibid.*, p. 606)

The Christians of the Middle East, therefore, are called to give a living sign of the unity of the human family. In the torn world of our day all the religions are required to play a positive role in the global struggle for peace and harmonious living together.

In order to convey the passionate eloquence, especially in this part of the Letter, we quote the French original:

> Le dialogue est une spiritualité qui nous transplante de l'exclusion & l'assimilation, du refus a l'accueil, du classement par catégories a la compréhension, de la défguration d'autrui au respect, de la condamnation a la miséricorde, de l'inimitié a la concorde, de la concurrence a la complémentarité, de l'antipathie a la rencontre et de l'hostilité a la fraternité. (*ibid.*, p. 606)

The patriarchs then single out 'fanaticism in any of its various forms' as 'the number one enemy of dialogue' and contrast the fanatic with the believer:

> ... le croyant est au service de Dieu, le fanatique met Dieu à son service. Le croyant rend un culte à Dieu. Le fanatique un culte à lui-même en s'imaginant qu'il rend un culte à Dieu. Le croyant écoute la parole de Dieu, le fanatique l'altère. Le croyant s'élève au niveau de Dieu et a son amour, le fanatique abaisse Dieu a son propre niveau. Le

> croyant craint Dieu, le fanatique menace les autres au nom de Dieu. Le croyant honoure Dieu, le fanatique met sa volonté a la place de la volonté divine. Le fanatisme est un mode du rejet simultané de Dieu et de l'homme. Dans le fanatique, l'énergie de la foi et de l'amour se transforme en énergie de l'hostilité et de la rancœur. Il croit rendre un culte à Dieu, quand il agresse celui qui est différent de lui par la religion, l'ethnie, la langue, la couleur ou le patrimoine. Dans le croyant, toutes ces énergies servent au contraire la rencontre, la collaboration et l'édifcation. (*ibid.*)

They leave no doubt that they want the dialogue with the Muslim majority to hold pride of place:

> Our dialogue is frst of all a dialogue with our Muslim brothers. Our life together for centuries constitutes a fundamental experience without return. These Churches want in fact to be a bridge between East and West, Christianity and Islam, because of the fact of our cultural proximity with the Muslim East. (*ibid.*)

Turning to the future, the letter deems it crucial that the Muslim side consider and treat the Christians as 'an inseparable part of the life of society and that the Christian side, adopting a correct vision of its own faith, arrive at 'a positive, sincere and decided engagement' with the whole of Arab society. Both sides are called to turn their mutual relationship into a positive one, accepting to live together in diversity. Hence the need for institutions of dialogue that will make possible regular encounter, in order to develop together the proper modes of exchange and co-operation, for the benefit of all.

This argument leads on to the central theme of the third letter of the patriarchs: *Ensemble devant Dieu pour le bien de la personne et de la societé. La coexistence entre musulmans et chrétiens dans le monde arabe* (Together before God for the Good of the Person and of Society: The coexistence of Muslims and Christians in the Arab World) (Patriarches 1994). The Letter begins with an appreciable degree of honest self-criticism about the past and present experience of coexistence. It singles out the factor that would obstruct a felicitous common future: Communalism, mutual ignorance, refusal to accept pluralism and difference, polemical deformation of religious discourse, before, finally, indicating the areas where this future positively has to be constructed: education in family and school, churches and mosques, publications and other mass media.

The third part of this letter, *Ensemble pour une societé égalitaire* (Together for a Just Society), offers elements of reflection in three areas that are held to be of crucial importance for constructing the future together; citizenship, the relationship between religion and politics and that between religion and violence.

Citizenship for all is a key issue for the Middle East: 'the law must guarantee the equality of all and it must protect everyone, whatever their religion or number. There exists the need to form a free, responsible and conscious citizen, capable of participating properly in public life and of putting the public before one's own—individual or corporate—interests. Our Arab societies still have much to do in this direction' (Patriarches 1994, p. 50).

On the sensitive issue of the relationship between religion and politics the letter wishes 'the bitter struggle' in this area between different religious movements and types of outlook to transform itself into 'a serious dialogue' (*ibid.*, p. 52). It is not adequate to remove religion from public life or to confine it to acts of liturgy and devotion only, 'because religion is dogma and life and this concerns the whole of human existence, private and public, individual and social.' (*ibid.*) But what has to be avoided at any cost is that religion would transform itself into political ideology and politics would instrumentalise religion. From there arise urgent questions, the answers to which need to be worked out in a 'vast and honest national dialogue' (*ibid.*, p. 55), among Christians and Muslims.

More specifically the patriarchs ask how the equality and equal status of Christians and Muslims in the Arab countries can be guaranteed and how the discrimination between citizens on the basis of their religious allegiance can be overcome, while at the same time retaining religion as an essential element of citizenship and of public life. The Christians, they insist, wish to be considered citizens in the full meaning of the term and not a minority that asks [the majority] for protection.

To link citizenship with religious values is not a bad thing. On the contrary, these values give a soul to citizenship. But in this case it is necessary that religion orients the person wholly to God and to the total respect of God's creature and of any given religious conviction, especially in the case of a minority religion. The laws of the state must guarantee these rights with the same rigour as they guarantee the rights of the majority or of the religion of the state. (*ibid.*, p. 55)

Human Rights, consequently are a key issue:

Human rights draw their sacred character from the sanctity of God who has created and willed the human person subject of rights and duties and has given him/her a living conscience by which he/she can seek the truth and arrive at it without constraint. There is no contradiction between the rights of the person and the rights of God. Therefore, who does not respect the creature of God does not respect the Creator. (*ibid.*, pp. 55–6)

Finally, the patriarchs address the issue of violence practiced in the name of religion, be it within one and the same religion or towards other religions. While condemning unambiguously any manifestation of moral and physical violence, especially when practiced in the name of confession or religion, they stress the absolute need to remove its causes. They mention for instance political, social and economic injustice, corruption, poverty and the spirit of dominating and humiliating peoples.

In the last part of the letter the patriarchs speak about relations between Muslims and Christians in a world-wide perspective. They mention the present climate of mutual suspicion, helped by the confusing habit of attributing to Christianity, by oversimplification, the unjust politics practiced in the region by certain western governments and by frequently identifying the 'Oriental Christians' with the West (cf. *ibid.*, p. 62). They also mention the existence in the Middle East of 'a collective memory of aggressive nature', brought about by ancient and recent wars with their efforts to conquer and exploit. 'The believers of the two religions must move from the logic of struggle and dispute to that of dialogue and collaboration' (*ibid.*, p. 64).

The negative facts, the letter insists, 'must not be allowed to obliterate the memory of the periods marked by creative interaction on the cultural level. It is these historical moments which we have to bring to life today and on which we must dwell, making of them the base of dialogue and positive encounter' (*ibid.*, pp. 62f.).

'The believers of the two religions must move from the logic of struggle and dispute to that of dialogue and collaboration' (*ibid.*, p. 64).

The Christians in the Arab world participate with the Arab Muslims in one and the same Arab culture, with all its constitutive elements. At the same time, together with the other Christians throughout the world, they profess Jesus as the Christ, as the Word of the eternal God. They are convinced to have to further rapprochement between the Christian and the Muslim world, transforming opposition and confrontation into positive collaboration, on the basis of mutual respect.

> The Christian Arabs tell the West that Islam is not its enemy but rather the partner in the dialogue, indispensable for the construction of the new human civilization. They tell the same thing to the Muslim East: Christianity in the West is not the enemy but the principal partner in the indispensable dialogue for the construction of a new world. (*ibid.*, p. 65)

2.1.2. The Apostolic Exhortation for Lebanon

Already in 1991 the Pope had announced the convocation of a 'Special Assembly of the Synod of Bishops, for Lebanon'. After numerous stages of reflection and sharing this Assembly was held during the months of November and December 1996. The final document: *Une ésperance nouvelle pour le Liban* (*A New Hope for Lebanon*) was solemnly signed and proclaimed by the Pope during his visit of Lebanon on 10 May 1997.

Not surprisingly, the document contains many of the points made in the three pastoral letters of the Catholic Patriarchs of the East, discussed above. However, in the light of the traumatic experience of the Lebanese war and the socio-historical texture of a plural Lebanon, some aspects of the text deserve special mention here.[21]

(1) *Solidarity with the Arab world*: the Catholic Church of Lebanon wishes to be open to dialogue and collaboration with Muslims of the other Arab countries, of which Lebanon is an integral part.

I would like to insist on the need for the Christians of Lebanon to maintain and to strengthen their links of solidarity with the Arab world. I invited them to consider their insertion into Arab culture, to which they have contributed so much, as a privileged 'locus' for pursuing, together with the Christians of the other Arab countries, an authentic and profound dialogue with the believers of Islam. Living in the same region, having known in their history moments of glory and of distress, the Christians and Muslims of the Middle East are called to construct together a future of *convivialité* and of collaboration aiming at the human and moral developments of their peoples. (EAL 93, pp. 214f.)

(2) *Being sincere partners in serving the common good and in furthering 'convivialité'* among all those who make up the country (Cf. EAL 14).

(3) *Removing the prejudices which are strongly anchored in the mentalities* and which contribute to maintaining a lack of mutual confidence.[22]

(4) Making a special effort to get to know better the others and *to assent fully to the fact of ethnic, cultural and religious pluralism.* This also must shape all stages of *education* (Cf. EAL 92).

(5) *Within this perspective religious dialogue retains uppermost importance.* It 'must help everyone to esteem, discern and acknowledge the greatness of the spiritual strivings of one's brethren [of the Islamic Tradition], an effort which leads to walking the path of the divine Will (EAL 91) [emphasis mine].

In all this an 'asceticism of listening and of speaking is required: to will and to know how to understand the deep meaning of the discourse and the action of the partner; to grasp the source of the [non-Christian] partner's experience and the human perspectives in which that person places herself; to express oneself in a manner that one's word can really be understood by the other and to behave according to the Gospel in a way that the witness of life renders credible the spoken word' (EAL 36).

2.1.3. The Latin Patriarch to the [Catholic] Christians of the Holy Land

On the occasion of the ninth centenary of the call of the Crusade at Clermont in 1095, Mgr. Michel Sabbah, the Catholic Latin Patriarch of Jerusalem, delivered at Clermont-Ferrant on 25 November 1995 a public lecture entitled: 'Les Chrétiens de Terre Sainte aujourd'hui et le dialogue des religions') The Patriarch states that the Crusades concern the community of the Latin-rite Christians of the Holy Land (Israel, Palestine, Jordan) in a special way. They belong to both Eastern and Western Christianity and, as Arab Palestinians, they also belong to the Arab world, the history of which has been to a large extent determined by Islam.[23]

The Patriarch makes clear his position on many of the basic questions regarding Christian-Muslim relations and dialogue in the Arab world and especially in the Holy Land (Israel, Palestine, Jordan): the religious meaning which the Christians of the Arab world—especially the relatively small number of them that lives in the Holy Land (*c*.3000.000)—attach to the Christian presence there; the small and vulnerable beginnings of a tripartite dialogue between Jews, Muslims and Christians and the political and moral conditions for its further development; the different levels of interreligious dialogue; the problems of citizenship and of religious rights, including the freedom to choose, change or abandon a given institutional religious allegiance.

Hinting at the complexity of the situation, the Patriarch judges that the main challenge which Christians and Muslims have to confront, is that of different faith attitudes. Without a new spiritual solidarity, he argues, felicitous and harmonious living together cannot exist.

> We must develop in ourselves the sense of a spiritual solidarity. This is to say, when I pray and put myself in the presence of God, I do not present myself alone, with my questions, joys and sorrows. Before God I present myself with all my Muslim brethren, as they adore and question, as they rejoice or experience sorrow. This is a necessary education for both Muslims and Christians, so that we, all of us, become able to encounter one another before God.

We would then be able to esteem one another and to collaborate in building a new society freed from mistrust and fear. Together we must move towards the day when Muslims and Christians will hear the same call from both mosques and churches, a call which will say: Christian, love your Muslim brother, and you, Muslim believer, love your Christian brother. (Sabbah. 1996, p. 179)

2.2. *North Africa*

2.2.1. Henri Teissier: Dialogue as 'Partage Humain' (1984)

In a recent essay on 'Changing Catholic Views of Islam'[24] I have briefly dealt with the Pastoral Letter of the Regional Bishops'

Conference of North Africa of 1979, enditled *Chrétiens du Maghreb: le sens de nos rencontres.*[25] It should be seen in the context of the distinctive situation of the Christian communities of North Africa. They constitute a small minority and are made up of small groups of persons, mostly foreigners, living in the Maghreb for professional reasons. French is the language they normally use and French is the religious culture prevalent among them. A tiny nucleus of lay persons, priests and members of religious orders, assume the responsibility of a more continuous presence.

This situation explains in part why the Church of the Maghreb in its relations with the Muslim majority gives pride of place to *coexistence*, encounter in daily life and collaboration on a simply human plane, minimizing the specifically religious aspects that characterize Church and *umma*.

In their pastoral letter of 1979 the bishops of the Maghreb speak of the Muslim(s) as such only tangentially, only in so far as they deserve to be respected in their allegiance to another faith and in the choice and liberty to live according to it (Troll, 1998, p. 35).

One of the authors of that letter was the present Archbishop of Algiers, Henri Teissier (*b.*1929; Bishop of Oran: 1972–81) who as a pastor, Christian theologian and student of Arabic and Islam has been for decades outstanding in his commitment to the deepening of Christian-Muslim relations in Algeria, North Africa and beyond. He can be considered an authentic and authoritative voice of the Catholic Church of Algeria and of the whole region of North Africa.

In 1984 Henri Teissier published Église en Islam. Méditation sur l'existence chrétienne en Algérie. He sees the unique feature of the present day Christian community in the Maghreb in that it lives its minority situation 'en terre d'Islam' 'not as an historical necessity or as something inherited, but rather by choice and vocation.' (Teissier. 1984, p. 12) This Church lives as a horst community. How should it, in the light of its faith, understand this situation and live it? What are, in the answers given to these two questions, elements which are of significance for the Muslim-Christian dialogue at large and, more generally, for the fraternal living together (*convivence fraternelle*) of individuals and groups of different origins and cultures?

Reading Teissier's pastoral-theological reflections on the life of his Church in the Algerian context, one sees that the 'non-confessional' approach to Christian-Muslim relations of the Bishops' Letter of 1979—with its emphasis on the fact of neighbourhood and professional collaboration as the place of encounter with 'the other'—was the result of the 'situation' of that Church and of a conscious pastoral choice. This non-confessional approach should in no way be attributed to a lack of awareness as to the important role which the Islamic religion plays in the life of the people.

Teissier explains: 'One must recognize that up to now in Algeria the contacts (*Les proximités*) between Christians and Muslims come about through the intermediary of various forms of collaboration in the service of men and women rather than by instances of religious search, organized dialogue or by organized joined prayers (*prière officiellement exprimée en commun).'* (Teissier, 1984, p. 153) Dialogue about properly religious questions takes place only when the partners have traveled together already by way of concrete collaboration. The confidence that has grown in this way between them allows them to communicate further in truth, starting from the questions which they put to themselves and about which they desire to share with partners of the other community.

In contrast, conversations on religious matters between persons who do not know one another, most of the time seem to lead to general statements without real, existential significance. Affirmations of that kind would be, for instance: true believers must struggle together against atheism; all religions invite men and women to do what is good. Some partners in such 'dialogue' may even indulge in apologetic, if not polemical declarations.

Not surprisingly, then, the Christian community of Algeria keeps a certain distance from the word 'Dialogue', at least in so far as this term would suggest *une activité abstraite et gratuite entre des spécialistes* (*ibid.*, p. 154) The Christians have become much more aware of a further, subtle difficulty, that of the vocabulary; in the majority of the cases the same words do not cover the same realities in one and the other tradition. For instance, the Muslim terms for prayer do not cover the reality of Christian prayer. Of even more serious consequence is the lack of true understanding on both sides with regard to expressions like inspiration (of Scripture), Islamic Law, Jesus' identity, etc. Using common terms for designating key elements of the Christian and the Islamic faith that differ in fact substantially as to their content, introduces ambiguity and confusion into Christian-Muslim conversation and discussion.

As Teissier states it, Algeria at the present point of its history, generally speaking, has other needs and preoccupations than Muslim-Christian dialogue.[26] Algeria is still deeply involved in recovering its true identity, its language and culture, including its religious dimension, all of which had been made to suffer traumatically—and in part even had been suppressed—during the colonial period. A handful of Christian-Muslim groups, sparsely dispersed over the country, practice a spiritual exchange. However, they are the exception and have grown out of existing friendships based on encounter in work and neighbourhood.

Hence most Christians in Algeria would speak about their deeper encounters with Muslims in terms of *partage d'humanité* rather than of Muslim-Christian dialogue.

> Christians in Algeria, like in many other places, have the experience that the encounter [between Christians and Muslims] is possible, real, enriching. But that encounter is not one of people standing for an ideology or defending a creed [*rencontre de porteurs d'idéologie, de defenseurs de credo*], rather it is one of believers who, living in and for the same country, fnd themselves united in having the same questions, and often in similar terms, about future, life, responsibility, suffering, God. (B. Lapize de Salée, quoted in Teissier, 1984, p. 156)

In short, the Catholic Church in Algeria perceives it as the vocation of its members, individually and as communities, 'to join (*rejoindre*) a history of salvation which God accomplishes in the life of individuals and of communities, in order to participate in it somehow, in solidarity: solidarity of work accepted together solidarity expressed in the links and in the exchanges which come about between Christians and Muslims, solidarity of prayer' (Teissier, 1984, p. 205).

2.2.2. *Pierre Claverie: Coexistence, Dialogue and Reciprocity (1986)*

The Iranian revolution and the proclamation of the Islamic Republic of Iran in 1979 very soon almost everywhere in the Muslim world led to a new consciousness of the relevance and power of Islam. During the 1980's North Africa experienced an increased political influence and visibility of the Islamist movements. The tiny but highly sensitive leadership of the local Church took stock of the new situation and made a critical assessment of Christian-Muslim relations and of dialogue. The earliest and most penetrating essay along this line was that of a bishop in Algeria, published in 1986 in the Bulletin of the then 'Secretariat for Non-Muslims'[27] under the title of 'Chemins du dialogue Islamo-chrétien'. The author was Pierre Claverie (1938–96), Bishop of Oran from 1981 until his death by murder in 1996).

Claverie begins by a wide-ranging reflection on the nature and the conditions for 'true coexistence', which he considers 'the indispensable condition for dialogue'. By dialogue he means 'those encounters that are wanted by believers who are not resigned to the divisions and conflicts that tear humanity to pieces' (Claverie, 1986, p. 23).

In the effort to promote harmonious Christian-Muslim relations today, Claverie argues, it would be a serious mistake, simply to appeal again and again to noble sentiments and moral maxims, without taking into account the real differences. We cannot make abstraction from the tensions and even bloody conflicts that, unfortunately, even in our day constitute at least one aspect of Christian-Muslim relations.

'True coexistence' is not a naturally given fact. Rather, the mere presence of an 'other' in our space easily gives rise to tension and to aggressive attitudes arising from uneasiness and fear. This applies especially in the communal sphere, when groups that share the same space organize themselves along distinct cultural and religious lines. Ignorance of the other further compounds the problem, because it leads to suspicion of the other's motives.

Claverie thinks that compared with other social groups making up a secular society, the 'Muslim group' distinguishes itself in that it has 'a project of society and for the society where it implants itself. Islam does not only belong to the domain of the individual conscience, rather it claims a direct socio-political impact on the life of the countries which adopt it or welcome it' (*ibid.*, p. 15).

In addition to this fact we observe that in societies built on secular political structures Islam affirms itself as an alternative constitutional model, and that everywhere, from Egypt to Senegal, and further Eastward Islamist movements try to impose on existing governments the strict application of the *sharī'a*. In fact, not a few

Muslim teachers of religion and religious law, presuming that the *s sharīa* is applicable to all, do all they can to make it prevail. This explains to some extent, Claverie remarks, the uneasiness of the non-Muslims.

> To this must be added that 'the sincere Muslim who also happens to be a friend, will not understand our uneasiness. Does this divine Law [i.e., the *shar'ìa]*, not provide the best guidance for every human person one could wish for? Is not every human being congenitally Muslim? Does the *shar'ýa* not offer the best guarantees for justice and tolerance? Does it not fulfll all anterior Revelations for the salvation and the well-being of all humanity? (*ibid.*, p. 15)

The correct Christian answer in this situation is neither to react with blind passion nor to close one's eyes to the real differences that exist. Rather: 'co-existence implies *a true knowledge* [of the partner] which is objective and demanding'.

At this point Claverie, with honesty and courage, introduces what would seem to be a crucial theme in our context: the fact that harmonious coexistence and dialogue are greatly conditioned by power relationships: 'But co-existence is also a *power relationship (rapport de force)* which continuously needs to be negotiated, short of letting it degenerate into oppression, exclusion and violence.' (*ibid.*, p. 16)

> These power relationships 'paralyse us collectively' (p. 18) They are 'due to cultural inequalities, to the aftermath of colonialism badly accepted on all sides, to open, or hidden, political and economic conficts with their inevitable religious legitimation *(argument)* so tragically illustrated by Lebanon. How can one serenely undertake to get to know the other side while one knows it to be dependent on groups which one—at times justifiably—suspects of domination and of expansionist manoeuvres and intentions. Here mistrust prevents the best intentions from being realised. Every Christian a priori is suspected of resuscitating the Crusades in new forms. Every Muslim a priori is seen as a fanatic or a potential terrorist. (*ibid.*, p. 18)

Claverie foresees already in 1986 'diffcult hours' for the Church in Algeria. But he maintains that the Church is 'one of the places where that negotiation between individuals and groups remains possible.

We entertain no ambition whatsoever of power or expansion. We only want to help in rendering possible a living together (*cohabitation*) in difference (.), not only *beyond* the differences. A living together that respects all the diversities and takes risks by granting them a place and a role. A *cohabitation*, fnally, that is based on an obstinate will to live together. (*ibid.*)

On the level of political relations the many efforts to establish confidence and to overcome fear are made difficult by economic and political concerns. Ideally, the believers of both religions should be the first to create the climate of confidence which disarms and incites to coexistence and to dialogue in the name of a common human destiny, beyond the frontiers and the walls that separate the political blocs. When Catholics and mainstream Protestants at present see the struggle for just and harmonious coexistence as the heart of their vocation and mission, this has nothing to do with a mere 'change of tactics', which would disguise underlying aims of proselytizing.

What is needed above all is real reciprocity. Both sides have to ask themselves whether they are 'really willing to coexist and to pay the price for it'. Such reciprocity in truth and justice for all concerned has to go hand in hand with critically discerning the objective reasons for the difficulties and conflicts that exist between the communities

Claverie, in writing this critical essay in 1986, was aware of the reaction his outspokenness might provoke. Hence he made it a point to stress that in calling into question certitudes about dialogue too easily assumed, and even taking the opposite view of apparently evident affirmations, he was guided only by wanting 'to be true and to be provoked into doing the truth, convinced that "whoever does the truth comes to the light"'.

> The questions which I put to myself, my fellow Christians and to my Muslim friends. refect, I believe, the complexities of our relations which often are concealed by a too simplistic discourse, be it vindictive or moralizing. If these observations and these questions have put a question mark behind too easily acquired certitudes and have unmasked the duplicity of certain attitudes, if they have taken the opposite view of seemingly evident

> affrmations, my intention was not to destroy or to attack. May the reader forgive me if he or she has been hurt. I myself have been hurt by too many instances of aggressive behaviour and discourse, on the one hand, and, on the other, by too many pious and vain appeals to illusory encounters where complacency is mingled with hypocrisy. My wish is that at least everyone may leave behind his illusions and pretensions and move out of the fortresses where he hides and destroys himself. (*ibid.*, p. 28)

As Christians we cannot betray our faith and our identity, refusing to stretch out our hand towards the others, whoever they may be, in order to understand, serve and love them better. Once we have lucidly observed and analysed the objective obstacles which made every relationship a risky adventure, we cannot refuse to commit ourselves [to improve that relationship] (*ibid.*)

In the present passionate climate, created by the political and religious authorities, it is diffcult for both sides to accept our differences lucidly and to live them peacefully. However, 'the Christians on their part, can at least see to it that they do not make others suffer the fate they do not want to suffer themselves: becoming oppressed minorities, dispossessed of their rights, their culture, being marginalized and rejected. Encounter and dialogue have that price. (*ibid.*, p. 31)

2.2.3. Henri Teissier: the Present State of Formal Christian-Muslim Dialogue (1989)

Less than three years after the publication of Claverie's critical essay, Henri Teissier was asked by the association *Crislam* of Madrid to contribute to the volume *Fede Adelante: Los problemas de fondo del dialogo islamo-cristiano*.[28] The editors of the volume, aware of a certain lack of openness and willingness to accept mutual criticism in most of the formal dialogue meetings, had asked the Christian and Muslim contributors, by way of written contributions to this collective work, 'to break the wall which prohibits an authentic expression' of views.

Teissier believes, therefore, that it is possible 'to state openly where the reasons are located and what are the chief reasons for the present freeze in the Christian-Muslim dialogue.'(Teissier, 1989, p. 95) The essay first enumerates four 'hindrances on the path of the Christian-Muslim dialogue' and then suggests five proposals for a solution.

The first obstacle is the lack of a truly critical assessment of the Christian and Muslim heritage. The Christian today approaches his Muslim partner in dialogue with the consciousness of the need for numerous qualifications due to the complex history of the formation and the development of his religious heritage. Much work on the Muslim tradition, too, has to be accomplished before the Muslim and Christian partners can arrive at a true exchange in depth.

> A new critical and scholarly view of the Muslim tradition can only be born from a long collective effort, comparable to that of Christian exegesis of the Bible or that of the critical history of the formation and development of the dogmas in the Christian tradition. Scholars formed at the university level, who because of their critical academic formation could contribute to this great work, are not lacking. But, in most countries, it would not be easy for then to communicate the results of this research in their communities. Public opinion would not allow them to do so. (Teissier, 1989, pp. 97–8)

The second obstacle is that the Christian and Muslim partners in dialogue do not receive equal support from their respective communities. There are some courageous Muslim pioneers of this dialogue, as for instance M. Talbi and A. Charfi, both of Tunisia. Yet their voices have not found a wider echo in their communities. Muslim educational institutions, authors and leaders of important movements generally do not echo the thought and attitudes of these pioneers.

> Extended work inside the Muslim community, parallel to that done on various levels in the Christian community, would seem to be needed to render authentic the encounters between the representatives of the two communities. for the moment, the conciliatory declarations published at the end of international dialogue encounters, are not accompanied by, and have not yet led to, any true change of the religious policies of those governments or organizations for whom the Muslim participants in these dialogues speak, particularly as to

> their statements about the legal position and treatment of the minorities. (*ibid.*, pp. 99–100)

Third, few are those Muslim scholars who feel impelled and free to get to know Christianity and the Christians as they understand and present themselves today. For instance, about such crucial and centrally important issues of Christian teaching as the Trinity, Incarnation and Redemption or the relationship between state and religion, generally speaking, Muslims do not consider it necessary to ask the Christians themselves about their understanding of these aspects of their faith. This is so, because Muslims are deeply convinced that they know the authentic Message of Jesus directly from the Koran

Hence, normally even highly educated Muslims are ignorant of the distinctively Christian vision of God, of the human person ad of salvation. And in case they are aware of it, they regard the differences as ultimately of secondary importance. In consequence they are tempted to interpret as a sign of stubbornness—and/or of a lack in 'ecumenical' outlook—the fact that Christians, even after having been exposed to the message of Islam, continue to consider the distinctive teaching of their faith as an essential part of that faith. 'We do have the right', Teissier insists, 'to expect from the Muslim the acceptance of the fact that "for the Christian" these doctrines are of absolutely central importance' (*ibid.*, p. 101).

A fourth serious obstacle to the development of Christian-Muslim relations, in Teissier's eyes, has to do with the difficulty of implementing the right of freedom of conscience. All partners in dialogue certainly must condemn proselytism, understood as 'indiscrete actions designed to turn away the partner in dialogue from her/his tradition without taking account of hishe/her personal history and fidelity to the call of God' (*ibid.*, p. 101).[29]

It is commonly realized in our day that it is impossible to reconcile respect of the human person and of God with oppressive practices that have existed and been justified in the past in Christianity, such as the Inquisition or the expulsion of the Moriscos. Mohamed Talbi says the same thing with regard to the *hadith* which prescribes the killing of a convert of Muslim origin. Certainly, Teissier states, except in a few Muslim countries the physical carrying out of the death sentence is no longer practiced, but the civil, social and, at times, even family 'death' of the convert is still a reality. And he adds: Christians find it unacceptable that on the one hand Muslims frown upon the participation of converts from Islam to Christianity in public, formal dialogue meetings and consider it even an affront to Islam, and yet, that Muslims on the other hand consider it normal that Muslim delegations in dialogue meetings quite often include converts from Christianity or other religions to Islam. The participation of converts is something that the Christian side finds not only acceptable but even helpful, since free and sincere conversions form part and parcel of the universe of both religions, past and present (cf. *ibid.*, p. 102).

Subsequently, Archbishop Teissier makes the following five proposals for the progress and credibility of formal dialogue meetings.

1. *To include in the agenda of dialogue the central faith convictions that are misunderstood by the partner in dialogue*, e.g. the core issues and great mysteries of the Christian faith and the centrality of the *sharī'a* within the Muslim faith.
2. *To seek dialogue with those responsible on the Muslim side on the subject of the principle of reciprocity.* This applies to freedom of cult, including public celebrations; freedom of conscience, including the freedom to change one's religious allegiance or to have none; examination of textbooks and other educational materials by mixed commissions consisting of competent Christian and Muslim scholars who have to look at the objective presentation of matters pertaining to Muslim and Christian culture and religion, in the past and at present.

   The contradiction that exists between the declarations made by the authorities in the Christian-Muslim dialogues and the actions—or lack of action—of these same authorities once 'back home' discredits dialogue. This contradiction was somehow acceptable during the frst years of dialogue, because the encounter had frst to get under way. It cannot continue, however, without rendering meaningless the good intentions of those who organize Christian-Muslim encounters. The problem of reciprocity can no longer be bracketed. short of removing all credibility from offcial dialogue' (*ibid.*, p. 103)
3. *To deepen the 'dialogue of life' wherever Christians and Muslims are already true partners.* As mentioned earlier (cf. 2.2.1.),

one has honestly to admit that frequently 'relations are better between persons of a (non religious) humanist culture that between representatives of religions.' To acknowledge this, means simply taking act of the role which religions play in dividing humanity and trying to overcome this fact by the joint commitment of persons of a 'humanist background'—be they practicing a religion or not.

4. *To further and support Christian-Muslim research by believers who are independent and of comparable scholarly and academic standard*. The collaboration and the publications of the 'Groupe de Recherches Islamo-Chrétien' (GRIC) as well as regular academic exchanges like the one between the Gregorian University and the Islamic Faculty of Theology of the University of Ankara (begun in 1985) move into this direction. Scholarly research into the history of one's own cultural and religious heritage should be supported by the communities concerned.
5. *To support the spiritual encounter of both traditions*. This type of encounter should not be restricted to meetings (and/or periods of living together) between Christian contemplatives and Sufis, but also include meetings between spirituality committed member(s) of the two communities whom everyday life has brought into contact. In our peculiar situation in the Maghreb, Teissier explains, there exist thousands of persons who see themselves close to another and who want to give this relationship spiritual expression and meaning: they pray for one another and find their fidelity to their own heritage strengthened by those belonging to the other community. However, such spiritual sharing again and again meets with a lack of understanding or even with direct opposition from religious authorities, on both sides, Archbishop Teissier is convinced that encounters of this type 'glorify God and His work in the hearts of sincere believers and thus 'unfreeze' the Christian-Muslim dialogue held on the level of the respective religious authorities' (*ibid*., p. 106).

As Teissier states at the end of his analysis, formal dialogue is only one form among other more elementary forms that communication between Christians and Muslims can take. Still, it remains true that 'those who hold positions of responsibility in the two religious communities have a great influence on the believers of their traditions. A lasting and pervasive progress in the Muslim-Christian relationship will hardly occur, if the religious authorities of Christianity and Islam do not commit themselves in this direction' (*ibid.*).

It is true that there exists between the two faiths a fundamental difference as to the Christian vision of the history of salvation and the Muslim conception of faith. 'Yet,' Teissier emphasizes, 'there is no alternative to pursuing the task, because, if believers do not become people of peace and those in responsible positions do not become people of people of dialogue, there is no future, either for religions or for humanity' (*ibid.*, p. 106).

2.2.4. Claverie: Solidarity between Believers to Overcome Radicalism (1994)

For more than a decade now, Algeria has been in the grip of continuous, dramatic tension and violence between Islamist groups and security forces of the government, in short: of civil war-like circumstances. The Islamists in their various formations are waging *jihād* against he military government that defends the given secular state. Both Henri Teissier of Algiers and the late Pierre Claverie of Oran, as bishops and theologians wrote about Christian-Muslim dialogue during these past years in other to provide discernment and guidance to the Christians entrusted to them. Their writings include elements of analysis of the overall situation as a basis for indicating the direction Christian-Muslim relations in Algeria should take.[30] On Pentecost 1994 Claverie in a compact text 'Croire au dialogue', with characteristic perspicacity and directness, states his vision of Christian-Muslim relations in the given Algerian situation. He speaks of the dream of his minuscule Algerian Church, after centuries of conflicts and 130 years of colonization, to make a new beginning, instituting '*un veritable dialogue pour mieux se connaitre, se comprendre et prendre en charge ensemble les défis communs que nous lançent les évolutions de nos societés.*' (Claverie, 1996, p. 21) Claverie is aware of the historical burden which the Church in Algeria carries. It forms a part of the Catholic Church, which for centuries was marked by 'a will to domination and which has sometimes, in the name of religion, committed crimes analogous to those which today cover Muslim lands with blood.'

The 'project' of a small and powerless Church to establish 'new relations', at this juncture, seems heavily burdened:

> Armed groups which claim to take their inspiration from Islam and call themselves fghters *(mujāhidīn)* for a cultural, political and economic revolution, have taken us as their target. They intend, as they themselves put it, to purify the Algerian soil of any presence they judge impure: of the Jews, the Christians and the unbelievers, according to their own words. In justifying this process of 'purifcation' they invoke history, accusing us of being the crusaders of a new war, waged by the West against Islam, of being agents of a cultural neo-colonialism which brings with it a perversion, to which they oppose the Arabo-Muslim heritage which, for them are the Shari'a and its prescriptions, as they interpret them. The Christians, by the way, are not the only victims of this operation: the Muslims who interpret that same heritage differently, also suffer their attacks. (Claverie, 1996, p. 22)

While Claverie is aware of the capital importance of the socio-economic factors for creating conditions conducive to positive relations, he remains convinced that 'it is the right vision of faith which ultimately must motivate persons to enter courageously into dialogical relations with the others, not beyond our differences but with them. Jesus enables me to recognize in the other the call to overcome my limits and my domineering arrogance, so as to discover in the other, what I still lack for being fully, authentically and generously human' (*ibid.*, p. 24).

Thus Claverie believes in the need for dialogue, even in 1994, i.e. a time of heightened tension in Algeria:

> Hence the key-word of my faith today is dialogue. Not out of tactics of opportunism but because dialogue is constitutive of the relation of God with human persons and of the relation between human persons. all sacred history takes place under the sign of broken and restored communication, in a dialogue in which God takes the initiative. For this very reason I have a grudge against the religions, and often also against my own Church, for practicing all too willingly an aggressive monologue and

> for cultivating their specifc identities. And I suffer when I see what a deplorable witness the religious faiths give when they pretend to subdue and control humanity, making it a slave to their laws. (*ibid.*, p. 24)

Dispersed in the monthly letters which Bishop Claverie continued to address to his diocesans during these past years up to his death in 1996, we find further significant and distinctive elements of his teaching on Christian-Muslim dialogue.

He formulates and applies the criteria that must underlie any fair and effective dialogue, strictly and 'mercilessly' to both his own Christian and the Islamic tradition. Analysing critically the phenomenon of politico-religious messianism he writes:

> The expectation of 'the Messiah to come' has mobilized generations of oppressed, despoiled, exiled, dispersed, massacred Jews. Was not the son of David to come and re-establish the kingdom of God on earth? For them the Davidic kingship remains the model and Jerusalem the symbol city. One can understand the messianism of Israel: the Alliance, the Promises and the Law exist precisely in order to make Israel the people which will lead all the nations to the Unique and True God. And one sees the ravages which this dream brings forth and sustains.
>
> For a long time the Christians—and especially the Roman Church— have held themselves the legitimate heirs of that messianism. More, they have proclaimed the kingdom of God as having arrived in the Church and in those kingdoms to which she delegated her powers. A tragical enterprise this was: it has carried along the worst and the best, during the tortuous course of a thousand-year-old history., from the Crusades to the Inquisition, as our friends smugly remind us: perverted religion, the yoke of which has been carried by too many peoples. And, in the name of Christian values revolutions have been born against the Church which warded them off. We are not yet completely recovered from these rifts.
>
> Today, the Muslims take up the torch, with the same simplistic convictions. Once again it is in the name of God and of His eternal Law that we are promised a world from which, it is claimed, will be banned all diffculties, because

> Islam embraces all the aspects of life. But how to make one's own these promises? Are they founded upon history? Evidently not, because Muslim history, too, carries along the worst and the best, as all the other civilizations. Are these promises founded upon scholarly evidence? The demonstrations of the pseudo-scholars convince only the ignorant or those who a priori are in complete support of them. Does one have to become Muslim in order to see these promises being realised? Some push us to do so. However, nothing we see or hear encourage us to do so. (Claverie, 1996, pp. 52–3; see also pp. 61, 94)

In 1989, at the beginning of a period of heightened tension and virulent confrontation not yet ended, between islamist groups and government forces, Claverie foresees that these developments will profoundly affect the dialogue of the Church with Islam. His analysis makes out, on the one hand, openings on the part of single Muslims, '*sensibles aux evolutions contemporaines*, who appeal to a new reading of the sources in order to find in them the inspiration capable of vitalizing contemporary Muslim society' (Claverie. 1996, p. 40).

On the other hand, he speaks of 'the irresistible wave, surging from a forgotten depth carrying a mad hope of reinstating a mythical Islamic polity, structured according to the *Shari'a*' (*ibid.*).

Claverie's advice is:

> Let us keep calm faced with the upheaval of political life. Let us not loose our judgement and let us be, above all, on the side of the little ones and the men and women who thirst for truth, justice, liberty and peace. Finally, let us not forsake the encounter and the dialogue with the Muslims in all their diversity. Let us not be discouraged by the signs of hardening attitudes and let us search continually for openings. Let us not shrink away from those who seek support from us in their struggle for overcoming the lack of understanding and for 'opening the frontiers of the spirit'. (*ibid.*, p. 41)

In March and April 1990, at the time when the (oppositional) FIS (*Front islamique du salut*) and the (governmental) FFS (*Front des forces socialistes*), after having been legalized in 1989, were preparing the first great demonstrations, Claverie wrote a pastoral letter in two instalments: 'L'étape présente du dialogue islamo-chrétien en Algérie'. Noting the rise of 'the religious factor' and the progressive islamisation of the context of life, even in the great cities, he discusses at greater length the themes developed by the president of the FIS, Madani Abbassi which dominate the political discourse of all parties. Claverie takes 'each one of these themes' to be conducive 'to deepen our knowledge of God and of His relations with the human person and with history, in other words, (to deepen our knowledge of) the function of religion in society' (*ibid*., p. 66). He singles out for discussion five of them: submission to God; *laicité*; democracy; woman; the other (the stranger), because, he suggests, 'they can become matter of a true dialogue with our Muslim friends' (*ibid*., p. 66).

After having indicated the historical context in which the concept of *laicité* developed and finally found acceptance in France, Claverie contrasts Muslim and Christian positions on the issue of the relationship of religion and state. The Muslims claim that the religious factor cannot just be conceived of as a private matter. Instead, it must permeate collective life in order to allow persons to make the right choices in the spheres of cultic and social life. The Christian side fears that full citizenship in an Islamically structured polity (in other words: the *dār al-Islām*) will be accorded only to the Muslim, whereas the members of the minorities are *de iure* considered and *de facto* treated as 'protected ones', the tolerated remainder of past religions which in a more or less short period of time cannot but find their destiny in being Islamised. Islamic tolerance, as conceived of by classical Islamic legislation, Claverie argues, cannot claim any more today convincingly to ensure what other societies in fact do ensure, also with regard to the Muslim minorities: the legal recognition of the latter's freedom, and an equal treatment as compared to the other social groups.

> Personally, I understand perfectly well that the Islamist condemns *laicité*, because it threatens the foundations of society in so far as society wants to remain a confessional one and to ensure the domination of one religious group, however tolerant. The neutrality of the state here [in such a confessional state] is unacceptable, as the president of the FIS says frequently. Accepting it would amount to renouncing to the effort of making respected the rights of God on His earth, the '*terre d'Islam*'. (*ibid*., p. 72)

Numerous are the questions *laicité* provides for Christian-Muslim dialogue:

> Do we have to think that the Muslim countries are and will always be, by nature and divine vocation, confessional societies, and that the Muslims dispersed all over the world, cannot conceive of an ideal society other than a Muslim one or as one on the way of becoming a Muslim one? Yet, *laicité* does not mean only neutrality of the state, it presupposes that the religions as such give up (the claim and the desire) to rule. In this area questions would have to be put also to the Christians, as to which kind of relationship they intend to establish between the religious and the political factor, and as to what place they intend to make for the other religions in a pluralist society of Christian tradition. (*ibid.*, p. 73)

Concerning democracy, the key question in Islamic political thought is whether 'it would be possible'—as M. Arkoun claims it to be—'to distinguish between religious and political power, the former governing the cultic and moral prescriptions on the basis of Koran and Sunna, the latter taking inspiration from religious orientations in the elaboration of a positive law that meets the demands of modern societies and is capable of being revised according to the economic, cultural and political data of the societies in question' (*ibid.*, p. 75).

> All that can enhance the respect—and not only the tolerance—of the rights of the minorities and hence their active and responsible participation in the future of the country, constitutes a positive step in the direction of just and true relations, which alone can provide the basis of a serene dialogue. (*ibid.*)

On the question of the rights of woman and their place in society, Claverie once more shows that for him critical questions to the partner in dialogue always go together with a critical assessment of one's own society, in this case, of the woman's position and rights in the Church, past and present. Discussing the theme of the 'other', Claverie stigmatizes the 'strategy of the assailed fortress' by which 'too often one exalts the myth of an ideal Islamic society by disfiguring the other, contrasting the

Islamic ideal with the negative myth of the failure of the other civilizations. What is needed instead is:

> The precise and realistic analysis of situations, of one's own and of that of the others. This would allow,. to bring to light the failures and success on both sides. This effort at demystifcation has to be undertaken again and again. One of the bases of dialogue consists in the realistic approach to the other in his/her being different. We are still for from this. (*ibid.*, p. 78)

Claverie proposes to Christians and Muslims to pool their resources in order to act together for the defense of human rights, without distinction of race, religion or opinion, as also for the training and education of the young, in a spirit of openness as well as in the appreciation of cultural roots, in the movements or associations that work for the rehabilitation of the handicapped or the promotion of persons and the like. It is in a shared action, in an enduring human relationship, he stresses, that we establish the bases for a dialogue. Coexistence in difference is more than ever the call of the hour' (*ibid.*, p. 79).

H. Teissier in 1996 observed that the protracted terrorist action of Islamist groups in Algeria had substituted to the traditional division of Muslim and non-Muslim another one: the Islamists on the one side and the victims of Islamism (moderate Muslims, agnostics, Christians and Jews) on the other. In this way Christians and Muslims, Teissier thinks, are not placed any longer in two separate camps.

> Today many Muslims feel themselves standing on the same side with the Christians. The ones and the others together take conscience of the threat to the dignity of man, the respect of woman, the liberty of the human communities and fnally to the religion, the sense of God and the promotion of true spiritual values. Even more important is the fact that the collaboration between Christians and Muslims appears as the putting into practice of a project of God for the human person which makes it grow and frees it, or simply as a human project which constructs a future for all. (Teissier, 1996, p. 14)

How close the ideal of the solidarity of all believers—Muslim or Christian—with the disadvantaged, was to Claverie's heart, is seen in the last of his published essay *'Les derniers et le règne de l'homme'*. (Claverie, 1997) There he states his conviction that true religion cannot serve as a guarantee for any power. True religion, on the contrary, is the critical ferment that is interior to all possible systems. It prevents them from closing themselves off in smugness and from making themselves the object of idolatry.

3. Conclusion

In the foregoing pages I have confined myself to presenting some aspects of Catholic teachings concerning Christian-Muslim dialogue. The essay thus remains strictly on the normative level. In no way have I attempted here to present an outline of the history of Catholic-Muslim relations.

The texts that form the basis of our analysis, from the point of view of the Catholic faith, vary considerably as to their authoritative character for Catholics: texts of an ecumenical Council, i.e., of Vatican II, encyclical letters, papal allocations and speeches, reflections and orientations on the part of dicasteries of the Roman Curia, letters of the *Conseil des Patriarches Catholiques* d'Orient and of the *Conférence Épiscopale Régionale de l'Afrique du Nord*, pastoral letters, addresses and also essays by individual bishops. Yet, all these texts emanate from the Catholic hierarchy and are consequently an authentic expression of the way in which those who, according to Catholic tradition, are the appointed successors of the apostles, at present guide the communities of Catholic believers in their relationship with the Muslims and with Islam.[31]

Furthermore, in this essay I have restricted myself in two important ways. Only the most relevant documents of the 'centre' (Second Vatican Council, papal encyclicals, documents of Vatican dicasteries) and of the Arab world (Catholic Patriarchs of the Orient and bishops of the Regional Conference of North Africa) have been taken into account. I did not present here an analysis of comparable, relevant Episcopal teaching in other regions where Catholics live together with Muslims, such as, e.g., sub-Saharan Africa, Asia East of the Arab world and Europe. I also did not analyze here Catholic statements and declarations on sub-episcopal levels, not to speak of the numerous shared Catholic-Muslim and Christian-Muslim Declarations of the past decades (see Haddad, 1997).

The encyclical *Ecclesiam suam* of Pope Paul VI, published on 6 August 1964, i.e. between the second and the third sessions of the Vatican Council, breathed the spirit of the theology that had prepared the Council and inspired its first two sessions. In its turn, this encyclical was to leave a palpable imprint on the subsequent debates of Vatican II and on the documents it produced.

It has been the aim of this essay to show the place which interreligious dialogue in its various modes occupies within the overall Catholic vision of the Church and her relationship to the religious world around her and to point out its theological presuppositions and the inner link between mission and dialogue.[32]

This overall vision of interreligious dialogue was significantly developed and globally propagated during the decades after Vatican II. From the beginning of his pontificate in 1978 Pope John Paul II paid special attention to Christian-Muslim relations, not least on the occasion of his frequent pastoral visits to countries where Catholics and Muslims are living together.

Whether the allocutions of the Pope are addressed to Muslim, Catholic or mixed audiences, they usually form part of elaborate diplomatic arrangements in often delicate and complex political circumstances. These naturally would seem to favour a polite, somewhat general, not too explicit, optimistically-coloured type of discourse. This explains to some extent a certain distance or, at times even, estrangement on the part of leaders of local Churches, vis-à-vis the discourse and the initiatives of the central Church authority with regard to Christian-Muslim relations and dialogue. Catholic leaders who live within Muslim majority societies, often detect in the statements and activities of the Holy See vis-à-vis Muslim governments, institutions and movements a tendency to refrain from addressing concrete problems and mentioning unpleasant facts: doing so could easily spoil the atmosphere of serene diplomatic relations.

Whereas the local Churches, 'on the spot' as it were, perceive Muslims and Islam from the places where they share life and try to practice good neighbourly relations, the Centre speaks in a global context. The difficult task of translating the noble principles and ideals into everyday reality largely is left to the local Churches.

I, therefore, chose to balance the overall presentation by moving in its second part to one specific region of Christian-Muslim relations: the Arab-speaking world. The particular history as well as the present socio-cultural realities of Christian-Muslim relations in the Arab Middle East on the one hand and in North Africa, on the other, produce in the teaching of Christian-Muslim relations and on dialogue significant new emphases. Not surprisingly, themes that are relatively little, or not at all, mentioned in the documents of the Holy See, gain prominence on the regional level.

The Catholic Patriarchs of the Orient speak on the basis of the centuries-old cultural kinship of Christian and Muslim Arabs in the Middle East. Their primary aim is to preserve and develop this relationship, while preserving and strengthening their own identities as Christians and Christian communities of the Arab East. They see dialogue above all as the privileged means to pursue this task.

Concretely they demand an open dialogue on such questions as the distinction between the religious and the political spheres of national life as it finds concrete expression in the legislation and in day to day running of e.g. the educational institutions, the mass media and the political parties. They ask for initiating and deepening dialogue on the concept and legal definition of citizenship, with the aim of arriving at a truly equal status for all citizens. They propose dialogue on the issue of violence perpetrated, and at times even propagated, in the name of religion. At the same time, the Catholic patriarchs are aware that honest dialogue on issues of harmonious 'living together' needs, as a condition of its possibility and eventual success, the development of new attitudes growing out of a reformed vision of faith, in other words, a new sense of spiritual solidarity beyond the confines of one's own (ethnic-cultural-religious) community.

The distinct history and peculiar composition of the minuscule Church of North Africa as well as the specific character of Christian-Muslim relations here, reflects itself in the discourse of the bishops of Algeria. They are aware of the difficulty of translating the lofty dialogical vision of the Vatican Council and of the Holy See's teachings on dialogue into the everyday realities of Christian life in Algeria. They prefer to speak of: *'partage d'humanité'*.

The bishops of Algeria view the life of the Christian in Algerian society as a true 'dialogue of life'. Simultaneously, they are convinced that the conditions for formal dialogue(s) about ideological and theological questions, at least in Algeria, hardly exist yet. In this context noble sentiments and moral maxims alone lead nowhere. First of all, the conditions for true co-existence have to be met and serious obstacles to it need to be removed. Furthermore, the bishops are aware of the fact that co-existence of groups (naturally including religious groups) is a power-relationship and as such has to be negotiated continuously.

It is not by accident that the most sober, if not pessimistic, analysis of the *status quo* (in 1988) of *formal* Christian-Muslim dialogues comes from the Archbishop of Algiers. He considers formal dialogue to be in a state of grave illness and immobility. Without applying as it were a whole range of costly and taxing remedies to the suffering patient, formal dialogue in Algeria and beyond, Teissier thinks that it will hardly regain health.

We are not surprised then to learn that the bishops of Algeria, faced with the protracted wave of violent and terrorist action on the part of groups acting in the name of Islam, increasingly place dialogue in the context of living and collaborating in solidarity with all those 'believers'—be they persons who practice religion or not—who are conscious of the threat to the dignity of the human person and the liberty of human communities.

The very crisis of Algeria with 'the pathological deviations of the armed Islamist groups' (Teissier, 1996, p. 14), Teisser judges, has given a new spiritual depth of Muslim-Christian collaboration, especially with those Muslims who suffer from the violence of the Islamists and who try to live Islam in quite a different way. Christians should be prepared, however, to encounter the Islamists as persons beyond their ideology.

This statement reminds us that dialogue, as a desire to establish mutual relationships of respect, by its very nature is unconditional. As a lived social reality, however, even if only between two persons, dialogue presupposes the willingness on both sides to enter into such a relationship. Moreover, as soon as one moves from individual relationships or that of small groups into formal dialogue between partners as members and even representatives, of institutions, existing legal and political structures with their underlying power relationships become relevant and in some sense determining.

In the effort to promote formal dialogue on a larger scale, a continuous listening will be needed, to the way in which the partners in dialogue perceive the other side and its willingness to engage in dialogue. Only recently have a few Christian scholars and scholarly institutions made it a point to engage on a regular basis in this kind of study and research, especially with regard to the Muslims' perception of Christianity and Christian-Muslim relations. These are distinct signs that a younger generation of Muslim scholars, whether citizens of Muslim majority countries or of countries where Muslims form a minority—in the East and the West—are beginning to study seriously and in an orderly fashion Christian faith. In that effort they also pay attention to Christian practice and religious thought, including the Christian teachings on, and perceptions of, interreligious dialogue. This essay hopes to serve such a promising endeavour.

Abbreviations

AG *Ad Gentes*. Vatican II 'Decree on the Church's Missionary Activity'. Bulletin Bulletin of the Secretariatus pro non Christianis (from 1990 onwards: Pontificium Consilium Pro Dialogo Inter Religiones) (Città del Vaticano). From the beginning of 1994 onwards continued under the title: Pro Dialogo.

DH *Dignitatis Humanae*. Vatican II 'Declaration on Religious Liberty'.

DM The Attitude of the Church towards the Followers of the Religions: Reflections and Orientation on Dialogue and Mission. Città del Vaticano: Secretariatus pro non Christianis, 1984.

DP Dialogue and Proclamation: Reflections and Orientations on Interreligious Dialogue and the Proclamation of the Gospel of Jesus Christ Vatican City: Pontifical Council for Interreligious Dialogue and Congregation for the Evangelization of Peoples, 1991.

DV *Dominum et Vivificantem*. The Holy Spirit in the Life of the Church and the World. Boston, MA 02130: St. Paul Books and Media. n.d.

EAL L'Exhortation Apostolique post-synodale, "Une espérance nouvelle pour le Liban" de Sa Sainteté Jean-Paul II. Aux Patriarches, aux Evêques, au Clergé, aux Religieux, aux Religieuses et a tous les Fideles du Liban (10 mai 1997).

ES *Ecclesiam Suam.*(1964) (Paths of the Church) Encyclical Letter of Pope Paul VI. Boston: Pauline Books and Media, n.d.

G Francesco Gioia, ed., *Interreligious Dialogue: The Official Teaching of the Catholic Church (1963–1995)*, Boston, MA 02130: St. Paul Books and Media, 1997.

GS *Gaudium et Spes.* Vatican II 'Pastoral constitution on the Church in the Modern World'.

NA *Nostra Aetate.* Vatican II 'Declaration on the Relations of the Church to non-Christian Religions'.

RH *Redemptor Hominis.* (1979) Encyclical Letter of Pope John Paul II. London: Catholic Truth Society, n.d.

RM *Redemptoris Missio.* (1990) Encyclical Letter of Pope John Paul II on the Permanent Validity of the Church's Missionary Mandate. London: Catholic Truth Society, 1991.

SELECT BIBLIOGRAPHY

Anawati, Georges C., 'Vers un dialogue islamo-chrétien', *Revue thomiste,* 64, 1964, pp. 280–326; 585–630.

— —, 'Exkurs zum Konzilstext über die Muslime', *Lexikon für Theologie und Kirche,* Das Zweite Vatikanische Konzil, Teil II, Freiburg: Herder, 1967, pp. 485–7.

Arinze, Francis, *Meeting Other Believers*, Herefordshire: Grace wing Fowler Wright Books, 1997.

— —. *Christian-Muslim Relations in the Twenty-First Century*, Washington, D.C.: Center for Muslim-Christian Understanding, 1998.

Caspar, Robert, 'Le Concile et l'Islam', *Etudes,* 324, 1966, pp. 114–26.

Chenu, Bruno, ed., *Sept vies pour Dieu et l'Algérie,* Paris: Bayard Editions, 1996.

Claverie, Pierre, 'Chemins du dialogue Islamo-Chrétien', Bulletin no. 61, vol. XXI/I (1986), pp. 12-31, repr. CLAVERIE, 1996, pp. 185–207.

— —, *Lettres et messages d'Algérie,* 2nd ed., Paris: Editions Karthala, 1996.

— —, 'Les derniers et le règne de l'homme', Enrico Ferri, ed., *Monoteismo e conflitto,* Napoli: CUEN, 1997, p. 243–54.

De Cherge, Christian, 'L'échelle mystique du dialogue', *Islamochristiana,* 23, 1997, pp. 1–26.

Dupuis, Jacques, Art. 'Interreligious Dialogue', in Latourelle, R. and R. Fisichella, eds., *Dictionary of Fundamental Theology,* New York: Crossroad, 1995.

Editors, *Pro Mundi Vita Bulletin,* 'The Muslim-Christian Dialogue of the Past Ten Years (68–78)', Part Three. Repr. in Richard W. Rousseau, ed.), *The Struggling Dialogue,* Scranton: Ridge Row Press, 1985, pp. 129–59.

FABC Papers, (no. 38), *Christian Presence among Muslims in Asia.* A Consultation of the Federation of Asian Bishops' Conferences. Nav Sadhana, Varanasi, India, November 26-December 4, 1983. The full text of all the papers, group reports, the final report and message in *Church and Islam.* Report of a Consultation, held 26 November–4 December 1983, Nav Sadhana, Varanasi.

Fitzmaurice, Redmond, 'The Roman Catholic Church and Interreligious Dialogue: Implications for Christian-Muslim Relations', *Islam and Christian-Muslim Relations,* 3, 1992, pp. 83–107.

G.R.I.C. (Groupe de Recherches islamo-chrétien), *Ces Ecritures qui nous questionnent,* La Bible et le Coran, Paris: Le Centurion, 1987.

Haddad, Juliette Nasri, *Déclarations communes Islamo-chrétiennes 1954 c.–1995 c./1373 h.–1415 h.)* Sous la direction de A. Dupré la Tour SJ et Dr. Hisham Nashabé, Beyrouth: Dar el-Machreq, 1997.

Lebatelier, Nasreddin, (Pseudonym for Jean Y. Michot), *Ibn Taymiyya Le statut des moines.* Trad. Francaise, en reference a l'affaire de Thiberine, Beyrouth: El-Safina Editions, 1997.

— —, (Pseudonym for Jean Y. Michot), *Ibn Taymiyya. Le statut des moines.* Trad. française, en référence à l'affaire de Thibérine, Beyrouth: El-Safina Éditions, 1997.

Michel, Thomas, 'Christianity and Islam. Reflections on recent Teaching of the Church', *Encounter* (Rome: P.I.S.Ai.), no. 112, 1985.

— —, 'Pope John Paul II's Teaching about Islam in His Addresses to Muslims', *Bulletin,* no. 62, vol. XXI/2, 1986, pp. 182–91.

Patriarches Catholiques D'orient, 'Un temps decisive pour les Eglises du Moyen Orient', *La Documentation Catholique,* no. 2037, 1991, pp. 938–42.

— —, 'La présence chrétienne en Orient: témoignage et mission', *La Documentation Catholique,* no. 2052, 1992, pp. 595–611.

— —, 'Ensemble devant Dieu: pour le bien de la personne et de la société' (La coexistence entre musulmans et chrétiens dans le monde arabe) *La Documentation Catholique,* no. 2113, 1994, pp. 320–36.

Pontifical Council For Interreligious Dialkogue, *Guidelines for Dialogue between Muslims and Christians.* Prepared by Maurice Borrmans. Tr. From the French original (publ. 1981) by R. Marston Speight, New York: Paulist Press, 1990.

— —, *Recognise the Spiritual Bonds which Unite Us.* 16 years of Christian-Muslim Dialogue, Vatican City: P.C.I.D., 1994.

Pruvost, Lucie, 'From Tolerance to Spiritual Emulation: An analysis of official texts on Christian-Muslim dialogue', *Islamochristiana,* 6, 1989, pp. 1–9.

Renard, John, 'Christian-Muslim Dialogue: a review of six Vatican II Church-related documents', L. Swidler, ed., *Muslims in Dialogue: the evolution of a dialogue*. Lewiston/ Queenstown/Lampeter: The Edwin Mellen Press, 1992, pp. 283–310.

Sabbah, Michel, 'Les chrétiens de Terre Sainte aujourd'hui et le dialogue des religions. *La Documentation Catholique*, 18 fevrier, no. 2132, 1996, pp. 176–80.

Tanner, Norman P. (ed.), *Decrees of the Ecumenical Councils*, vol. 2 (Trent—Vatican II), London/Washington (DC): Sheed/ Georgetown Univ.

Teissier, Henri, *Eglise en Islam: méditation sur l'existence chrétienne en Algérie*, Paris: Le Centurion, 1984.

——, 'Pour un renouveau du dialogue islamo-chrétien', *Islamo-christiana*, 15, 1989, pp. 95–107.

——, 'Un alleanza fra credenti per vincere l'integralismo', *Mondo e Missione*, Aprile 1996, pp. 11–14.

Troll, Christian W. 'Changing Catholic Views of Islam', in: Jacques Waardenburg (ed.), *Islam and Christianity: Mutual perceptions since the mid-20th Century*, Leuven: Peeters, 1998, pp. 19–77.

NOTES

1. For a typology of interreligious dialogue from a post-Vatican II perspective, see Sabah, 1996, p. 178
2. Boston: Pauline Books & Media, 1997, p. 694 (abbreviated here as G). The Italian edition: *Il Dialogo interreligioso nel Magistero Pontificio* (Citta del Vaticano: Libreria Editrice Vaticana, 1994), p. 879, offers documents published up to 1993. Both publications include excellent indices (general, geographical and analytical). The beautifully illustrated and expertly composed volume *Recognize the Spiritual Bonds which Unite Us.* 16 years of Christian-Muslim dialogue by the Pontifical Council for Interreligious Dialogue (Vatican City, 1994) constitutes a valuable companion volume to Gioia, as far as Christian-Muslim Relations are concerned.

   Gioia's edited volume presents first the texts of Vatican Council II that relate to interreligious dialogue, then the texts belonging to what he terms the 'solemn magisterium', i.e. relevant encyclical letters of popes Paul VI and John Paul II. These are followed by numerous texts belonging to the 'magisterium', consisting here of a considerable number of papal allocutions addressed to a great variety of audience in Rome and throughout the world. Finally, Gioia's volume produces the relevant documents of the dicasteries of the Roman Curia, parts of legislative documents such as the Code of Canon Law and the Code of Canons of the Oriental Churches as well as extracts from documents of the theological commission. The magisterium of the Church, in other words, the 'teaching authority of bishops' comprises besides the teaching of the bishop of Rome that of other bishops and their regional and national conferences.

3. In a later essay we hope to make an analogous study of significant variation of Catholic teaching on Christian-Muslim dialogue in Asia, in Africa and elsewhere.
4. For an explanation of the Roman Catholic teaching on the biblical foundation, the various forms of the exercise and the subject matter of the magisterium see Francis A. Sullivan, art. *Magisterium*, in Latourelle. 1995, pp. 614–20.
5. Within the limits of the present essay the part dealing with interreligious dialogue as such as to confine itself to the documents of the Holy See.
6. Jacques Dupuis, art. 'Interreligious Dialogue' in R. Latourelle & R. Fisichella (eds.), *Dictionary of Fundamental Theology*, New York: Crossroad, 1995, p. 518.
7. The English text of Gioia by a serious mistake has left out the adjective 'true'.
8. See Anawati, 1967 and Caspar, 1966, passim.
9. Important references in this context are: RH 14; DV 53, quoted in G 170; DP 30f.
10. Card. Jozef Tomko, Prefect of the Congregation for the Evangelization of Peoples, in the press conference on the occasion of the release of the document *Dialogue and Proclamation* on 20.6.1991 printed as introduction to the document (*DP*, p. 208).
11. The allocation of John Paul II to the Roman Curia of 22 December \ 1986 was totally dedicated to defending the holding of the Day of Assisi and to expounding its deeper theological meaning. It can justifiably be considered the key theological document of this pope's pontificate. Of special importance would seem to be the following phrase: '. the Church is called to work with all her energies. so that the wounds and divisions of men. may be healed'. It means also that the entire human race, in the infinite complexity of its history, with its different cultures, is 'called to form the new People of God to which, in various ways, being or are oriented both the Catholic faithful and the others who believe in Christ, and finally all who have been called to salvation by the grace of God' (LG 13) (G 567).
12. The same document stresses: the Church's commitment to dialogue is not dependent on success in achieving mutual understanding and enrichment (see DP 53).
13. 'Christianity and Islam. Reflections on Recent Teachings of the Church', *Encounter* Rome, PISAI, 1985, no. 112, p. 6.
14. Cf. esp. G 339 (Ankara 1979).
15. The Pope does not, however, downplay the fundamental differences:

'Loyalty demands also that we should recognize and respect our differences. Obviously, what is most fundamental is the view we hold on the person and work of Jesus of Nazareth.' (*G* 474) [Casablanca 1985]).

16. Here I follow closely Th. Michel's summary of John Paul II's teaching on Christian-Muslim dialogue ('Pope John Paul II's Teaching about Islam, in his Addresses to Muslims' in *Bulletin* (Secretariatus, Roma) XXI/2: 182-91. Here specifically p. 187f.). However, I shall add elements from later statements.
17. Cf., e.g. *DP* (1991) 42–3; also *G* 744 (Senegal 1992): 'We Christians and Muslims must be people of dialogue. this commitment to dialogue means, first of all, 'a dialogue of life,' a positive acceptance, interaction and co-operation by which we bear active witness, as believers to the ideals to which God has called us.'
18. In Troll, 1998, pp. 32–4. I have discussed the pioneering and influential work by Maurice Borrmans (M. Afr.) prepared for and published in the name of the Pontifical Council for Interreligious Dialogue (Pontifical Council, 1990).
19. The Council of the Catholic Patriarchs of the East comprises the Patriarchs of the following Churches: the Coptic Catholic Church, the Greek Catholic Church, the Syrian Catholic Church, the Maronite Catholic Church, the Chaldean Catholic Church and the Armenian Catholic Church. The Patriarch of Jerusalem for the Latin Christians also belongs to this Council which was formed in the early 1990's at a moment when the Lebanese and the Gulf Wars were still very fresh in the memories of the peoples of the Middle East.
20. That is how I render the French term of the original: 'confessionaliste'.
21. According to the rules regulating synods of bishops valid in the post-Vatican II Church, the results of the reflections and discussions of the bishops of a given region, together with priests, religious and lay representatives are taken up in the final synodal document which is then signed and proclaimed by the Bishop of Rome.
22. Part of this effort is also the courage to forgive and to put an end to points of ancient discord and enmity (Cf. EAL 14:89). 'After the years of suffering and the long period of war which Lebanon has experienced, its people and the governing authorities are called to perform courageous and prophetic gestures of forgiveness and healing of memory' (EAL 114).
23. See: *La Documentation Catholique*, 18 fevrier 1996, no. 2132, p. 176
24. In Jacques Waardenburg, ed., *Islam and Christianity: Mutual perceptions since the mid-20th century*, Leuven: Peeters, 1998, pp. 21–77.
25. Text in *La Documentation Catholique* (Paris), no. 1775 (2 December 1979), pp. 1032–46.

26. This statement would need to be slightly modified with regard to other parts of the Maghreb.
27. Reprinted in Claverie. 1996, pp. 185–207.
28. Madrid: Crislam, Darek-Nyumba, 1988, pp. 17–28. Here we refer to the reprint of the French version in *Islamochristiana*, see Teissier. 1989.
29. Teissier here refers to 'Le sens de nos rencontres', *La Documentation Catholique*. 1979k, column 1175, 1043, 10/2; cf. also DM 18.
30. For Claverie I refer to the monthly letters he as Bishop used to send to the faithful of his diocese, especially I refer to the ones written in March and April 1990, entitled 'L'étape présente du dialogue islamo-chrétien en Algérie' (Claverie. 1996, pp. 63–79) and for Teissier in an essay: 'Un'alleanza fra credenti per vincere l'integralismo' (An alliance between believers for overcoming integralism'), see Teissier 1996.
31. The Volume *Interreligious Dialogue. The official teaching of the Catholic Church*, edited by Gioia (see G), for instance, distinguishes: Teachings of the Council; Solemn Magisterium; Magisterium of Pope.; Documents of the Dicasteries; Legislative Documents. We have added texts of the ordinary magisterium of catholic patriarchs and bishops.
32. It would, however, need a further, distinct sutyd to highlight the various factors that have contributed to convince the bishops, including the Bishop of Rome, of the need for a dialogical approach in the Church's interreligious relations, and which finally made the call to dialogue an essential and integral part of official Catholic teaching in our day.

7

Who is Christ for Me—In the Context of Encountering Muslims and Studying Islam?

1. My Encounter with Muslims and with Islam

You have asked me to speak about emphases and peculiar features of my Christian vision (which as such implies a distinct vision of the mystery of Christ), after years of living in various Christian-Muslim settings and constellations, in and outside Europe, years spent largely in meeting Muslims and in listening to the voices of Islam past and present, in the spirit of critical study and dialogue. Muslims and Islam have indeed become an important and integral dimension of my life and thought.

In fact, the study of aspects of Islamic culture(s) and religion for me always has been part of the living encounter with Muslims. In this encounter Islam has constantly challenged and put into question my Christian beliefs and practices, my Christian faith. I had to make ever anew the effort to answer the question: 'But you, who do you say I am' (Mt 16:15)? Obviously, this question concerns the totality of the faith vision peculiar to us Christians. The answer given to it determines the conception we have of God, of His relationship with the human person, created in His image and of relations between individuals and Communities in culturally and religiously plural settings.

---

* This essay was first published in 'Who is Jesus Christ for me—in the Context of Encountering Muslims and Studying Islam?', in *Who is Jesus a World of Many Faiths?* Report of the Swanwick Christology Conference, September 1999, London: CCIFR/ CTBI, 1999, pp. 16–36.

2. The Basic Religious Act and the Core Meaning of Islam

In the beginning of my encounter with Muslim believers, and hence with the Koran, I became interested in the latter's portrayal of Jesus and his mother—my first public talk to a Christian audience in fact dealt with Mary in the Koran. However, very soon I realised that it is not the figure of the prophet 'Isa, nor that of Moses, for that matter, but rather that of Abraham, who—of course after 'the seal of the prophets', Muhammad—occupies the central place in the Koran and even more so in the practice of the Muslim faith. The faith and unconditional obedience of Abraham represent the pure monotheism which Muhammad felt called to restore once and for all. The whole ritual of the *hajj* would seem to be as it were a 'sacramental' re-living of Abraham's faith and obedience just as *'Ìd al-kabīr,* the 'Great Feast', the 'Feast of Sacrifice', re-enacts Abraham's willingness to sacrifice his son in obedience to God's mysterious Will. Thus the pilgrim throughout the *hajj* continuously utters the *talbýyah,* the prayer of readiness to do the Will of the Lord: *labbayka Allāhumma labbayka:* What is Thy Command? I am here, O God! And, again and again the pilgrims add:

> O God, shower Thy Blessings upon Muhammad,
> And the family of Muhammad,
> As Thou didst shower Thy Mercy upon Ibrahim,
> And the family of Ibrahim,
> Thou art Praised, Glorious!
> O God, beatify Muhammad,
> And the family of Muhammad,
> As Thou hast beatifed Ibrahým,
> And the Family of Ibrahým,
> Thou art Praised, Glorious!

Let me begin, therefore, with putting before us the central part of the rite of the Pilgrimage, the *wuqūf,* together with a small number of selected prayers as the pilgrims recite them at that point of the Hajj. As far as I can see, nothing makes more palpable and expresses more precisely and concisely the core of Islam than the *wuquf,* the rite of the 'standing in front of Allah of all pilgrims in the Valley of 'Arafat by high noon on the ninth day of the *Dhū al-hijjah,* the last month of the Islamic calendar. It would seem to be here that we touch the pulse and listen to the heartbeat of Islam. It is the reality of Muslim faith and practice superbly expressed in that rite, which throughout the past four decades has inspired, enriched and challenged me as a Christian fellow-believer deeply interested in Muslims and Islam. Any inner dialogue with these must, I submit, start and return again and again from the reality of Muslims' faith and attitude densely expressed in the rite of *wuqūf* during the hajj. It is here, where true believers in God, whether members of the *umma* or not, can continually 'communicate', notwithstanding—and without in any way minimizing—all the essential differences that obtain between the two universes of faith and practice, of vision of God and of divine-human relationship.

A. Kamal Writes in the the Sacred Journey

'This is the Hajj. These are the supreme hours. Here by the mountain, the pilgrim will pass what should be, spirituality and intellectually, the noblest hours of life. The letters of the Faithful will cover the undulating variety as far as the eye can see. The immense congregation with the sacred mountain as its center is the heart of Islam. This is the day of the brotherhood, the day when God is revealed to His servants. We are promised that in these hours by 'Arafāt God will send down His forgiveness and mercy on those who are deserving and they will feel his presence. This is the day of brotherhood and heartbreak—heartbreak that we have not yet learned to cling to his solidarity where we dwell and labour in valleys and on mountains far from 'Arafāt. This is the day of promise, the guarantee of what Islam shall be when Muslims everywhere achieve the oneness today only known at 'Arafāt.'[1]

Lex orandi—lex credendi: the prayers pronounced on this occasion teach us the basic faith and spirituality of Muslims. They lay open, as it were, the heart of Islam. Here some extracts:

[*Tauhīd*, God: Creator, eternal, good and powerful; Muhammad, His chosen model]

> There is no deity except God, without companion! For Him is the Kingdom and the Praise He maketh to live—but dieth not! And in His hand is goodness.
> And He is All-Powerful!
> Our Lord, thou hast granted that we may stay here.
> Following the path of Thy Friend,

And following the footprints of Thy Chosen
From all Thy creatures,
Our Prince, Muhammad,
Upon whom be Peace and Blessings

[God giver of forgiveness, guidance, merciful liberator from eternal death]

And I seek of Thee, Our Lord, Thy forgiveness,
And that thou art pleased with me.
After which there can be no anger;
And guidance, after which there can be no error,
And a good and, and liberation from the fre, and reward with Paradise,
And to be remembered by Thee
When I am in misfortune,
When the mortals of the world forget me, and the earth covers.
And I am parted from my loved ones
And all is severed
O Most Glorious! O Bestower!
O Most Merciful of those who show mercy!

[Humble prayer of forgiveness from sins]

I am miserable and poverty-stricken...
Lamenting and confessing and knowing my sins,
Seeking from Thee as the humble seek
And I implore of Thee with the supplication of an abject sinner,
And I pray to Thee the prayer of a blind and frightened man,
The prayer of him who submits his neck to thee,
And weeps thee,
And is prostrate before There.

[Prayer for transforming grace]

Our Lord, create in my heart light,
in my ears light,
in my eyes light,
in my tongue light,
At my right light,

Above me light,
And create light in my soul –
And for me glorify light

[Prayer for real, effective faith]

Lord of all,
And King of all,
And Predestinator of all –
I pray to thee to grant me:
Wholesome knowledge,
And virtuous deeds,
And real Faith!
And grant that we may experience:
The repentance of the Faithful,
The submission of the submissive,
And the deeds of the virtuous,
And the conviction of those who are convinced,
The felicity of the God-fearing,
And the High Degree of the successful!

[The servant utterly ready to obey any divine command]

What is Thy Command? I am here, O God! (*labbaika!*)
Happiness attend Thee!
And all good is in they hands.
And I repent unto Thee!
Amen.[2]

3. The Scope of this Paper and Acknowledgements

In what follows I try to give a short account of the essential and distinctive features of my Christian faith as it has developed in the encounter with Islam. I shall present the relevant points not in their quality as basic dogmas of the Catholic Christian faith as one would find them in any catechism, rather I intend (a) to indicate the emphases of my Christian faith and practice, given the peculiar context of Christian-Muslim dialogue in which it has developed and (b) to indicate the basic structure, the inner logic that holds together these various emphases. Concretely this means: I shall try to show which place Christ occupies in my overall vision of faith and why my religious vision and my intelligence of faith centers on Christ and, through him, on the mystery of the triune

God of love. In the course of this exposition I shall only here and there explicitly refer to elements of the message of Islam. However, the challenging context of the Islamic message, as testimony of the Truth claiming continual attention, conversion and adherence, will be present effectively throughout this presentation as it has been throughout my adult life. Put differently, I shall expose the emphases and the inner logic of my faith and my central beliefs 'in the presence' as it were of believing and theologically reflecting Muslim interlocutors. As a Christian who tries to explain his distinctly Christian beliefs in the context of Islam I know myself standing in a larger crowd of co-religionists belonging to practically all ages since the appearance of Islam. Christians who have tried to give account creatively and faithfully in the context of Christian-Muslim encounter. I am thinking especially of the tradition of Arab-Christian theological thought. Following this tradition I take as my basic plan the divine design of God for humanity. It is the structure of all the eastern and western anaphoras[3]: they speak about the design of God for humankind as it realizes itself in Jesus Christ.

PART ONE

4. God Creates the Universe and Man Because He is the Giver of Good

4.1. The Motive for God Creating the Universe and Man

Meditating the universe in its grandeur and order the Christian tradition concludes—indeed together with the Jewish and the Islamic tradition—that there exists a Creator. What is God's motive in creating us? Creation certainly did not come about by mere chance. Also, God certainly did not create because He was bored and was looking for a companion. He also did not create just for a joke, *'abathan,* as it were. (The Koran insists on this point, using this very term, cf. Q 28, 115.) Certainly God was 'motivated in creating. By which motive?

We can say, together with all the Christian Arab theologians, God has created us out of goodness, mercy, compassion, love. They express this by the following Arabic terms; *ra'fah, rahmah, lutf, jūd,* and sometimes *hubb,* although this last term is used much less frequently, because it does not figure in the Muslim vocabulary designating God. In any case, the overall answer is: God created because He is by nature generous, He is essentially *al-Jawwād* (the Giver of good), the Bestower. This is the motive of God in creating man and the universe together with and for man.

This attribute *al-Jawwād* (in some of the many respective lists it figures as one of the 'beautiful names of God' in the Muslim tradition) is one of the terms normally used by the Arab Christians in rendering the phrase of Saint John: '*God is love*' (1 Jn 4, 8 and 4, 16). They translate '*Allah huwa i-Jawwād*', i.e. God is the Bestower *par excellence*. And they start from this notion, when they expose their vision of the Christian faith

God out of His goodness has created the universe and man as the responsible master of it, in other words, as the representative (*khalīfa*) of God on earth, as the one responsible here on earth for the universe.

Starting from the action of God in the universe, I discover His nature, His essence. I ascend from His acts to His being and recognize Him as good, the only good, as Christ tells the young rich man (Lk 18, 19). God as the Giver of good par excellence. Whatever is good here on earth, it derives from the goodness of God, as the letter of James teaches: '*Make no mistake about this, my dear brothers, all that is good, all that is perfect, is given us from above; it comes down from the Father of all light* (Jas 1, 16-17)

4.2. God Takes the Initiative and Continuously Seeks Man

In the light of the history of the God-man relationship as traced by the biblical Scriptures, we affirm the extraordinary fact that God is constantly in search of man, long before the latter searches God. God again and again takes the initiative, pursuing as it were man with his love, even when man forgets or even opposes God. If man searches God, it is always in response to God's initiative. As Jeremiah puts it (cf. e.g. 20,7): '*You have seduced me, Yahweh, and I have let myself be seduced; you have overpowered me: you were stronger*' (cf. also the images of the shepherd [Ez 34] and of the vine [Is 5; Ez 17,6-10], expressing the same ardour and drama of God's initiatives)

The first letter of John repeatedly states the fact of the anteriority of God's love: '*Love consists in this: it is not we who loved God, but God loved us.*' (4,10). *And: 'Let us love, then, because He first loved us'* (4, 19).

St. Paul expresses the same in his own way: '*So it is proof of God's own love for us, that Christ died for us while we were still sinners*' (Rm 5, 8). And again: '*He [the Son of God] loved me and gave himself for me*' (Gal 2, 20).

John of the Cross has taken up this idea poetically in the canticle *The Dark Night of the Soul* where he speaks of God and man as the hunter and the game, and where he asks himself, who of the two is the hunter and who is in pursuit of the other.

5. The Incarnation Completes Creation and Indicates Its Meaning

5.1. The Act of Creation Continues, and Achieves Itself, in the Gift of the Incarnation

If God is essentially the Bestower, he will never cease to bestow. It is not thinkable that He should have given all in the beginning in the act of creating and that He would suddenly cease to bestow. To believe in God the Creator means to believe that God continues to create and re-create now and always. God continuously takes care of the world created by Him, especially of the human person and each person individually. In this way God is faithful to Himself, to His deepest being

In the line of this approach, the Arab Christians set out to present the 'necessity' of the incarnation: God is the Giver. By Creation God seeks the human being because He desires to give Himself to it. He desires to share Himself and to unite Himself to the human person, the apex of His Creation.

Now if God is the Giver *par excellence,* it is necessary that He bestow what is the most precious and valuable in the world. It is not thinkable that he would give as it were a good of secondary value. But what is the absolutely best that exists (*ajwad al-mawjūdāt*)? The best that exists is evidently God.

If then God is God—that is, the Bestower per excellence, *al-Jawwād,* then He will give not less than Himself. With Yahyā ibn 'Adī (Christian philosopher, *d.*974), one can say; the giver gives the best of the beings: *Al-Jawwād yajūd bi-ajwad al-mawjūdāt*)

5.2. Reply to a Possible Objection

Yahyā ibn 'Adī, at this point of his argument, makes an objection to which he replies himself. Two things could prevent this self-gift of God: on the part of God, the incapacity or the refusal of God to give Himself, on, the part of man, the impossibility to receive this gift.

On the part of God such incapacity is unthinkable, because it would mean that God cannot give Himself, in other words that He is not omnipotent, but rather that there would be in him an *'ajz* (weakness, deficit)—something that is impossible in God. Equally impossible is a refusal on the part of God, because it would mean that God does not want to give Himself, which is contrary to his nature of Giver of Good, of *Jawwād*. And there would exist in God a kind of avarice (*bukhl*), which again is impossible. If God, then he wishes to give Himself to man and He can do so. On the part of God nothing hinders this Gift, on the contrary.

On the part of the human person, in a similar way, God's uniting Himself to man is possible. Because the only thing that could render impossible the union (*ittihād*) of God and man would be an essential opposition (*tadādd* or *mudāddah*) between the two. Now, it is impossible that such an opposition should obtain between God and man, because God has created man and the contrary cannot bring into existence its contrary.

Rather, the act of creation implies a link between God and the human person, a link of love. There is then a certain compatibility between the two. This is in effect confirmed by Holy Scripture which tells us that God created Adam and Eve, '*in His image and likeness*' (vgl. Gn 1, 26). Now, who says 'image' says: what is called image, carries in himself something of the other, which is more than a mere compatibility.

5.3. *One and the Same Movement Unites Creation and Incarnation*

This presentation of the 'necessity' of the incarnation is clear, beautiful and above all deeply Christian: in the same movement God creates man (which leads Him to communicating Himself to man) and '*takes flesh*' (in order to become the other, man)

Another Christian Arab, al-Safī ibn al-'Assāl, took up this argument in 1239 in a simple and clear fashion. He says: In the same way in which God by creating man has perfected him, in the same way by incarnating himself does he perfect His love (*jūd*) and perfect the perfection (*kamāl*) of man. Here one could coin the telling phrase: *Allāh huwa Ajwad*!

It is then one and the same movement which links the two actions or manifestations of God. If one admits the creation of the world by God (the starting point of all believers, not least, Christians and Muslims), then one must also admit the incarnation. By Creation God bestows something, whereas in the incarnation God bestows Himself. To say that God incarnates Himself means to say that God is so much in search of man that He wants to unite Himself to him, and that He does so intensely that, finally, He realizes this union in the incarnate Word (we are fully aware, that only *post factum* we realize the incarnation to be the end (*finis*) and objective of Creation.

Let us try to see now, at which point exactly does this vision depart from that of our Muslim interlocutors?

5.4 Muslim Perceptions of God and God-Human Relations

Studying the history of Islamic religious thought and listening to different contemporary Muslim thinkers have taught me that there exists a great variety of Muslim perceptions as to the Love of God (*gen. subjectivus*, i.e., Love on the part of God) and consequently of God's relationship to man. I confine myself here to mentioning two positions

(1) Fazlur Rahman (1919-1988) in his well-known *Major Themes of the Koran* (Minneapolis/Chicago, 1980) states about God's power and lordship in relation to his 'infinite mercy': 'His power, creation, and mercy are. not only fully co-extensive but fully interpenetrating and fully identical: '*He has imposed the law of mercy upon Himself*' (6,12), and '*My mercy comprehends all* (7,156). 'God exercises His greatness, power and all-comprehensive presence primarily through the entire range of the manifestations of mercy.' (pp. 6, 7) However, 'God's mercy reaches its logical zenith' in guiding man (*hidāyah*) by way of 'sending messengers,' 'revealing books', and showing man 'the Way.' The prospect of final Judgement helps man 'to develop that inner torch (called *taqwā*) [i.e. reverential fear of God] by the Koran whereby he can discern between right and wrong'. (p. 9)

In Rahman's reading of the Koran the 'all-powerful, purposeful, and merciful God 'measures out' everything, bestowing upon everything the range of its potentialities.' Thus He ensures the orderliness of nature and at the same time 'expresses the most fundamental, unbridgeable difference between

His own divine nature and the nature of man: the Creator's measuring implies an infinitude wherein no measured creature—no matter how great its powers and potentialities (as in the case of man)—may literally share. It is precisely this belief in such sharing that is categorically denied by the Koranic doctrine of *shirk* or 'participation in Godhead' (pp. 12f.)

The divine mercy of the Koran in the thinking of Muslims like Rahman remains a function of all-powerfulness in the image of a—however benevolent—ruler or patriarch. To imagine God as bestowing Himself upon the human person amounts to 'lack of *taqwā*.' According Rahman states: 'For the Koran, then, Jesus can be as little an incarnation of God as Muhammad itself or, indeed, any other prophet.' (p. 169) As incontrovertible as the fact is that the Koran regards Jesus and his followers 'as exceptionally charitable and self-sacrificing', this does not gainsay the other teaching of the Koran: Jesus' divinity and the Trinity are unacceptable. The Christian doctrine of the incarnation, in the light of sura 112 ('which', as Rahman states, 'has been rightly regarded by the Islamic tradition as presenting the essence of the whole of the Koran' [p. 10]),

> 'Say He is Allah the One!
> Allah, the eternally Besought of all
> He begetteth not nor was begotten
> And there is none comparable unto Him!'

And in the light of sura 3, 64

> Say, O People of the Scripture! Come to an agreement between us and you: That we shall worship none but Allah, and that we shall ascribe no partner unto Him, and that none of us shall take others for lords beside Allah. And if they turn away, then say: 'Bear witness that we are they who have surrendered unto Him).'

The belief in the divine sonship of Jesus Christ is nothing less than *shirk* [the capital sin of associationism].'

Hope for a change of this situation, Rahman adds, depends on whether 'recent pioneering efforts continue to yield a Christian doctrine more compatible with universal monotheism and egalitarianism.' (p. 170)

(2) But what about Sufi perceptions of God and God-human

relations? They are far from uniform. Generally speaking, it is no exaggeration to say that they always have been marginalized by the official doctors of Islam. From the beginning of my encounter with Islam I have been conscious of the danger for a Christian of either identifying the Sufi approach with Islam, forgetting that it is far from being accepted by all Muslims as an integral dimension of true Islamic faith and practice, or of considering Sufism a sect, in other words, something separate or alien to true Islam.

Always fascinated by the remarkable 'mystical dimension of Islam' (A. Schimmel) I have also become convinced that although Sufis do not add anything essential to what Christians have in their religious culture—if only they be familiar with it—the Christian believer can and should draw (spiritual) profit from it. How? By 'reflecting' the light of Sufism in the mirror of a Christian thinking, not in order to annex it but in order to see its image, to understand it, recognize and appreciate its values. And what is this Christian thought which functions as reflecting mirror? It is simply a genuine Christian life-experience rooted in the sacramental life of the Church and a Christian thought nourished from the Old and New Testaments and, finally, openness to all that these sacred biblical texts have inspired in the great Christian mystics. Along with advancing in my Christian spiritual formation I discovered values in Sufism—in all its variety—highlighting central truth of my own spiritual tradition.

Leaving completely aside here the elaborations of esoteric and theosophical Sufis and the rich tradition of Sufi poetry of later centuries, we take just one example, Ibn Mansur al-Hallaj of Baghdad (857-922 ce), who among the Sufis of the classical period is perhaps the one to have meditated most profoundly the question that presents itself not only to the Sufis but to all thinking believers in the One God who speaks to men: How is it possible that God, the absolutely Transcendent, can all the same speak to humans, in a language understandable to them commanding them to recognize Him in His unicity and to observe His commandments, obeying Him as their Lord?[4]

A Sufi is essentially a Muslim believer who—practicing asceticism *(zuhd)* by which he becomes detached from worldliness—intends to discover himself as he is in the hands of God. The Sufi is highly conscious of God as creating him within the pact *(mithāq)* which binds him to God, his Lord. God, in the very act of creating man by His word: *kun,* demands of him to recognize Him as Lord and to come to Him in total freedom. When the Sufi puts his whole person to listening in the depth of his being to the revealed Word of God, he desires to arrive at hearing in the intimate secret of himself *(sirr)* the sound of the command *kun* which bestows existence.

In this perspective Al-Hallaj arrives at the following answer to our question:

> Whereas created human nature *(nāsūt)* insofar as it is creature is infnitely apart from the divine nature of the Creator insofar as it is creative (i.e. *lāhūt)*—since these two natures by defnition are distinct and separate— the divine creative being *(lāhūt),* in contrast, encloses in itself the effect of its act of creation. This is *nāsūt,* i.e. Humanity that manifests its [the divine creative being's, i.e., *lāhūt's)* sublimeness. There exists in effect a pre-eternal relation between *lāhūt* and *nāsūt,* and Humanity *(=nāsūt)* as manifestation of Divinity *(lāhūt)* is for the human creature which eats and drinks, the place of the truthful Witness in which it [i.e. Humanity = *nāsūt]* unites itself to the unique Word which proclaims the divine Unicity and Lordship and which, at the same time, creates the being which it [i.e. Humanity] is, in its authentic purity. (R. Amaldez, p. 27)

Such a meditation on the enigma which constitutes the first part of the *shahāda: la ilāha illā Allāh* (which we find literally in the prophets of the Old Testament, cf. e.g., Is 45, 21) will hardly leave the Christian indifferent, who will rather regard with respect and sympathy the effort made by Sufis like al-Hallāj to respond with an undeniable spiritual depth

The Christian doctrine responds to the same problem by a meditation of the mysteries of Trinity and incarnation. Put very shortly: The Word of God is His Word, the second person of the Trinity, made flesh in Christ Jesus. Jesus is 'the faithful witness' (Rev 1, 6) who declares in front of Pilate. 'I came into the world for this, to bear witness to the truth; and all who are on the side of truth listen to my voice' (Jn 18, 37). And: 'these who were born not from human stock or human desire of human will but from God himself (Jn 1.13). Thus, the believer in God the Truth can through Christ, with him and in him, render the same authentic testimony as Jesus. Born from God he will be son of God by adoption. It is man in the authenticity of his humanity that has been created in the Christ, by and in him (cf. Col 1, 15-17). The truthfulness of Christ's witness is based on the reciprocity of the two testimonies that of the Father and of the Son, and man can, through, in and with Christ, give an equally authentic and truthful testimony. But to make sure of the authenticity of this testimony Christ has sent His Spirit (Jn 15, 26-7)

6. God is Triune Communion Because He is the Giver of Love

We said: the two actions of God, creation and incarnation, flow from His very nature of being Bestower, Giver par excellence. The *process ad extra* (in creation and incarnation) flows from the *process ad intra* (the Trinity), as the great medieval Latin thinkers said: This continual, inner-divine Gift which manifests the mystery of the Trinity of Persons in the absolute unity of the Substance, is prolonged outside, as it were, in Creation, and it perfects itself in a unique way in the incarnation.

We are thus led to discover the Trinitarian nature of God, rising from his actions (creation and incarnation) to His being Love = Trinity). Because God is Gift not only as to outside Himself but also and above all as to inside Himself. The *procession ad intra* signifies simply the internal dynamics of God. God is in Himself a dynamic and dynamising (energizing) unity.

In the beginning we set out to speak of Christ and Christology. Our question was: Who is Christ for you? But in effect I cannot speak about Christ without speaking about the Trinity, because Christ is at the heart of the Trinity. All flows from the Trinity which I discover starting from where I see its effect: i.e. from the work of God in the Word, in Jesus Christ. In examining God's work in Christ I am lead to say: it is God's nature to bestow, to be the Giver. Now, who says gift, says plurality. That is the pivotal idea of the Treatise of Unity *(Maqāla fi l-tawhīd)* written by Yahyā ibn 'Adī in 941. He says in substance, without mentioning the Muslims: 'There exist believers who conceive of the unity of God as of a tautological unity: he is one because he is one. There is another way of conceiving of the unity, that which integrates plurality *(al-kathra)* and otherness *(al-ghayriyya)*. Now, the *tawhīd* of the Christians is a *tawhīd* of otherness, and that is the true *tawhīd*, much richer in content than the tautological *tawhīd*.

It is probably Yahya himself who has invented the word 'otherness', formed from the eternal *ghayr*, a term which did not exist before him, says Samir Khalil. One may easily object: God is indeed the totally other, according to the Koranic formula: *Laysa ka-mithlihi shay'un*. But Yahyā's point here is this: God is the totally other not because he is one in the sense of an absolute monotheism, a numerical unity (which applies to all single beings), but rather because his unity includes otherness (and this is true only of God).

No other being is one and multiple in its very essence. In this sense, the God of the Christian faith is truly unique and one can say really only of such a God: *Laysa ka-mithlihi shay'un*.

This vision is not just a beautiful theoretical abstraction, as if the Trinity was something abstract. The mystery of the Trinity has concrete consequences for my everyday Christian life. It leads me to a distinct vision of inter-human relations based on giving and sharing which however in no way would exclude a meaningful hierarchy. This applies especially to the structure of the family (between the spouses on the one hand and the parents and children on the other, as one can see in the texts of Saint Paul). However, political society and the Church's social structures become dictatorial and oppressive of personal identities if they are not founded on belief in a God who is Love, that is: giving and sharing.

The incarnation then is at the center of the movement of God towards man, and all the same time is its perfection.

7. Consequences of the Incarnation

Three consequences of the incarnation would seem to be particularly important in the context of Christian reflection in the mirror of Islam

7.1. The Habitual Union with God is Possible for All

In Christ, the Word incarnate (*kalima munzala*), the union of God and humanity, the union of God with each human being becomes real and possible. Every Christian, in so far as he or she really lives the faith authentically, is a kind of 'Sufi', a mystic united to God. What in Islam is a privilege, granted to a restricted elite (*khāssa*), in Christianity is the natural way offered, at least in principle, to every believer. What in the Muslim religion is characteristic of a small group of Sufis (i.e. the continuous union with God) is basic norm of the Christian's life, by being sacramentally incorporated in Jesus Christ through and thanks to the mystery of the incarnation.

7.2. The Absolute Value of the Human Person

Furthermore, through the incarnation man acquires a hitherto unknown value, because God has made him a participant in His nature, and already now he is the temple of the Holy Spirit. In this perspective the concrete and most effective way to defend on this earth and promote the 'rights of God' (*huqūq Allāh*) is to defend the human rights. Through the incarnation God and the human person are identified with one another to such an extent that I can no longer distinguish between the rights of the human person and the rights of God (*huqūq al-insān* and *huqūq Allāh*)

It would seem that in general the Muslim is more sensible to the 'rights of God' (always difficult to specify) than to the 'rights of the human person.' This is so not simply in consequence of merely socio-cultural factors but because the Koran underlines in a radical way the absolute transcendence of God. In Jesus Christ incarnate, the Transcendent has made Himself immanent

7.3. The Holy Eucharist 'Prolongs' the Incarnation

In the Christian vision the incarnation prolongs and completes itself in the Eucharist. This has been stated well by Arab Christian thinkers but is known also from more recent theological spiritual writing. In the words of medieval Arab theologians God has made Himself Word, the Word has made Itself flesh, the flesh has made Itself bread. The Eucharist is the final completion of this 'movement' begun in God. It is also the concrete expression of the whole *kenôsis* of God, 'arriving' as it were in our daily life.

Furthermore, the Eucharist (without denying its 'substantial' reality) becomes efficacious in the believer who receives Communion. We start from the lived reality of faith: the believer who receives Communion in the Eucharist communicates with God in Jesus Christ. The believer realizes absolute mystical union in communicating, i.e. receiving the flesh and blood of Jesus Christ.

This coming of God into the 'flesh' as it were of our daily lives, is the Gift of God, the Giver of good (*al-Jawwād*) who bestows

Himself in the incarnation and in consequence, in the Eucharist in order to transform me and making me participant in His life and goodness. St. Irenaeus of Lyons (*c.*130–*c.*200) put it thus: 'God has made Himself human so that the human person may become God'. The Incarnation of God and the divinization of the human person meet one another.

Once again, in contemplating the mystery of the Eucharist I discover the deepest aspect of God's nature: LOVE. And we have known the love of God in this that He has handed over to us as a gift His own Son who has delivered Himself for us on the Cross and continues to deliver himself to us in the Eucharist. Once again it is this dynamic of the 'going out of oneself' and of 'handing over of oneself'. In the Eucharist this amazing divine dynamic comes to the fore clearly and absolutely: the dynamic of divine *kenôsis*.

PART TWO

8. Kenôsis: A Key Phrase of Christian Faith

8.1. Theological Considerations

Christian reflection naturally seeks a summary, an essential concept which expresses the very essence of the theological totality of revelation and salvation in such a fashion as to eminently expose, so to speak, the 'heart' of God, the essential reality that forms and moves everything else? Christian Revelation itself, it would appear, offers us with just such a concept, a concept that has proved effective in the life of such outstanding Christians as Francis of Assisi (c.1181/82-1226) and Mother Theresa of Calcutta (1910-1997): the *kenôsis tou Theou*, God's self-emptying love. Are we correct in thinking that a presentation and explanation of this key concept of our Christian faith might assist us and the Muslim to perceive the core of the affirmation of our Christian faith?

When te4h Apostel Paul introduced his letter to the Philippians with the exhortation: 'Make your own the mind of Jesus Christ', he did not just present an ascetic appendix to our faith, but rather indicated its core.

> Who, being in the form of God
> Did not count equally with God
> Something to be grasped

But he emptied himself
Taking the form of a slave.
Becoming as human being are;
And being in every way like a human being.
He was humble yet,
Even to accepting death, death on a cross.
And for this God raised him high,
And gave him the name
Which is above all other names;
So that all beings
In the heavens, on earth and in the underworld,
Should bend the knee at the name of Jesus
And that every tongue should acknowledge
Jesus as Lord.
To the glory of the Father. (Phil 2, 6-11)

As other religions also maintain, God loves both men and women and He is merciful to sinners. However, this offer is largely rejected, and thus a drama unfolds which leads to the refusal of the message of mercy as well as of the repentance this message demands and ends in the ignominious crucifixion of the Savior. At this point all seems to be lost, because Jesus is the 'eschatological' deliverer and giver of salvation. After Jesus, God's 'own beloved son' (cf. Lk 20, 13), no new offer on the part of God is possible. But exactly at this turning point the unexpected occurs: God turns the rejection on the part of sinners of the ultimate deliverer of salvation, 'his own beloved son,' into their redemption: *'The stone which the builders rejected has become the cornerstone'* (cf. Lk 20, 17, quoted from Ps 118, 22). The cross, therefore, becomes the sacrament of salvation, the 'place' of resurrection to new life, in the power of the Spirit and through the Son of the Father.

The Son's offering of himself for sinful humanity is the act which St. Paul defines as *heautón ekénôsen*: He emptied himself. The letter to the Philippians states this offering of self directly of Jesus. But the oblation of self on the part of the Son ('for us' [Eph 5, 21), 'for the Church' [Eph 5, 25). 'for me' [Gal 2, 20) is inconceivable without Him being offered by the Father ('for us all' [Rom 8, 32]): 'who was handed over to death for our sins and raised to life for our justification' (Rom 4, 25). The two concepts (a) *paradidónai* (to transmit, hand over, extradite) which in its noun form becomes *parádosis* (tradition, extradition) and (b) *kenôo* (to empty self) and its substantival form *kenôsis*, theologically define one and the same 'act' or 'action', and that is the 'center or focal point of the content of revelation and faith,' 'the one foundation of Christian revelation.'

I should think that this kind of theological approach could be of significant 'use' in our meeting in faith with Muslims and our task '*to give account of our faith* (1 Peter 3, 15), when they request that we do so.

Jesus proves Himself to be the Son who alone can reveal the Father, because '*no one knows the Father except the Son*' (Matt 11, 27). The 'revealing' concerning which the Matthaean text speaks is not only the communication of an intimate knowledge in words; rather, it is Jesus in his entirely (*Gestalt*) who reveals the Father, so that He can in reality affirm: '*He who has seen me, has seen the Father* (Jn 14, 9). Faith alone can assist in such 'seeing'. In the full Johannine sense of the expression 'to believe' it, is not only to acquiesce in a 'dark' mystery, completely inaccessible to the human spirit, but rather a *Wahr-nehmen* (per-ceiving; comprehending). *Ein-sehen (in-tuire,* recognizing), a spiritual contemplating which is mediated through '*the Spirit of truth who does not speak of his own accord but will say only what he has been told.*' (Jn 16: 13-15). This is to aver that he will speak only from the Father and from Christ!

Therefore, God in himself and God for us form a totality. Thus Karl Rahner has formulated the principle: 'The 'economic' Trinity is the 'immanent' Trinity and vice-versa. If with St. Paul we would wish to understand the incarnation of the Son of God as self-emptying out of Love, we must presuppose that there exists in God a kind of 'movement' that urges him to such self-emptying. This 'movement' cannot be but the inner-divine love which is itself a kind of 'self-emptying', 'a giving or offering of self': The Father does not cling to His own being; rather He completely bequeaths to another, to the Son who possesses it only by owning it totally to the Father in gratitude (*ver-danken*), in a response qualified by an immeasurable depth (*Hin-gabe*); which profoundly denotes 'a giving of self.' This is, truly, a personal turning to one another of the first and second person, the fiery breath of their mutual love, the Holy Spirit.

One cannot comprehend the meaning of 'person' as long as one considers interpersonal love in God superfluous or impossible on the ground that God is only One and that, therefore, the divine unity of being, God, has no need of 'becoming' one through Love. In fact, there exists no higher or nobler spiritual act than personal love which is possible only by the free self-offering of persons to one another. This activity, although it corresponds completely to the *nature* of God, must as yet be distinguished from it on the 'thought level'; that is 'formally in thought'. God is in himself love through the *perichôresis*, the *circumincessio*, which is the self-giving into each other (*das Ineinanderverströmen)* of the Divine Persons.

The origin (der Ur-sprung), *however, of any other* 'selfemptying of God' (*der Selbstentäusserung Gottes)* is by way of creation and sanctification *(Begnadigung*), and by way of incarnation and the offering of self unto death for others' The 'not-clinging-to-oneself' of the Divine Persons, *die Ur-Kenôse*, is the *Ur-impuls* for the not-clinging-to-Himself of God in His creation, in the 'marriage-bond' with Israel and, finally, for the son's not-clinging to His godhead, to his divine power and to His glory, but rather the entire and unqualified giving of self, and thus suffering, dying, rising from the dead and ascending to the right hand of the Father in heaven.

It is of utmost importance for a deeper understanding of God constantly to keep before us these correspondences, because they constitute the presupposition for any 'justified' knowledge of God. It begins 'from below', in creation and the concrete historical Jesus whose transparency for God reveals the 'above', the inner life of God. Thus it becomes possible for any human knowledge of God to change, as it were, the perspective (point of view) and really to begin to understand creation, incarnation and the Cross from the viewpoint of the Tri-unity of God. Moreover, it is precisely there where we were transported in our contemplation of the human person and the Jesus event in time and place. With this, indeed, we glean profound wisdom into the logic of the incarnation.

We are searching for the culminating point of all theology, the position from which God and all that He does 'comes into view', and we discover it exactly here: it is the *kenôsis* of our Tri-une God as One-and-all, as the genuine expression of the absolute freedom of the divine love.

At this point it is possible to distinguish seven modes of the divine *kenôsis*:

1. the Ur-*Kenose* in God, which is the generation of the Son and the breathing of the Holy Spirit;

2. the *kenôsis* of God in creation which we could detect in relation to the incarnation;
3. towards which it is ordered;
4. the *kenôsis* of Jesus Christ on the Cross;
5. which is sacramentally continued in the Eucharist;
6. the *kenôsis* of the Holy Spirit in the minds-and-hearts of human beings; and
7. the participation of Christians and of all brothers and sisters of Jesus Christ (i.e. all human beings), in spirit and life, in the *kenôsis* of Christ Jesus.

In sum, we Christians believe in the *kenôsis,* i.e., the self-emptying, self-giving love of the triune God.

8.2. Practical Implications

The notion of *kenôsis,* like most theological concepts is abstract. If excerpted in isolation from the historical Jesus Christ-event, it definitely risks remaining bland and distant. However, in the life of Jesus an in that of His saints we see *kenôsis* lived out before our eyes.

The Koran states that 'the Messiah would never disdain to be the servant of God'*(lan yastankifa al-masýhu an yakuna 'abdan)* (4, 172, cf. 19, 30; 43, 59). It would suffice to change one word of the Koranic text, namely, putting instead of *yakūn, yasīr,* and we would have the text of Phil 2, 7: Christ did not consider it below His dignity to become *doulos* = 'abd = servant, slave. However, the idea of Paul could not enter the Koran because it presupposes the divinity Christ. For the Koran all are servants/slaves excepting Allah.

For Paul, in contrast, Jesus the Christ—notwithstanding his divine condition—chose to empty Himself of His Godhead out of love of us, in order to become one among us, even the least of humans, a slave *('abd).*

This is the total submission to the Will of the Father, it is the most perfect obedience, submission *(islam)* in all its depth to the will of the Father. In this sense Christ is the true Muslim *(muslim),* totally 'given over' to the love of the Father. He can realize this because He is God. And He invites and alone enables the Christian to follow Him in this, to live the same. This is the deep meaning of the Passion-Death Resurrection (that is, the Paschal) mystery of the *kenôsis* of Christ.

This *kenôsis* of Christ should have a fundamental importance in the life of the individual Christian and of the Church: it signifies the refusal of power for power's sake and the understanding of authority as service, as Jesus teaches the apostles

> You know that among the gentiles those they call their rulers lord it over them, and their great man make their authority felt. Among you this is not to happen. No; anyone who wants to become great among you must be your servant, and anyone who wants to be frst among you must be slave to all. For the Son of man himself came not to be served but to serve, and to give his life as a ransom for many.' (Mk 10, 42-45, almost identical with Mat 20, 25-28)

St. Luke places this teaching at the eve of the death of Christ as if to give it the value of last testament. In his vision, the motive of such an attitude which contradicts all normal usage in the world, is Christ Himself. 'For who is the greater: the one at table or the one who serves? The one at table, surely? Yet here am I among you as one who serves!' (Lk 22, 27)

This is the key teaching of the Gospel and—as history amply demonstrates—it is most difficult to accept and live. In St. John's gospel the reality of Christ's choice to be the Servant of all and his call to follow Him precisely in this, finds expression in the washing of the feet: When he had washed their feet and put on his outer garments again he went back to the table. 'Do you understand' he said, 'what I have done to you? You call me Master and Lord, and rightly; so I am. If I, then, the Lord and Master, have washed your feet, you must wash each other's feet. I have given you an example, so that you may copy what I have done to you' (Jn 13, 12-15)

Christ is conscious of being the Master and Lord, to have the power and authority over his disciples, and yet he chooses to be their servant. This should be of heightened significance in the context of Christian-Muslim relations. Why? I perceive Islam as a religion of power, a religion which seeks, in the name of God with all legitimate means, to take power and having once attained it, in the name of God, to hold on to it. There exists in Islam a tactics of power and a great ability to arrive at the final goal, in the name of God. This is not a reproach (in as much as the means employed be honesty and respectful of the freedoms of the others). It is rather an observation.

The individual Christian and the Church should be fully conscious of their call to be sons of God in Christ and of the fact that they have received all in Jesus Christ, the Alpha and Omega of history. Beyond insisting on the basic rights of all our fellow humans, individuals and groups, we are called as individuals and as Church to give the witness of self-less service on the pattern of Christ. Christians as individuals, as groups and as Church will have to discern ever anew what are the proper ways of living their vocation to service in given Christian-Muslim circumstances.

9. Speaking About the God of Our Faith in Parables

My personal experience over the past years in teaching Christian themes on Muslim faculties of theology in Turkey has convinced me that the most adequate way of speaking about the heart of our Christian faith—it is understood that I have always been invited by Muslims to do so—is through the narrating of stories and parables, the way in which Jesus also taught. I have repeatedly told the following parable in the context of personal conversation, either in small groups or even in classroom teaching. It will become immediately evident that my parable is an adaptation and modification of Jesus' parable about the 'prodigal' son (or, better of the loving father) in Luke 15, 11-32 and of the master of the vineyard in Luke 20:9-18.

There lived a wealthy and widely respected banking director in Frankfurt. He was married and had several children. They resided in a magnifcent villa in the lovely green and quiet outskirts of the city. They lacked nothing. But one day the youngest son disappeared. In fact, his busy father had not noticed that his son had become friends with a group of youths in the neighbourhood. These were youngsters who were given to drugs and dreamed of a life of errant independence, far away from straight German society. Without informing his father, one day the son had disappeared, he left for the Goan coasts of Western India. He lived there off the money, which his father had put into a special account towards his university education.

This sudden and sly departure saddened and hurt the father. It took some time for him to discover his son's whereabouts. He wrote him letters after letters, but his letters never brought him any reply. This is what he wrote

My dear son,

I think of you constantly. I do not know why you left me. Perhaps I have been too busy with my work and thus failed to be with you as much as you would have liked and deserved. Maybe it is precisely this that made you feel unwanted and lonely at home. But whatever may have happened, please do come back. And please be sure that I have pardoned you and desire to be close to you, to spend much time with you. All you have to do is to come back. I think of you all the time, every day, and I long for the day of your return home!

The son did not respond in any way to the father's plea. But one day the father learned of some friends of the family who intended to spend their holiday in India. He immediately contacted them and informed and told them about his son in Goa. He mercifully implored them to visit his son whilst there were there. 'Here is his address. Please go and personally tell him in my name how very much I yearn for his coming back home. Because of his absence and silence I suffer deeply in mind-and-heart. Please try to persuade him to believe that in no way do I harbor any grudge against him. On the contrary.

The family's friends went to India and met the son. Their unexpected visit surprised and profoundly moved him. At fst he was inclined to return back to Germany with them. But as much as he tried he found it diffcult to separate himself from his friends and their frivolous lifestyle; this in spite of the fact that he was left with practically no money and so was compelled to beg.

When his friends back in Frankfurt informed the father about this, he said to himself. 'I myself must go to India, to be reunited with my son. In any event, life without him has become meaningless for me. I'll resign from my position and become a 'hippie' like him. Just to be with him will be my joy in life. When he sees and understands my concern and deep love for him frst hand, he will surely not remain unmoved. As I see it, this is the only way, hopefully, that he will be able to freely to decide to return home with me.

But his family, friends and associates in Frankfurt protested. 'How can you abandon your important position in the bank, which is crucial to the economy of the State; just because you want to join your incorrigibly ungrateful son? Forget it! You're exaggerating. Haven't you already done all that's possible and expected of you as a righteous and merciful father? You discovered his whereabouts. You sent him letter after letter. Even messengers! You have not forgotten him. Your way of acting now is outrageous, even scandalous, not worthy of your high standing. Furthermore, your son is intelligent enough to understand your many invitations and you generous offer to forgive him in spite of everything he had done. Now let him act like a responsible person; he knows quite well what to do.

Still the father insisted: 'Everything that I have done has had no effect on my beloved son. It is clear to me that he lacks the courage to return home alone. When he sees me, touches me, hears my voice, surely he will be moved it's ready up to me now to take the initiative I'll become like him and join him. He will surely repent I know my son.

To conclude, the father, the affuent and renowned banker, resigned from his honourable position. Now prepared, he put his back-pack on his shoulders and so made the long journey to the shores of Goa in India.

When they eventually met his son was completely overwhelmed, deeply ashamed. His frst reaction was again to reject his father, but his father just stayed on, without uttering many words. Eventually the son's resistance began to soften. But one day he went to his father who lovingly embraced him and so both returned home. Together they lived in joy and peace for the rest of their lives.

So, if we wish to understand God's greatest 'greatness', as Christian faith perceives it, it is exactly here. It was revealed in Jesus' parable, indeed in his life. God, Jesus' Father, in the life of his Son has brought to light this divine magnanimity. It exceeds all human comprehension of imagination, especially when God, in Jesus, makes Himself equal to us human beings, sharing with us every aspect of our human condition except sin. Thus God in Jesus through the power of the Holy Spirit enables us to transform our hearts-and-minds, making us participants of his triune, divine life of love for ever.

Allāhu Akbar—Allāhu Asghar—Allāhu ajwad—Allāhu Mahabba

God, the ever greater—God, the ever smaller—God the ever more generous—God is Love

10. Jesus Christ—The Liberator5

Jesus Christ is free and makes his disciple free from all constraints and all dimensions. Paul expresses this clearly:

'But now that faith has come [.] there can be neither Jew nor Greek, there can be neither slave nor freeman, there can be neither male nor female—for you are all one in Christ Jesus' (Gal 3, 25a.28)

Or as Colossians 3, 11 states:

> 'Now there is no room for distinction between Greek and Jew, between the circumcised and the uncircumcised, or between barbarian and Scythian, slave and free. There is only Christ: he is everything and he is in everything.'

10.1 Christ Frees Us from Any Sharì'ah

When Paul says: 'There is no longer Jew nor Greek, he underlines the fact that Christ has freed man from the Jewish Law as he now frees him from the *sharī'ah.* There is no need to remind us of the detailed prescriptions of the Jewish Law as taught and authoritatively proposed by the teachers of the Jewish Law, the *fuqahā*' of the time. One understands the revolution brought by Jesus and the scandal it provoked. This Law, as taught and practiced by established religion in Jesus' time, in His view ultimately paralyzed man's movement towards God. Christ frees us and all humankind of any *sharī'ah.*

The Christian who lives in Islam-determined societies becomes vividly aware of the centrality of this point, even more so in the context of the vigorous efforts over the past decades towards a world-wide revival of Islam in terms of reinstating integrally the *sharī'ah,* including its political component. At this point it is worth underlining that the movements of political Islam, whilst they do not represent the whole spectre of the *umma,* certainly are, and understand themselves to be, an authentic form of Islam in that they continue in the context of our times a respected and powerful tradition of interpreting the normative sources of Islam.

The major concern of the leading figures of the Islamic revival as, for instance of Khomeīni, Maudūdi and more recent Islamist thinkers of the type of Rāshid al-Ghannūshi is conformity with the detailed and comprehensive prescriptions of the *sharīah.* One of their constant basic concerns is how to fulfill the legal prescriptions of the *sharīah* (esp. regarding 'the five pillars') integrally and in a ritually pure manner *(halāl)*. This concern clearly takes precedence over the content of the ritual actions themselves. The same could be said of the catechism taught to children in the mosques the world over. Concerning alimentation, buying and selling, sexual relations etc. there are numerous rules which should make sure that the act performed will be *halāl and* not *harām*. And if by leaving out detail, the prayer has become illicit, what must I do in order to make it a licit performance. The study of these books which address themselves to all sincere followers of Islam, represent authentic Islam. The Christian believer in close and regular contact with practicing Muslims becomes aware of how much Christ liberates his followers from the straightjacket of the Jewish Law and any other Law resembling it as to matter and spirit. In this way I have come to appreciate better the passionate mind and language of St. Paul, someone who after having tried to live this kind of religion uncompromisingly, met Jesus Christ as Liberator from the Law.

10.2. Christ Liberates from All Discrimination

Similarly, Christ liberates his true disciple from any ethnic-racial, cultural, social, sexual or even religious discrimination. Clearly the Koran and the Tradition condemn any ethnic-racial discrimination. As a Hadith says 'I have come to bring together while and black, yellow and red'. However, the Koran makes a net distinction—of grave judicial consequences—between believer and non-believer. More exactly, it distinguishes three categories of men: the Muslim (member of the *umma* and called 'believer', *mu'min*), the Jew and the Christian or *dhimmī* and the others.

The Gospel, in contrast, does not know, in a comparable way, of such a categorization, not even on the religious level:

> You have heard how it was said, *You will love your neighbour and hate your enemy*. But I say this to you, love your enemies and pray for those who persecute you, so that you may be children of your Father it heaven, for he causes his sum to rise on the bad as well as on the good, and sends down rain to fall on the upright and the wicked alike (Mk 5, 43-45)

And a little afterwards:

> You must therefore set no bounds to your love, just as your heavenly Father sets none to his' (Mt 5, 48)

In this way Christ invites his disciples in treating people not to distinguish between good and bad, just and unjust (the *abrār* and the kuffar), in order to act in the image of God the Father.

10.3. Christ Inaugurates A Truly Universal Fraternity

The notion of brotherhood either applies universally or not at all. To say that all the believers are brothers and at the same time implying that they are not brothers with the non-believers, equals gainsaying the notion of fraternity. From the moment I exclude one single person in principle, there is no more universal brotherhood.

Now Christ teaches that there is absolutely no frontier or barrier between human beings. In a sense this is quite uncomfortable. Ephesians formulates this teaching in its own inimitable way.

For He [Jesus Christ] is the peace between us, and has made the two into one entity and broken down the barrier which used to keep them apart, by destroying in his own person the hostility, that is, the Law of commandments with its decrees. His purpose in this was, by restoring peace, to create a single New Man out of the two of them, and through the cross, to reconcile them both to God in one Body; in his own person he killed the hostility (Eph 2, 14-16)

The universally of Christ's message thus understood distinguishes it from any other. Christ comes to bring a liberating message which tears down all barriers and walls. It says: Ultimately there is not, and there must not be supposed to be, any duality of: God and Man, man and man, believer and unbeliever, man and woman (we could think of Q 2, 228 which says that there obtains between man and woman a degree of difference (*daraja*) or the verse (Q 4, 34) which affirms that men have superiority or authority (*qawwāmun 'ala*) over women, and so on). There is only God who is all in all, in Jesus Christ.

Christ brings to humanity with himself the message of absolute, total liberation.

10.4. Christ Liberates from Death

This same message expresses itself finally in the tearing down of the ultimate wall, the wall of death which Christ Himself destroys. This is the absolute and total liberation. The Koran states: 'They did not kill him, nor did they crucify him, though it was made to appear like that to them.' (sura 4, 157). One can interpret this verse in various ways: however, whatever the interpretation may be, the Muslims in the diversity of their opinions are agreed in the denial of Christ's death and crucifixion. Now, if Christ has not died, he is not risen. As Paul reminds us: '*And if Christ has not been raised, your faith is pointless*' (1 Cor 15, 17).

Quite clearly, this point is fundamental. The death of Christ, for us, as well as for anybody else informed about history, cannot be doubted. The resurrection of Christ, in contrast, is an act of faith which can be refused or accepted. Its meaning is basic for us. Once all the walls (as e.g. religious, theological, cultural, psychological, etc.) have been torn down by the passion of Christ, the last wall (which is the wall of death) is being destroyed by His divinity, by the fact that He is God and Man in one being.

Furthermore, by this passion-resurrection, Jesus Christ—who through the incarnation identifies with every human person—raises all and everyone towards God, His Father, as he has promised Himself: '*And when I am lifted up from the earth, I shall draw all people to myself*' (Jn 12, 32).

In Greek, being lifted up has a double meaning (as the Gospel according to St. John frequently employs words of double meaning). It gives expression to the lifting up of Jesus on the cross as well as of his being lifted up to heavenly glory.

11. Conclusion

In this talk I have referred to various different doctrines. I have pointed out the emphases of my Christian faith in the context of encountering Muslims and Islam. However, ultimately the Christian faith flows from, is sustained by, and wants to lead to, only one mystery, that of the self-giving Love of God. All statements the Christian faith makes about God refer to different manifestations of the one movement of God's self-giving and self-emptying love in which shines forth His divine glory and power. Consequently, all the Christian faith has to say about the human person's true nature and vocation is summed up in the one commandment of unconditional love of God and neighbour. The 'commandment' is really the invitation to all and everyone to allow themselves to be transformed by God's grace into participants in divine life, the communion of triune Love.

The teaching of Jesus Christ in Mt 5, 48: 'You, therefore, must b perfect, as your heavenly Father is perfect.' (Bible of Jerusalem: 'You must therefore set no bounds to your love, just as your heavenly Father sets none to his.') seems to ask for the humanly impossible. And indeed, taken to be a legal prescription, this command would be absurd. However, what Christ tells us is this: no limits are set to your spiritual growth, because the energy, the model and the aim of such growth is the triune God Himself. He invites us and enables us through His Spirit to grow ever more into being living images of His Son. The only real failure on our part would be lack of confidence and faith in God.

The essence of my Christian life is *Sendung* (being sent) as Jesus Christ was sent. Which concrete form this *Sendung* (mission) takes will depend on the particularities of a given situation. If it is not informed by self-giving love and deep respect for the freedom of the other as other, it lacks in the qualities of the One, in name of whom it claims to speak. Hence Christian *Sendung* (mission, apostolate) will be marked by deep respect for everything that has been brought about in human beings by the Spirit who blows where it wills, and it will be aware of the dangers of manipulation and exploitation of ignorance in so-called missionary efforts. Life-in-mission may take most varied forms, depending on the given situation and the special personal vocation: a silent presence of service, of patient listening and research, of exchange of ideas and ideals, of struggle for a more adequate understanding of the truth, of work for peace but also the service of *parrèsia,* that is, of the courageous announcing of the good news of God's mystery of love as it has been revealed to the Church for the benefit and joy of all.

The aim of God in sending Christ and hence the aim of all God does in preparation for it, in other words, the aim of God creating and guiding through the prophets, is stated by Christ, His Son in all clarity: 'I have come so that they may have life and have it to the full' (Jn 10,10). And this endless life consists in this: 'to know the only true God and Jesus Christ whom He has sent' (cf. Jn 17, 13).

NOTES

1. Ahmad Kamal, *The Sacred Journey*, London: Allen and Unwin, 1961, p. 69.
2. Kamal, *op. cit.*, pp. 69–81 *passim*.
3. The central prayer in the Eucharistic Liturgy, containing the Consecration, the Anamnesis [that is the commemoration of the Passion, Resurrection, and the Ascension of Christ], and the Communion.
4. We could also have taken as example the life and teaching of the great Indian Sufi Sharafuddīn Yahyā Maneri (1263–1381) whose deep as well as balanced spirituality has been effectively presented in English by the translations and studies of Paul Jackson SJ. See, for instance, his *Sharafuddin Maneri: The Hundred Letters*, London: SPCK, 1980. However, al-Hallāj's reflections concerning the nature of God and the relationship of the revealing god to the revealed Word are directly relevant to the topic of this essay.
5. Here again, I follow closely Samir Khalil Samir—see bibliography.

BIBLIOGRAPHY

Roger Amaldez, *Réflexions chrétiennes sur la mystique musulmane*, Paris. O.E.I.L., 1989.

Muhammad Ata'ur-Rahman and Ahmad Thomson, *Jesus: Prophet of Islam*, rev. ed., London: Ta-Ha, 1996.

Edmond Farahian, SJ & Christiaan van Nispen tot Sevenaer, SJ, *'Approaches biblico-theologiques de l'Islam'*, in: Peter-Hans Kolvbenbach, SJ et al, *Understanding and Discussion*, Rome: P.U.G., 1996, pp. 31–57.

Jacques Jomier, *Dieu et l'homme dans le Coran. L'aspect religieux de la nature humaine joint* à l'obeissance *au Prophète de l'islam*, Paris: Cerf, 1996.

Id., *Jesus, the life of the Messiah*, Madras: Christian Literature Society, 1974.

John Paul II, *Encyclical Letter Redemptoris Missio: On the Permanent Validity of the Church's Missionary Mandate*, London: Catholic Truth Society, 1991.

Journées Romaines XVII (Proceedings), *Qui est le Christ pour nous, Chrétiens, Vivant avec les musulmans?*, Rome, PISAAI, 1991 [for private circulation].

Peter-Hans Kolvenbach, SJ *et al.*, *Understanding and Discussion: Approaches to Muslim-Christian Dialogue*, Rome: Editrice Pont. Univ. Gregoriana, 1998.

Karl-Josef Kuschel, 'Christologie und interreligiöser Dialog Die Einzigartigkeit Christi im Gespräch mit den Weltreligionen' in *Stimmen der Zeit (München)*, 209, 1991, pp. 387–402.

Oddbjørn Leirvik, *Images of Jesus Christ in Islam*, Uppsala: Swedish Institute of Missionary Research, 1999.

Christian van Nispen tot Sevenaer, SJ see: E. Farahian, SJ.

Fazlur Rahman, *Major Themes of the Koran*, Minneapolis/Chicago: Bibliotheca Islamica, 1980.

Karl Rahner, 'Einzigkeit und Dreifaltigkeit Gottes', in: Andreas Bsteh (ed.), *Der Gott des Christentums und des Islams*, Mödling: St. Gabriel, 1992, [Beitrage z. Religionstheologie 2], pp. 119–36.

Neal Robinson, *Christ in Islam and Christianity. The Representation of Jesus in the Koran and the Classical Muslim commentaries*, London: Macmillan, 1991.

Semir Khalil Samir, 'Qui est le Christ, pour moi qui vie on milieu musulman?' in: *Journées Romaines* XVIII, pp. 55–64.

Olaf Schumann, *Der Christus der Muslime*, Köln/Wien: Böhlau Verlag, 1988.

8

Mosque and Church: Their Contribution to Inter-Religious Harmony and Reconciliation

Twelve Muslims and twelve Christians from various parts of India and a few Christian and Muslim guests from abroad met from 9 to 11 October 1978 in Tughluqabad on the outskirts of New Delhi. They were guests of the Indian Institute of Islamic Studies on its new magnificent campus there.

The aim was to explore, in the light of the message of the Bible and Koran, the possibilities of a common commitment to harmony and reconciliation, not only between Muslims and Christians, but also among all religious and ideological groups in India

The Seminar was organized by the Indian Institute of Islamic Studies together with the Henry Martyn Institute, Hyderabad, and it was co-sponsored by the Dialogue Commission of the Catholic Bishops' Conference of India who had been asked to invite six of the twelve Christian delegates.

The discussion revolved around three pairs of working-papers, each pair giving the Muslim and the Christian perspective on a given topic. The first couple of papers dealt with the Koranic and with the Biblical understanding of inter-religious harmony and reconciliation. The second asked what it is that makes a community in the Koranic and the Biblical perspective, and what is the place of mosque and church in the life of that community. The last two

* This essay was first published in *Vidyajyoti Journal of Theological Reflections*, Vol. 43, No. 1, January 1979, pp. 16–24.

papers, finally, searched for ways and means to promote a new inter-religious harmony and reconciliation.

During the past few years quite a number of Muslim-Christian meetings have been held, not only on an international level, but also on the national one. Dr Samuel Bhajjan, the Director of the H.M.I., mentioned five such meetings in India, the first of which was held as early as 1965 in Nagpur. Nevertheless, the present Seminar marked a new beginning in that it was co-sponsored by the Roman Catholic Church and, above all, because of the remarkable break-through in Muslim-Christian relations in recent years, through such important international meetings as, e.g., those of Tunis, Tripoli (Libya) and Cordoba.[1]

In this article we shall present a few points from the papers and discussions of the Tughluqabad Seminar, depict the background of the development of Muslim-Christian dialogue on the international level and look towards the future development of Muslim-Christian dialogue here in India.

The Wider Context

The topic of the Tughluqabad Seminar makes it clear that it is not as isolated individuals that Christians and Muslims meet. Each individual is shaped by and in turn helps to shape his own community. Again communities cannot remain isolated but necessarily define themselves and their action in relationship to other communities. We have become more aware of this dimension of dialogue. The credit for this goes to a great extent to a number of inter-religious meetings, inspired and organized by the WCC during the past few years.[2]

An unprecedented meeting in Colombo, in April 1974, brought together fifty Hindu, Jewish, Buddhist, Christian and Muslim delegates to reflect on the 'Living Together' of the various religions within the one world community. They tried to single out the factors and tendencies in the various traditions that may prevent or hinder true togetherness. They spoke of 'those 'blocks' that have for one reason or other been part of our religious traditions in the past', and saw the need 'for a reconstruction or rebuilding of our communities consistent with the new dimension that is introduced in our faiths, namely, loyalty to the whole of mankind and not only to one component within it.'[3]

Already in Colombo practical ways of working together were

listed. Yet the more limited Christian-Muslim meeting in Hongkong, seven months after Colombo, in January 1975, was able to explore in more detail the possibilities of developing 'good will, consultation and working together in South-East Asia.'[4] The participants of the Hongkong meeting realized that in the past and even in the present time 'attitudes of exclusivism, of condescension or of hostility have characterized relations between Christians and Muslims in SouthEast Asia.'[5] They saw such attitudes of exclusivism contradicting the true character of either the Christian or the Muslim faith, and pointed out the wide gap existing in both Communities between the high principles of religious teaching and the actual practices of their adherents. The Hongkong meeting delineated 'the theological bases for Muslim-Christian relations and for the relations of both with all neighbouring religions and ideologies.'[6] At the same time, it marked out in a concrete way 'areas of common concern in social and political contexts.'[7]

Flaws in Organisation and Method

Reading the Hongkong memorandum now, one cannot help regretting that its texts—as well as number of related texts[8]—was not made available to all the participants of the Tughluqabad Seminar. This would have helped create in them a much more pronounced awareness as to the areas of concord and of conflict between Muslims and Christians in India. The Tughluqabad Seminar, by confining itself, at this stage, to the Christian and Muslim communities, had hoped thus to facilitate an initial understanding between these two communities. There is much that binds and that separates these two communities in a special way. However, it would help to open the door to a wider dialogue. It came as no surprise when towards the later stages of the Seminar, several delegates demanded that the kind of dialogue initiated here should be extended systematically to the other religious communities of India.

It would also have helped much had the inquiry into the Koranic and Biblical message regarding inter-religious and inter-community dialogue been preceded by an analysis and discussion of the actual relations obtaining here and now between Muslims and Christians in various parts of India in the experience of each participant. Since this was not attempted, the Seminar remained—

at least during the working sessions—largely on the level of discussions, personally engaging yet somewhat diffuse and merely intellectual, not sufficiently animated by the awareness of an urgent need to improve or heal a given situation.

Some Salient Points

Many points from the six papers presented would warrant special mention here.[9] In our present context we confine ourselves to a few points made by Muslim participants.

Professor Syed Vahiduddin, the former Head of the Department of Philosophy at Delhi University, addressed himself to the question, often raised by non-Muslim observers, whether the Koran really provides a basis for inter-religious dialogue as advocated today?[10]

At first sight, the Koran seems to be highly intransigent. Does it not posit a universal claim and present its message as *the* way to salvation which, if rejected, becomes a way to eternal perdition? How can inter-religious harmony be understood, in the Koranic perspective, as a state of affairs where various religious communities not only tolerate one another, excluding any violence and aggressiveness, but also positively appreciate one another and think and work together towards the common, material and spiritual, good? Does the Koran really accept such an objective? Does it not rather ask the believers to proclaim its message everywhere and at every time as the unique and exclusive way to salvation?

S. Vahiduddin here stressed the need to distinguish clearly between that Koranic ethos which is the ethos of 'primordial' Islam from the detailed teachings and actions of 'historical' Islam. The former presents the perennial message of monotheism and its exigencies, announced by the prophets in various ways throughout history and, in an unsurpassable way, enshrined in the basic message of the prophet, Muhammad, the Prophet of Islam. The latter, besides involving a religious commitment at a personal and existential level, is a civilization and an institution and, as such, prey to possible alienation from the original Islamic ethos. At other levels we can speak of 'cosmic' Islam, expressing the idea of the subservience of all nature to divine order (amr, cfr. Sura 13) or of Islam at a personal, existential level, understood as a response to the call from *al-ghaib*, the Mysterious, the Hidden.

The Koran, S. Vahiduddin stressed, besides calling men to adherence to historical, institutional Islam, tries to inculcate the Islamic temper in *all* its hearers, Muslim or not. Even the rejecters of the historical frame of reference of the Koran are made to feel their affinity and continuity with the same tradition. Thus the Koranic references to the pre-Islamic figures, like, e.g., Abraham, Moses, David and Jesus, are included to show us the way towards developing inter-religious harmony in a positive way.

There is, furthermore, what has been termed 'Koranic humanism'. Man is seen as God's vice-regent, with the mysterious freedom to sin. The unity—not uniformity—of mankind is seen as the direct corollary of God's unity. Any attempt, therefore, at the annihilation of one member of mankind is tantamount to an assault on mankind as a whole. Different patterns of belief and behaviour to be found among men, have a sanction in divine planning. Man will be judged not by his conformity to outward patterns but solely by the 'works' he does.

In the Koranic vision of God and man, the personal relationship God entertains with every man, his creature, is of basic importance. God is very close to *every* human being, 'nearer than the jugular vein', as the Koran (50, 16) puts it. God's tender mercy (*rahma*) embraces all, and every human being can respond to him in prayer and service.

However, this Koranic idea of God in his relationship to man, has been tragically betrayed in Islamic history. 'In order to find Islam in the Koranic perspective, we have to go back to that sense of transcendence of *al-ghayb* which the Koran inculcates or, in other words, to flee back to him in order to hear his voice unhampered by historical hurdles.'[11] We have to judge later historical interpretations and implementations again and again by the original framework of the Koran. And, S. Vahiduddin stressed, in this common reference to transcendence, Muslims and Christians (and 'even those who fight for the cause of Allah anonymously, without knowing that they are fighting for his cause') can and must—in the sense of Q. 3, 52—pursue a common endeavour.

The second pair of papers dealt with the idea of community in Bible and Koran. Much was said about the possible revitalization of the function of the mosque within the Muslim community and also about the Biblical idea of a Church as leaven of society. But little advance was made in answering whether Koran and Bible are really concerned with or can be seen as demanding the structuring of the wider, pluralist community we experience today; whether they give us guidance for the building up of this wider community as Muslim send as Christian believers.

The Christian paper touched upon the permanent tension in Christian thinking and practice between an inclusive and an exclusive outlook and attitude, but the subject was not dealt with in depth.

The Key Paper

The contribution of Professor Ziaul Hasan Faruqi, the Principal of Jamia Millia Islamia, New Delhi a graduate of the prestigious Darul ulum in Deoband, U.P., and of McGill University, Montreal is best suited to convey the tenor and main thrust of the discussions of the Seminar. It certainly belies the summary view expressed recently by Christians, here and there, that the Muslims themselves are not really interested in dialogue, and furthermore, that Islam as a whole represents a closed system and is opposed to any acceptance of religious pluralism.[12] Such indiscriminate, overall judgements recall similar statements one used to read about Roman Catholicism up to some twenty years ago.

Z.H. Faruqi states that no religious community can any longer afford to be indifferent to other religious groups. Each religious group has to seek the cooperation of others and to try to find ways and means for a durable inter-religious harmony. We have to choose, 'either to learn to live as members of a world-community composed of various cultures or not to live at all'. We have to learn to live as partners, to develop a 'mutual appreciation of each others' heritage based on the conviction of equality of all as human beings in the eyes of God'. In simple words: We have to meet each other looking into each others' eyes and with open hearts.

We how can this change of outlook and attitude take place without necessarily injuring the specific religious, moral and social life of the communities to which we deeply belong and who have made us what we are?

Z.H. Faruqi envisages action on both the intellectual and on the practical plane. On the former the *first* step should be to acquire a good and objective knowledge of various religious traditions. 'Centres of learning should be established by all religious traditions where it may become possible to 'study' various religious traditions, preferably according to the phenomenological approach'. A *second* step should be to revise thoroughly our traditional exclusivist attitude. 'We have to learn to respect other religious traditions as being as valid as our own'. Self-righteousness must cease. The particularism of the various religious traditions is understandable on historical grounds. But today we are all called to rediscover the universalistic trends present in each great religious tradition of the world. We must allow the original spirit of our respective religious tradition to assert itself as against the primacy of particular dogmas, rituals and ceremonies. In other words: a new theological approach is demanded that truly considers the whole of humankind as one community. 'Without a new theological approach to include all the world religions as the religious heritage of mankind and to find a respectable place for all religions in one's religious consciousness, the dream of inter-religious harmony will ever remain unrealized'. The *third* step must be an ever-increasing dialogue between adherents of the world-religions. Dialogue here is seen as the effort 'to establish a religious relationship with a person of another faith'. In the context of world religions it means to listen to each other's experience of their respective religious traditions and to share in a deeper union of mutual openness, even where perceptions and expressions remain in an irreducible difference.

Shared practical action, according to Z.H. Faruqi, should be built on the common perception of what is *ma'rūf* (lit. 'what is known' and hence: 'what is according to the acknowledged norm, what is accepted'), good, beautiful, just and the like.[13] Thus, for instance, 'all agree that honesty is a virtue and dishonesty a vice. All agree that service to parents, kindliness towards neighbours, care of the poor, and aiding of the oppressed are things good in themselves and none holds different views about them. The quality of justice is acclaimed by all, even if it has to be enforced against one's own self, relatives and co-religionists.

Therefore a 'dialogue' can and must be initiated in the world of action. If the *mar'ūf* is one and the same, then what bars us from uniting and working together for a just social order, against all kinds of injustices, social economic and political, from cooperating in doing things that make life good and beautiful?

Such a dialogue on the practical plane would go a long way to make religion assertive, dynamic and purposefully relevant in civil life.

Practical Suggestions

Z.H. Faruqi's paper certainly offered to the Seminar a framework for more specific considerations in the Muslim-Christian context in India, and for possible concrete action. But it was read and discussed only in the penultimate session of the Seminar. The participants were not yet quite prepared for effective decision and action.

It nevertheless emerged from the discussion, and especially from interventions in the final session, that certain initiatives have to be taken now. Both Muslims and Christians feel that much needs to be done in the field of teaching, especially in those institutions where the leaders of the communities are formed, such as seminaries, *madrasas* and institutes of Islamic Studies. A number of Christian faculties of theology and philosophy and seminaries have recently started to institute basic courses on Islam and on Muslim life in India, as part of their normal curriculum. Muslim participants, as, e.g., Professor Iqbal Ansari, Director of the Institute of Islamic Studies. Aligarh University, expressed the conviction that in their curriculum, too, room should be made for the teaching of the Christian religion as Christians see it. True, the traditional syllabus of *madrasas* provides here and there for information and discussion of elements of the Christian faith, but all this from the point of view of traditional Islamic thinking and theologizing

The need was felt, furthermore, to collaborate in working out basic textbooks and anthologies on Christianity and Islam for use in higher religious Muslim and Christian educational institutions. It should become normal to invite Muslim lectures to Christian institutions for participating in teaching on Islam and vice-versa.

Apart from the crucial work of introducing these changes in the training of our respective religious leaders, there is the wide area of initiatives to be taken on the local level. The participants of the Tughluqabad Seminar experienced during the three days of living together much mutual cordiality and frank conversation. The final session culminated spontaneously in a common silent prayer. At that point, when the participants were about to disperse, it seemed to us that a new starting point had been reached. There is very much need for this and similar groups to meet again and again and then to spread this attitude and way of proceeding on the local level.[14]

But the most important proposal, made in the last session, was to set up a small permanent Muslim-Christian committee, acting (a) as a watchdog over inter-community relations and as possible court of appeal in case of conflicts; (b) promoting and planning further meetings of this kind and spreading relevant mutual information via the media; (c) fostering the teaching of Islam in Christian institutions of religious learning and vice versa, and to check, in a scholarly manner, any educational material used in private or public educational institutions as to its fairness in dealing with matters pertaining to either Christianity or Islam; (d) to initiate and foster theological thinking about central question touching the faith and the ethical teaching of both religions.

Unfortunately, this committee was not set up. Somehow the final session was deprived of some of the key participants. Thus the Seminar did not have the determination to translate its insights and the felt needs of the hour into practical and effective terms.

The proposals, however, are so obviously an expression of real needs that they are bound to find realization soon, in one way or another. This, at least, is our firm hope.

NOTES

1. For reports and other important meetings of this kind of *Islamochristiana* (Roma, Pontifical Institute of Arabic Studies, 1975ff), nn. 1 ff, and *Bulletin* (Secretariatus pro non Christianis), passim.
2. Cf. *Christians meeting Muslims*. WCC papers on 10 years of Christian-Muslim dialogue (Geneva, World Council of Church), 1977.
3. *Ibid.*, p. 105.
4. *Ibid.*, p. 119.
5. *Ibid.*, p. 120.
6. *Ibid.*
7. *Ibid.*, p. 122.
8. The Seminar showed that basic information about significant development in inter-faith dialogue, even among the religiously interested and educated, is still very largely lacking.
9. The Seminar showed that basic information about significant developments in inter-faith dialogue, even among the religiously interested and educated, is still very largely lacking.

10. A number of recent Muslim voices strongly advocating dialogue with Christians especially, but also with other religious communities, could be quoted here. Cf. Muhammad Talbi, 'Islam and Dialogue', in *Islam and the Modern Age*, vol. IX, no. 2, May 1978, pp. 1–18; vol. IX, no. 3, August 1978, pp. 35–46; Zafar Ishaq Ansari, 'Some Reflections on Islamic Bases for Dialogue with Christians and Jews in *Journal of Ecumenical Studies*, vol. XIV, 1977, pp. 433–47.
11. What is here put in quotation marks has been take from the unpublished papers of the Seminar.
12. See the famous letter to this effect, sent by Bishop Paul Bassin, head of the Latin Rite Church in Lebanon, to Cardinal Pignedoli. Cf. *Rheinischer Merkur*, 13 January 1978, p. 19.
13. On this point see also the essay by A. Roest-Crollius, 'Mission and Morality. *Al-amr bi-l-ma'arūf* as Expression of the Communitarian and Missionary Dimensions of Koranic Ethics', *Studia Missionalia*, vol. 27, Roma, 1978, pp. 257–81.
14. The orthodox Muslim religious leaders (*'ulama*) in India have yet to be touched by the dialogue movement. One big practical difficulty is the language barrier. Who of the Christian partners is fluent in Urdu? Few, except some Protestant ministers. Very few *'ulama* know English well enough to lead a theological conversation in it. In some of the southern regions the situation is, of course, different.

9

Christian-Muslim Relations in India: A Critical Survey*

Introduction

Recently, from 28-30 March 1979, the first Catholic All-India Consultation on Dialogue with Muslims took place in Cathedral House at Agra. It had been convened by the Dialogue Commission of the Catholic Bishops' Conference of India (C.B.C.I.). Dr. Bhajjan, the Director of the Henry Marty Institute (H.M.I.), the renowned Protestant pioneer Institute of Islamic Studies in India, together with two of his colleagues, were present. Archbishop Dominic Athaide of Agra, who hosted the Consultation, rightly called it 'a milestone in the history of the Church of India'.

At this juncture it is good to assess critically Christian-Muslim relations in India in the light of the radical transformation of these relations in the world at large. However, a mere enumeration of select activities and events in this field would hardly be satisfying. The wider and deeper issues at stake as well as the specifically Indian predicament of the Christian-Muslim encounter need to be elucidated. In the Republic of India the vast Hindu majority together with the Muslim, Sikh, Christian and other smaller minorities, are called to strive, all together, for a better future within the democratic, secular framework provided for by the Constitution of January 1950.

---

* This essay was first published in *ISLAMOCHRISTIANA*, vol. 5, 1979, pp. 119–43.

1. The General Background and Some Basic Data

1.1. Islam in Post-Partition India

Islam in India finds itself—especially after the Independence of 1947—in a peculiar if not unique situation. The Muslims of the Indian Republic today count almost seventy million, that is, they constitute something like eleven per cent of the total population.[1] Their geographical distribution is rather uneven. The range is from areas of concentration with a proportion of anything between sixty and ninety per cent to large areas with only about one per cent of Muslims. Like other Indians, the Indian Muslims are predominantly a rural people. In 1961, seventy-three per cent of the total Muslim population were rural which amounts to nine-and-a-half per cent of the nation's rural population.[2]

The Partition of the Indian Subcontinent in 1947, brought about by the Muslims themselves, proved an event that can hardly be overestimated is its consequences. It brought about the Islamic Republic of Pakistan, and later, in 1971, led to the birth of a third nation on the Indian Subcontinent, the People's Republic of Bangladesh. At the same time, the Partition of 1947 drastically decreased Muslim weight in politics and other areas of social life within the Indian Republic. A total of at least six million Muslims migrated from India to Pakistan. Excepting those hailing from East Punjab (about eighty per cent), a high percentage of the emigrants originated from urban areas, comprising the bulk of the Muslim bourgeoisie who with all their forward-looking potential had been in the forefront of the Muslim League movement in undivided India. It was that movement and its two-nation ideology that brought about Partition.

As a result of Partition, the Muslims of India, generally, lost their eminence as well as their leadership. They became, moreover, suspect in the eyes of the majority community, especially when prominent Indian Muslims were switching their allegiance to Pakistan right into the 1950's. This in turn has resulted in the re-emergence of a largely inward-looking leadership with pietistic learning and in the weakening of the open-minded dynamic forces.[3]

Yet claiming the allegiance of eleven per cent of the total Indian population, the Muslims are still by far more numerous than any other minority group and they have inherited an indigenous 'thousand year tradition of imposing dimensions' in all walks of life.[4] The most characteristic feature of the Indian Muslims' position, 'the fundamental feature of their own current development', as W.C. Smith put it, 'is the fact that they share citizenship in the new (secular) republic with an immense number of other people'[5] On the religious level they are called to reconcile their faith with modernity. The inevitable fact that they have to share political power with others, to live with others as equals in democratic participation, presents an unprecedented challenge to them. 'It raises the deepest issues both of the meaning of man's being and of social morality. It raises the deepest issues of the significance of revelation, truth, and the relation to other people's faith'[6]

More concretely, the Indian Muslims are asked today 'to what degree and in what forms and with what ideological bases' they will 'set themselves to working for the welfare of the whole Indian community? How will they visualize the material and spiritual welfare of Indian Islam as integrated with the activity and loyalty of the non-Muslim Indians?'[7] The challenge may well seem overwhelming, especially to a community recently drained of so much of its intellectual leadership. But, in the end, the problems of Indian Islam do not differ essentially from those facing the whole Islamic group today, namely how to live as an important religious minority within the secular world of today—in brotherhood with those of other forms of faith.

1.2. Christianity in Post-Partition India

Compared to the Muslims the Christians in India form a much smaller minority. They make up only about two and a half per cent of the total population and thus number approximately sixteen million today. They are even less evenly spread over the country than the Muslims. They are concentrated in the southern States, especially in Kerala and Goa, and reach higher numbers in some of the larger urban centres (e.g. Bombay, Madras, Poona, Hyderabad and Calcutta) as well as in tribal areas like, for instance, those of North-Eastern India

The Indian Christians as a community were hardly affected by Partition. Whereas most of them had not participated actively in the struggle for independence, they did not oppose it actively either. As compared with the Muslims, there was less of a problem for them in accepting the democratic and secular character of the Indian Republic as outlined in the Constitution. In areas of old Christian settlement, like Europe and the United States, Christian thought already for considerable time had tried to come to terms with the concept and reality of democracy, of secularism and the like. The secular Constitution therefore was not alien to Christian experience and thought at large, both Protestant and Catholic

Furthermore, the status of being a minority is not in itself as problematic for a group of Christians as it is for a group of Muslims. The history of Christianity, especially that of its formative period of the first three hundred years, provides an accepted model of dynamic Christian life of faith in community without the support of a 'Christian' political structure or state. As is well-known, the case of Islam is totally different. The decision for the Medinan state and its initial development belong to the formative and normative period of early Islamic history.

The main endeavour of Indian Christianity in the decades since Independence has been to strengthen its sense of community, its coherence and identity. To this end it has tried to shed the traces of its colonial and foreign dependence, to indigenize Church personnel, to indianize Christian life, expression and thought, to strengthen the community by educational and social services and to witness to Jesus Christ not only by the word of preaching but by service, especially in the educational, medical and social field. Significant new membership of the Church has been won during these decades among the tribals, the Harijans and Hindu low-caste people.

The powerful Protestant missionary movement during the nineteenth and twentieth century had led to conversions from Islam. In many Protestant Churches, therefore, we find to this day a substantial element of Urdu culture and the cherishing of other important elements of the great Indian Muslim heritage. The Catholic Church in India, after the end of the Jesuit mission at the Mughal court,[8] had no such tradition of a determined evangelical outreach to Islam. Catholic missionary activity and thinking during the nineteenth and twentieth century was predominantly concerned either in the tradition of Robert de Nobili (1577-1656) with conversions from upper-caste Hinduism, or from the scheduled Hindu castes and the Adivasi populations.

2. Christian Outreach to Muslims Before the Age of Dialogue

2.1. *The Meaning of Dialogue*

Dialogue is an ill-defined term. We take it here in a very wide sense, as an approach to adherents of another religion that is not predominantly centred on and shaped by the aim of inducing conversions (in the sense of change of institutional allegiance), but rather gives positive meaning to the religious encounter between religions or adherents of religions as such. Dialogue denotes in fact 'a complex process that is characterized by (a) sincere effort by men of good will to purify their knowledge of religions other than their own from all prejudice, misunderstanding and distortion, and to learn from the experiences and insights of the members of these religions, (b) an exploration of the ways in which the adherents of different religions may develop fraternal relations expressive of mutual reverence and human solidarity, (c) a combined effort of men belonging to different systems of belief to arrive at a working consensus on conceptions of transcendence and human values and ideals that may be responsive to the religious aspirations and concerns of contemporary man'[9], (d) The All-India Seminar in Bangalore, 1969, in its description of dialogue, dwelt on its spiritual dimension. It 'is spiritual and religious communion, the experiencing in common of the religious reality. It consists in experiencing religiously the fact that we, though specially chosen and blessed by God in Christ, are, together with the non-Christian partners, seekers after a deeper realization of God, and witnesses to each other of his mystery and his love, and that therefore we are at once at the deepest level of life. We meet on the ultimate ground of existence. Therefore we can share both what is common and what is different, intimate and personal'[10] It is clear that a relationship between Christians and Muslims on these lines would scrupulously avoid any unfair comparison or caricature, syncretism, covert attempts of proselytism, complacent static co-existence, defensive and hostile attitudes towards secular neighbours.

2.2. *Forerunners of Christian-Muslim Dialogue*

2.2.1. The Jesuit as the Mughal Court

The overall tradition of Christian-Muslim relations in India has certainly not been characterized by the attitude and outlook described in the previous paragraphs. The European missionaries carried into India all the ignorance and prejudice regarding Islam that have prevailed throughout the centuries in Europe[11]. Some Protestant missionaries have detected an affinity between scripture-centered, iconoclastic and puritanical Islam and the original impetus of the Reformation. They therefore approached Islam with some respect. Post-tridentine, largely south-European Catholic missionaries, in contrast, if open to positive religious values outside Christianity at all, would rather be inclined towards Hinduism and its world of ritual and symbol.

Edward Maclagan and Arnulf Camps[12] have acquainted us with the facts of the Jesuit presence at the Mughal court from 1579 A.D. onwards till the end of the seventeenth century. What element of dialogue can we discover in the broad sweep of the Jesuits at the Mughal court for about a century? Clearly, the first missions had no idea of dialogue at all: they had one clear objective, known to friend and foe alike—convert the emperor and, through him, the people. In all their discussions their whole purpose was to discredit everything Islamic, thinking that thereby the Emperor and others would be forced to submit to the superiority of Christianity. Once, in a discussion with Fr. Montserrate, Abul Fazl (1551-1602)[13] maintained that there was spiritual nourishment in the Koran, but the priest would not agree. Having failed in their objective, the fathers gradually turned their attention to providing spiritual succour for the few Christians at the court, running schools and making a few converts here and there, mainly among the ordinary people. On the Muslim side, the divines were of the same mentality as the priests, but Akbar and Abul Fazl in particular, showed an openness to discussion which would reflect no small credit on a modern proponent of dialogue.

Strangely enough, the Jesuits at the Mughal court did end up writing an extremely important chapter in the history of religious dialogue in India, for that was precisely what circumstances thrust upon the fathers there. We see this beautifully illustrated by the deep friendship that existed between Fr. Busi and the eldest son of Shah Jahan, Dara Shikoh and which provided a matrix for fruitful dialogue. It seems to me that more detailed research into the activities of the Jesuits actually stationed in the court during these years would highlight the fact that the relationship was illustrative of what was normal, not exceptional.[14]

2.2.2 Henry Martyn (1781–1812)

Henry Martyn (1781–1812), the pioneer Protestant missionary among the Muslims of India and Iran, became famous for his 'Controversial Tracts'[15], prepared for the disputation with Muslim divines. Yet, his overall approach to Muslims was much broader than is evinced by the tracts. He had strong reservations as to the aptness of disputations and controversies for conveying the Christian message. At best, he thought, they would arouse a spirit of inquiry. By contrast, he felt that personal talks with a small circle of interested Muslims produced what he called 'mutually responsive notes'. He saw it as his main endeavour to share the religious experience of the forgiveness and peace attained through Christ. He purposely set out to appreciate whatever was best in his Muslim acquaintances and ascribe such to the activity of God[16]. He stressed the need to direct attention to the sacred Scriptures of Islam and Christianity themselves rather than to later, scholastic elaborations and insisted on the need for fostering lasting friendship with the enquirer. Finally, he stressed the centrality of God's work in the souls of men and consequent reverence and respect for souls.

2.2.3. G.C. Pfander (1803-65) and G.A. Lefroy (1854–1919)

A little later, there appeared on the Indian scene a man of great influence on the manner of Christian witness to the Muslims: Carl Gottlieb Pfander (1803–65), the author of the widely distributed, controversial work *Mizan al-Haqq* (The Balance of Truth)[17]. The public debates between him and Muslim scholars and the literature they produced set the tone for decades. These debates sowed the seed of enmity and hatred of Indian Muslims and they started to suspect the missionary efforts of the Christians as a plot to destroy Islam in India. Dr. S. Bhajjan describes the legacy of this approach thus: 'Muslims, do know that Christians have been preaching to them for the last hundred and fifty years. They are also aware of the fact that many Muslims have been converted to Christianity. They think that Christian missionaries from the West came to destroy the religion of Islam and help the foreign powers, especially the British, to conquer and subjugate India. Indian missionaries preaching to Muslims are considered paid workers of the foreign missionaries and incapable of studying and understanding Islam. The image of an Indian Padre in the mind of a Muslim has been that of an arrogant, ignorant, deceitful, and number one enemy of Islam'[18].

It must not be forgotten, however, that already in the nineteenth century a number of Protestant missionaries came to adopt a quite different attitude. The Anglican Bishop of Lahore, George A. Lefroy (1854–1919) of the Cambridge Brotherhood in Delhi, for example, detected and wished to explore the positive religious message of Islam: its witness in its very social and political structure to 'the knowledge of God which given strength to human society'[19] The older controversial literature he qualified as 'very hard indeed, as though intended to confute the enemy rather than to win a disguised friend'[20]

In the last quarter of the nineteenth century, in fact, the growth of liberal thought produced a reversal of the aggressive attitude of missionaries. New awareness of Eastern religions, the growth of humanistic and agnostic thought in Europe, and the changing relationship of Britain to her colonies, effected a profound change in missionary attitudes.

2.2.4. Sayyid Ahmad Khan (1817–98)

The great reformer of nineteenth-century India, Sayyid Ahmad Khan, merits a special place in the pre-history of Muslim-Christian dialogue. In an age poisoned by imperial domination and fierce religious controversy and, in fact, from some years before the upheaval of 1857 onwards, he practiced and advocated friendship with Christians, openness to each other's cultural heritage, and a sympathetic approach in scholarly studies of each other.[21]

In *Tabyīn al-kalām,* the unique fragmentary Commentary on the Bible in three parts (Part 1: Introductory Discourses, Part 2: Commentary on Genesis 1-11 and Part 3: Matthew 1-5) published in the early 1860's. Sayyid Ahmad Khan tried to demonstrate against contrary views both of Christian and Muslim controversialists that the present-day Scriptures of Jews and Christians can and must be viewed by Muslims positively, as witnessing to *tawhīd,* the chief message of all authentic Scriptures. The biblical Scriptures are not totally corrupted and therefore have not to be rejected entirely. Through them God has reiterated *tawhīd* throughout the ages, and they continue to be relevant to Muslims if only read critically, that is, uninfluenced by the distortions of an erroneous Christian interpretation and in the light of the Koran's unambiguous message of *tawhīd.*

Although largely rejected as unorthodox at the time, Sayyid Ahmad Khan's general attitude and many of his insights have made a considerable impact on later Indian Muslim generations.

2.2.5. A Catholic Pioneer: Fr. Victor Courtois Sj (1907-60)

After the closure of the Jesuit mission at the Mughal Court, the Catholic Church did not take any thought-out and concerted missionary initiative among Muslims in India. Ignorance and prejudice regarding Islam and Muslims prevailed. In the South—until this century, the predominant area of Catholic missionary presence—Tipu Sultan's (1749-99) policies towards Christian communities in the Carnatic (as well as certain excesses during the Mappila rebellion earlier in our century) did much to establish in the Catholic mind there the image of the fanatic, intolerant and cruel Muslim[22].

Yet, one remarkable exception must be noted here, the work and ideas of Fr. Victor Courtois SJ Calcutta. Up to the time of Vatican II, V Courtois has been the only Catholic in India to propagate consistently the need for an apostolate among Muslims and, as part of an overall vision, to evolve a concept of the methods to be used, the attitudes to be fostered.

V. Courtois saw it as his foremost task to make the Indian Church aware of the Muslim dimension of its apostolic mission. From September 1946 until his death in December 1960 he edited and wrote, almost single-handedly, the *Notes on Islam. A Bulletin of Information about Islam with special reference to India.* The subtitle constantly read thus: A HELP TO A BETTER APPRAISEMENT OF ISLAMIC CULTURE. The *Notes* first appeared bi-monthly, then, from 1953 onwards, quarterly. Their foremost objective was to acquaint the reader with 'what Islam is, whence it comes and whither it goes. to present the religion of the Koran as objectively as possible, its Institutions, its beliefs, its evolution'[23]. The *Notes* deliberately strove to remain expository and abstain from polemics'[24], [.] 'to avoid', in other words, 'all unpleasant controversy [.]'[25]. 'Enlightened knowledge must meets take away the sharp sting of prejudice and open the way to more sympathy and regard'[26].

V. Courtois looked with admiration at the great Ramon Lull (1232-1315) who 'studied Islam trying always to discover not what divides but what unites. It is the spirit which must be revived today, a spirit of intellectual fairness and charity. Prejudices, indeed, against one another are still common among Christians and among Muslims. Untrue and grossly distorted statements disparaging the other's religious belief or practice are still found in books of recent dates or heard in conversations in Christiandom as well as in the world of Islam'[27].

Commenting upon a detailed 'curriculum of Islamic studies' for Christian seminaries, which he had proposed in his *Notes*. V. Courtois remarked: 'Insistence should always be made not on what separates Christians from Muslims but on what may [.] bring them closer to each other and to the heart of Christ. We study them not as enemies but as Brothers. To study we shall add much prayer'[28]. 'The discrete fruit of mutual understanding and knowledge', so Fr. Courtois was convinced, 'must needs be mutual friendship'[29]

A sustained effort is needed towards 'a friendly exchange of views with the idea of bringing about mutual understanding and concord'[30]. This however must not be confused with 'the tendency of some well-intentioned speakers to slip over difficult problems: to ignore the differences between Islam and Christianity is not to solve them, nor is it a step towards better mutual understanding. These difficulties must be faced squarely in order to be understood and appreciated'[31]

The mainspring for V. Courtois' call for a wider ecumenism between the religions, and especially Christians and Muslims lay in a clear perception of what unites all men most deeply: the common Fatherhood of God, which in turn he saw as the basis for the brotherhood of all men. He also stressed much the Heart of Christ as the centre of the hearts of men and the fulfillment of their deepest and best aspirations.[32]

We find on the very first pages of the *Notes* a remarkable openness to 'the riches of those (Muslim) hearts'. This openness leads V. Courtois to wish 'that in them we may recognize the features of our Heavenly Father and love them as Brothers. Were they better known, they would surely be better loved, and where there is love there is God. *Ubi Caritas et Amor ibi Deus est*'.[33]

The concept of the periodical *Notes on Islam,* the choice of articles and the selection of the news reported and analysed in it, make it clear that its editor perceived Islam as the international spiritual *and* socio-political reality it remains to this day. He did not succumb to the temptation to stress one or the other side of the over-all reality of Islam disproportionately, at the cost of other important aspects.

He, further, had a keen perception of the living and dynamic character of Islam and 'the profound revolution which is slowly changing the Muslims' Weltanschauung'[34]

The revival of Islam which V. Courtois witnessed and reported, in his eyes, gave the lie to all those who only decently declared Islam to be caught up on an irreversible process of disintegration. Islam had been thought wrongly to be dead irreversible process of disintegration. Islam had been thought wrongly to be dead. 'A true Muslim Renaissance has begun'[35].

V. Courtois kept strictly to the repeatedly stated objective of the *Notes*: to contribute to a better appraisement of Islamic Culture. Simultaneously he worked, reflected and wrote to promote a better knowledge of Christ and his teaching among Muslims. But he kept this work outside the sphere of the *Notes*.

However the *Notes* did report about Christian-Muslim 'conversations', that is, the beginnings of what has now developed into a world-wide dialogue movement. He advocated Muslim-Christian cooperation and reported about its earliest beginnings.

The *Notes on Islam* succeeded well. They gained international recognition and were increasingly read by Muslims, especially in India and Pakistan. They must be regarded as one important prophetical voice that brought the Catholic Church to the great landmark in Christian-Muslim relations, the declaration *Nostra Aetate* of Vatican Council II.

With his untimely death, this unique voice of the Indian Church fell into abrupt silence.

3. The Henry Martyn Institute and the Dialogue Approach

3.1. Earlier History

In contrast to the lone effort of Victor Courtois on the Catholic side, the Protestant Churches in India can look back to a great continuing tradition of outreach to Muslims, from the beginnings of Serampore College at the end of the eighteenth century and Henry Martyn onwards. This outreach is characterized by an approach that aimed primarily at conversion and Church expansion[36]

Here we are interested to see when and to what effect the

specifically dialogical approach entered Protestant missionary thinking and practice. To this end we have to look at the Henry Martyn Institute (named until the end of 1959 Henry Martyn School) of Islamic Studies. Its publication, the quarterly *Bulletin of Christian Institutes of Islamic Studies*, mirrors best the spirit and development of Protestant missionary thinking vis-à-vis Muslims in India.

The Bulletin's history goes back to the year 1911 when, under the inspiration and leadership of Dr. Samuel M. Zwemer (1867-1952), the 'Lucknow Conference on behalf of the Muslim World' was held. The Conference proposed the setting up of centres of study of Islam in different regions of the Islamic world. In India, an All-India Missionaries to Muslims League was founded, with its *News and Notes*, a Newsletter published occasionally for private circulation. Discussions for setting up a centre of Islamic studies in India were started only in the late 1920's (by the National Christian Council Executive). This led to the founding of the Henry Martyn School in Lahore in 1930. Its object was the training of missionaries and national evangelists for work among Muslims. The School in Lahore took over the Newsletter and continued to publish it quarterly under its old name 'News and Notes'. 'News and Notes' was first published as *The Bulletin of the Henry Martyn School of Islamic Studies* from Aligarh, where the Henry Martyn School had moved in 1960taking the name of 'Henry Martyn Institute of Islamic Studies'.[37]

3.2. *The Beginnings of the Dialogical Approach*

Going through the back numbers of the *Bulletin*, a first breaking in of the ideas of the then nascent international dialogue movement is clearly noticeable in the late 1950's[38]. Dr. Kenneth Cragg, during his visit to India late in the year 1958, made a strong and lasting impression. He lectured extensively and also actively took part in deliberations on the future of H.M.I.[39]. The Editorial of the April-June 1959 issue pointed out the new situation created by the new means of rapid international communication, in other words, by international exchanges of ecumenical leaders creating an 'evangelistic ecumenicity'. The then editor, Rev. Ian H. Douglas[40] introduced for the first time in the *Bulletin* the concept of dialogue: 'Even if Christian-Muslim meeting on the world-wide level in a long way off, there is real hope of the true dialogue here and there at the highest intellectual level. And the preparation of Christians in study conferences under able leadership increases the possibilities'[41]. But together with this and answering 'an even greater need. is that of encouraging meeting between its [the Church's] ordinary members and their Muslim neighbours. If the results of the high level conference can filter down to affect Christian-Muslim relationships at the grass roots level, the gain will be great indeed'[42]. I.H. Douglas defined the purpose of H.M.I. 'to assist the Church to realize and fulfill its evangelistic obligations to Muslims by fostering among Christians an adequate and sympathetic understanding of Islam'[43] Both in the *Bulletin* and in *Religion and Society, the Bulletin of the Christian Institute for the Study of Religion and Society,* Bangalore, we notice from around 1959/1960 onwards an opening to the dialogue approach and the willingness to a radical reappraisal of traditional approaches. Kenneth Cragg's *The Call of the Minaret,* first published in 1956, found an echo in both Journals. Rev. John B. Carman, in a review article 'Cragg's Call to Understanding', asked whether Cragg's 'humble invitation to a great invitation' can be broadened or at least repeated, to summon Christians to such a meeting with Hindus and Buddhists.[44] In the same article we notice a new stress on the need of openness to the presence of Christ's word in the non-Christian traditions even before the advent of the Gospel. 'As we try here in India to present the universal Christ in a way which will be relevant to both Muslim and Hindu, we do so in the confidence that he who has given us the Word to proclaim is the same Divine Word who has already prepared, and continues to prepare, the way for his coming in this land and among this people'[45].

We also notice in the early 1960's, for the first time in the *Bulletin,* articles including the need for a better understanding of central Muslim concerns and a deliberate abstaining from disparaging 'comparison'[46]. Now, the *Bulletin* also began to open its pages to Catholic thought and reflection on Islam and Christian-Muslim encounter[47]. Finally, from 1966 onwards, prominent Muslims began to write in the pages of the *Bulletin*[48].

It goes to the credit of Dr. Sam Bhajjan, the present Director of H.M.I., himself a notable Urdu poet and writer with a deep knowledge of Sufism and of the Persian literary tradition, to have stressed in the pages of the Bulletin and elsewhere the paramount importance of Urdu language and literature as a meeting–place for Muslims and Christians in India. From 1963 onwards he introduced in the Bulletin the important section 'From the Urdu Press'. In 1967 he and Dr. G. Adelphi, Lucknow, started the Urdu Quarterly *Humā* which ever since has reached a great number of Muslims, especially those brought up exclusively in the traditional type of education. The correspondence pages of *Humā* carry on a dialogue on a scholastic level with a numerous and most important section of the Muslim community, the *'ulamā* and the Urdu-knowing Muslims. Each issue of *Humā* states clearly on the final page the seven 'aims and objectives' of the Journal:

1. To create among Christians the taste for a serious study of Islam
2. To provide Urdu knowing evangelists with material that can help them in the friendly exchange of ideas with their Muslim friends
3. To publish articles that may help Christians to acquaint themselves with Muslim beliefs and help Muslims to acquaint themselves with Christian beliefs.
4. To awaken the desire among the Christian and Muslim minority to adopt a sympathetic and friendly attitude and to foster mutual understanding in religious and social questions.
5. Notwithstanding a number of fundamental differences between Christian and Muslim scholars, to prepare the way for formal dialogue and exchange of views in a regular manner.
6. To invite Christian and Muslim scholars to write and publish in the pages of *Huma* research articles about religious aspects of Islam and Christianity
7. To publish translations of books concerning Islam and Christianity that are highly respected in both religious communities.

Huma reserves twenty to twenty-five pages in each issue for Muslim writers. Many Muslims who were in the beginning reluctant to contribute articles for a Christian paper gradually started writing for *Humā*. This has becomes the safe of it among the Urdu-knowing Muslims. This dialogue through exchange of articles on common concerns has been regularly going on through *Humā* on one side and various Urdu papers on the other:

3.3. The Work Towards and in Dialogue

The Henry Marty Institute with its headquarters in the centre of the capital of Andhra Pradesh, Hyderabad, with a full-time staff of three to four persons, in collaboration with its various regional secretaries, pursues a number of activities that are an essential preparation for dialogue or directly involve it. (1) Courses on Islam are organized in theological colleges and seminaries. From 1966 onwards Catholic institutions were included in the program. A Catholic Indian scholar of Islam. Fr. Andreas D'Souza O.F.M. Cap., several years ago became member of the staff. (2) Area committees have been organizing Training Institutes in various parts of India to assist the local congregations and church leaders to understand their Muslim neighbours more fully and to relate to them more effectively in a Christian spirit. (3) Summer Schools have been offering an introduction to Islam. (Since 1978, the Catholic JAMI group, in collaboration with H.M.I., offers a summer course in Urdu plus introduction to the basics of Islam,). In all these programmes (1-3), Muslim scholars and teachers are involved actively. (4) An elementary correspondence course on Islam as well as courses on Christianity are offered, in both English and Urdu.

As early as in 1963, H.M.I. sincerely started talking about formal Christian-Muslim dialogue. The main stimulus was concern for deteriorating communal harmony and peace in India and Pakistan. Muslims were invited to start dialogue with Christians on issues common to both communities. After some hesitation a handful of Muslim intellectuals—mostly professors educated on western lines—showed interest. Although there was not much enthusiasm in evidence, on the part of the churches, many teachers in theological colleges and seminaries encouraged the H.M.I. staff to start such a movement. The hesitation on the part of the *ulamā* was that they thought the Christian invitation to Muslims for dialogue was just another method of the Christians to proselytize Muslims. One Muslim paper wrote a strong-worded editorial, warning Muslims of the dangers involved in starting a dialogue with Christians. It termed the efforts of the H.M.I. for dialogue as a 'new trap of the old trappers'.

Finally, a first three-day dialogue meeting on the question of 'faith and works' was organized in Nagpur in 1966. It was sponsored jointly by the Indian Institute of Islamic Studies (founded in 1963 in New Delhi) and by H.M.I. then stationed in Jabalpur (Madhya Pradesh) and was attended by twenty Muslim and Christian scholars. Some Muslim participants wrote favourable comments in Muslim newspapers, advocating a better understanding between Muslims and Christians. The ice was broken once and for all.

After this first dialogue several dialogues on the same pattern were organized in subsequent years, some of them together with Muslim institutions such as the Jamia Nizamiyyah in Hyderabad and the Indian Institute of Islamic Studies in New Delhi. The topics chosen were: Religion in the Modern Age; Man, His Nature and Destiny[49]; Salvation; God and Secularly; Social Justice; Woman in Great Religions. Some of the meetings were held in English and Urdu, the one on Social Justice completely in Urdu.

However, the H.M.I. and its *Bulletin* have never worked out a defined, unified view or policy of how to approach Muslims. Hence a certain tension has remained characteristic of the *Bulletin*, between an evangelization-proclamation approach at the one and a truly dialogical approach at the other end of the spectrum. Dr. S. Bhajjan writes: 'The H.M.I. does not recommend or favour any particular approach. We of the Institute are free to present any approach and discuss any kind of dialogue. However we have some guidelines that we try to put before our listeners: (1) We emphasize that when Christians and Muslims meet in dialogue we do not meet as enemies to defeat each other. We must say of the bitter rivalries in the past centuries that in many ways the only final solution is to forget them. (2) Our meeting is not a more sophisticated form of the old polemical debates. (3) We are not meeting as rival debating teams, athletics in place of military engagement. This is not a case of a Muslim team and a Christian team but a meeting of people some of whom are Muslims and some Christians. (4) Nor are we seeking any propaganda advantage. (5) Nor do we gloss over real difficulties. True friendship exists only where there is mutual understanding and the willingness to face the difficulties without fighting. Christians and Muslims are woefully ignorant with regard to each other and therefore the keeping open of communications in an all-important objective'[50].

4. Catholic Initiatives

4.1. Recent Catholic Awakening to Dialogue with Muslims in India

As late as 1975, Fr. Albert Nambiaparambil C.M.I., the Secretary of the C.B.C.I. Commission for Dialogue, in a survey article on 'Dialogue in India. A challenge to redeem hope', had this to say on dialogue of Catholics with Muslims: 'This entire field remains almost totally unexplored. By and large, a cloud of ignorance and suspicion continues to prevail[51].

The overall effort made by the Catholic Church in India to examine seriously its response to Vatican II (closure in 1965), culminated in the holding of the All-India Seminar held in Bangalore in 1969. This seminar achieved a breakthrough as to the recognition by the Church of India of the need to enter on a large scale into dialogue with the great I Indian religious traditions. The following areas were singled out for special concern: (1) change in our attitude towards other religions and education towards this on various levels; (2) demand for a theology of dialogue; (3) need for experts for training in dialogue, for research and the promotion of dialogue on the scholastic level and for advising the Christian Community at large; (4) setting up of centres for dialogue; 5) production of suitable literature; (6) developing the Christian ecumenical dimension of this work; (7) cooperation with non-Christians in the secular field[52].

With regard to the Muslims the report of the general workshop on dialogue and evangelization became aware of the need to initiate dialogue with the Muslims of India. It urged 'that scholars be set aside to study the Muslim religion, social life and culture in India, hoping by this means to come to a better understanding of this great people'[53]. Clearly, the first step the Indian Church had to take was that of getting to know its Muslim neighbours—no easy task when one considers the rich, multi-faceted nature of Indian Islam.

After an interval of another four years—as a follow-up of the International Theological Conference of Nagpur of 1971—the All-India Consultation on Evangelization (Patna, Oct. 1973) marked a further important step forward. It set up a special workshop (n. III-2) 'Evangelization and dialogue with Muslims'. For the first time, a group devoted to approaching Muslims came together. Fr. J. Wijngaards of the Mill Hill Fathers presented (in absentia) a

perhaps somewhat too ambitious but nevertheless truly prophetical plan concerning a future Catholic Apostolic outreach to the Muslims.

The resolutions of the group were basic. The need was stressed for courses, especially in seminaries, on Islam and on the approach to Muslims and Islam. The founding of a Catholic Institute to provide such courses was recommended. Finally, a note of caution was sounded against an Indianization 'that tended to be exclusively Hinduization'[54] These resolutions, however, were bound to remain on paper as long as the whole Church in India did not have more than one person officially set aside for this work.

The Research Seminar on non-biblical Scriptures held in Bangalore in 1974, again organized a special workshop on Islam. Its report is remarkable in that it expresses the conviction that Islam has a positive religious message, of special significance for the Christian Church in India: 'The self-communication of God. is partially recorded in the Koran which is acknowledged by Muslims as normative in Islam. Therefore, there are traces of divine influence in it. In some sense Islam in India may even he said to have been entrusted with the continuation of the O.T. task of conveying its experiences of the transcendence and majesty of God, shown so distinctively in the deep sense of reverence for God by Muslims in their prayer life. We Christians have something to learn from this attitude which may lead us to a new awareness of God's greatness and power'[55].

4.2. The Work and Approach of the Dialogue Commission of the C.B.C.I.

From January 1973 onwards the Dialogue Commission of the Catholic Bishops' Conference of India (C.B.C.I.) in the person of his full-time Secretary. Fr. Albert Nambiaparambil has vigorously worked to prepare the Catholic Community on all levels for dialogue.

It took its inspiration from Pope Paul VI's address delivered in Bombay in 1964, on the occasion of the Eucharistic Congress. 'We must meet not only as tourists, but as pilgrims who set out to find God, not in buildings of stone but in human hearts. Man must meet man, nation meet nation, as brothers and sisters, as children of God. In this mutual understanding and friendship, in this sacred communion, we must also begin to work together to build a

common future of the human race. Such a union. must be built on a common love that embraces all and has its roots in God who is love'[56]. Realizing 'that a good deal should both be done and undone if a dialogue worth the name is to be carried on between Christians and Muslims'[57], the Commission has been organizing with the help of the H.M.I., numerous three day courses in different parts of the country, covering the basic tenets of Islam, areas of misunderstanding of convergence etc. Wherever possible, participants in the courses visited mosques during their prayer-time. These courses were meant for all the Churches, and participants were from various Churches. Muslim took active part in these courses, as teachers and witnesses to their faith.

So-called 'get-togethers' on dialogue bring together participants, delegates from different dioceses of a region for two or three days to study the nature, scope, demands, difficulties, risks and concrete possibilities of inter-religious dialogue in the particular region. 'They try to relate the call to proclaim the Gospel to the call to be dialogue-pilgrims on earth. They hear leaders of other religions expound their own ways of life or their own religion as a way of life, share their feelings and hear the opinions of Christians'[58].

In the 'live-together' 'Christians and followers of other religions, come together in prayer, meditation, and shared reflections. They share the same life-style, share the costs of the occasion. They discuss topics of common concern. Much time is spent in prayer, songs and bhajans (i.e. religious songs in the Indian tradition). the topics are personal and the emphasis is always to keep it at that level'[59]

The first multi-lateral 'Live-Together' was held at Aligarh, the seat of the famous Muslim University, from October 25th to 27th, 1974. Of the thirty-three participants, thirteen were Muslims. The initial plan of having a bi-lateral (Muslim-Christian) live-together was altered on the suggestion of Muslim friends into holding it on a multi-lateral basis. The Muslims felt that this would help to foster better communal harmony. Aligarh is a very sensitive spot in India, and has been repeatedly the scene of bitter communal riots.

A Nambiaparambil reported at the time: 'The experience of dialogue ran into three days, through seven sessions. Each session began with a prayer and ended with prayers, said by participants from each religion. The topics proposed for shared reflection and prayer were: 'what does my religion mean to me?'; 'challenges to my religion'; 'my religion and social concern'; 'prayer in my life'; 'the hope that is n me'; 'steps to foster unity, understanding and collaboration among religions'.

'Some salient features which characterized the meeting are worth recording here. There was on the part of all a return to their own religious tradition and inheritance to draw light, inscription and motivation for social concern, for hope for meeting the challenges of the day. There was—as in previous bi-lateral life together—a conscious effort to focus on those elements which are common and unite the various religious traditions, and to go beyond the divisive separating factors. It took some time in fact to realize that the differentiating elements too can and must contribute to mutual enrichment. Towards the end of the meeting, the participants having moved away from the reflex of self-defence, the focus slowly shifted to the terrible gap that exists in all of us between theory and practice, to a heart-searching confession of common guilt. These were, perhaps the richest moments of the live-together. Preoccupation with self have given way to a common awakening of religious experience. Again, while at the early stage of the dialogue some seemed to conceive the aim set before us as the search for a universal religion, all slowly moved to the realization that dialogue must spring from each partner's deep commitment to his own tradition—an attitude to be constantly maintained even at the cost of disagreement on dividing factors'[60].

Aligarh has kept the bold initiative alive. The local branch of the Inter-Faith Association, founded by Archbishop D. Athaide of Agra, in February 1979, brought forty Hindus, Muslims, Jains and Christians together for a spiritual weekend. This most recent dialogue meeting was different from the other dialogues organized by the Association at Aligarh till now. The purpose of it was common prayer and meditation, while the previous ones were more of discussion and talks. The whole week-end was an experience of prayer and reflection. The organizing committee had held several preparatory meetings with the believers of the different faiths, and discussed with them the common forms of prayer that would be acceptable to all. As a result it was agreed that during the prayer session of the week-end, no object would be used to represent God, no language sacred to a particular tradition would be used for the singing of bhajans and no names for God which were unacceptable to any particular group of participants (e.g. OM) would be used in prayer and bhajans.

Participants, both Hindu and Muslim, who were interviewed for a feed-back said that in no way did they felt that their faith was compromised by this spiritual week-end. All found it an enriching and new experience, and spontaneously decided to have such prayer meetings more often[61].

We have given the Aligarh dialogue meetings as an example. Numerous other ongoing activities of the same kind could be quoted here, e.g. Fr. Leo D'Souza's multi-lateral meetings in Lucknow, the capital of U.P., Fr. Aelred Pereira's activities in multi-religious sharing in Bombay, again a place of high Muslim concentration, Br. Cyriac's inter-religious meetings in Hyderabad, the fortnightly prayer-services for people of all religions in Ashirvad dialogue centre and in Dharmaram Centre for World Religions in Bangalore and so on.

It is on the basis of such initiatives of the past ten years or so, that C.B.C.I. Commission on Dialogue with the help of the staff members of Vidyajyoti Institute of Religious Studies in Delhi was able to publish the *Guidelines for Inter-religious Dialogue.*[62] They provide, besides a historical note, theological perspectives and pastoral guidelines, fairly detailed information on dialogue activities in India, i.e., a list of Centres, Ashrams, Groups and Movements. Later this year the Commission is going to publish an Indian re-edition of the *Guidelines for a Dialogue between Muslims and Christians* of the Secretariat for Non-Christians in Rome, with an additional chapter on the Muslims of India and points to be kept in mind when engaging in dialogue with them.

On being asked, many of the persons actively engaged in initiating multilateral dialogue in India admit that—on the whole—a sizeable and regular Muslim participation has not been forthcoming. They attribute this partly to lack of interest or to hesitation on the Muslim side but even more to a lack of sympathetic knowledge, contact and sensitivity towards Muslims and their religious tradition, among themselves. Many Ashrams and Dialogue Centres are built, furnished and run in such a way as to make it difficult for Muslims to feel at home there. Wherever, on the other hand, informed sympathy and sensitivity towards Muslims existed, Muslims have responded positively.

5. Muslim Initatives

5.1. *The Islam and the Modern Age Society*

The previous paragraphs should not create the mistaken impression that the Muslims of India have been solely passive partners in dialogue. Earlier we mentioned Sayyid Ahmad Khan's outstanding contribution. As to more recent times, we have seen that the I.I.I.S. from the year of its foundation in 1963 onwards, continuously has cooperated with the H.M.I. in organizing dialogue meetings. The *Islam and the Modern Age Society*, founded by the late Dr. Abid Husayn (d.1978) in 1970, likewise has been keeping up a strong commitment to dialogue on the intellectual level. The Quarterly of the Society, in its first issue (May 1970), introduced itself as the organ of a group of 'persons in the East and the West who. are in search for a philosophy of life calculated to reconcile the conflict between individualism and collectivism and between material and moral values', who aim at 'a new synthesis of reason and revelation'. It continued: 'They feel it to be the most pressing need of the modern age and a challenge to all the great religions to find, in their respective ways, and if possible, in cooperation with one another, to work out such a synthesis'[63]. (sic!) Under number four the programme of the Society includes 'Discussions of the way in which Islam and other religions can cooperate to meet the challenge of the growing skepticism and unbelief throughout the world'[64]. Motivated by such preoccupations, the Society has organized a number of important national and international seminars, e.g. the Seminar on Inter-religious Understanding (Oct. 17-20, 1971), New Delhi.[65] The quarterly also reprinted most of the papers of the famous Christian-Muslim in Broumana/Lebanon (July 11-18, 1972) and produced a detailed report of it. Unfortunately, with the death of the two outstanding promoters of its ideas and ideals, D. K.G. Saiyidain (1904-71) and Dr. Abid Husain 1896-1978), the activities of the Society have come to a virtual standstill.

5.2. *The Tughlaqabad Seminar on Mosque and Church*

Not long after its transfer to the new magnificent campus on the outskirts of Southern New Delhi, the I.I.I.S. hosted in Oct. 1978 a meeting of twelve Muslims and twelve Christians hailing from various parts of India. The aim was to explore, in the light of the message of the Bible and Koran, the possibilities of a common commitment to harmony and reconciliation, not only between Muslims and Christian but also among all religions and ideological groups in India.

The Seminar 'Mosque and Church. Their contribution to interreligious harmony and reconciliation' was organized jointly by I.I.I.S., by H.M.I. and by the Dialogue Commission of the C.B.C.I.[66]. The Seminar highlighted the new awareness of the community dimension of dialogue. International meetings sponsored by the W.C.C., like the one in Hongkong in January 1975, earlier had delineated 'the theological bases FOR Muslim-Christian relations and for the relations of both with all neighbouring religions and ideologies'[67]. At the same time, it marked out in a concrete way 'areas of common concern in social and political contexts'[68].

Two key papers by prominent Muslim participants merit special mention here because of their pleading from a decidedly Muslim point of view for accepting and promoting inter-religious dialogue, especially with Christians. Syed Vahiduddin, former Head of the Department of Philosophy at Delhi University, pointed out the Koranic basis for interreligious dialogue as advocated today: the Islamic temper and ethos that transcends historical, institutional Islam and in fact does not cease to challenge and call into self-questioning; further, 'Koranic humanism' that follows directly from the way the Koran views man's dignity, grounded in his being foremost and essentially related, by the act of creation, to the God of mercy. S. Vahiduddin stressed that in their common reference to transcendence. Muslims and Christians (and even those who right for the cause of Allah without knowing that they are fighting for His cause) can and must—in the sense of Q. 3:52—pursue a common endeavour.

Professor Ziaul Hasan Faruqi, the Principal of Jamia Millia Islamia, New Delhi, a graduate of the prestigious Dar al-ulum in Deoband, U.P. and of McGill University, Montreal, in his paper made a strong plea for the need for religious communities to open up to one another in dialogue and to thoroughly revise traditional attitudes and teachings. We have to choose either to learn to live as members of a world-community composed of various cultures or not to live at all. We have to learn to live as partners, to develop a 'mutual appreciation of each other's heritage based on the conviction of equality of all as human beings in the eyes of God'[69].

To bring about this change of attitude and outlook, Z.H. Faruqi envisages action on both the intellectual and on the practical plane. On the former, the *first* step should be to acquire a good and objective knowledge of various religious traditions. A *second* step should be to revise thoroughly our traditional exclusivist attitude. The original spirit of our respective religious tradition must be allowed by us to assert itself as against the primary of particular dogmas, rituals and ceremonies. 'Without a new theological approach to include all the world religions as the religious heritage of mankind and to find a respectable place for all religions in one's religious consciousness the dream of inter-religious harmony will ever remain unrealized'.

The *third* step must be an ever-increasing dialogue between adherents of the world religions. Dialogue is here seen as the effort 'to establish a religious relationship with a person of another faith'. In the context of world religions it means to listen to each other's experience of their respective religious traditions and to share in deeper union of mutual openness, even where irreducible differences remain in perception and expression.

A shared action, according to Z.H. Faruqi, should in built on the common perception of what is—Koranically speaking—*ma'rūf*, that is, good, beautiful, just and the like. If the *ma'rūf* is one and the same for all mankind, then nothing should bar us from uniting and working together for a just social order, against all kinds of injustices, social, economic and political, from cooperating in doing things that make life good and beautiful.

It clearly emerged from this Seminar that certain initiatives have to be taken now, many of them by way of concerted action. Both the Christians and Muslims at the Seminar felt that much needs to be done in the field of teaching, especially in those institutions where the leaders of the communities are formed, such as seminaries, *madrasas,* and institutes of Islamic or Christian studies. A number of Christian faculties of theology and philosophy and of seminaries have recently started to institute basic courses on Islam and on Muslim life in India as part of their normal curriculum. Muslim participants as e.g. Prof. Iqbal Ansari Director of the Institute of Islamic Studies in Aligarh University, expressed the conviction that in their curriculum, too, room should be made for teaching the Christian religion as Christians see it. True, the traditional syllabus of *madrasas* provides here and there for information and discussion of the elements of the Christian faith, but all this within the framework and outlook of traditional Islamic thinking.

The need was felt, furthermore, to collaborate in working out basic textbooks and anthologies on Christianity and Islam for use in higher religious Muslim and Christian educational Institutions. It should become normal to invite Muslim lecturers to Christian institutions for participating in teaching on Islam and vice versa.

Apart from the crucial work of introducing these changes in the training of our respective religious leaders, there is the wide area of initiatives to be taken on the local level. The participants of the Tughluqabad Seminar experienced during the three days of living together much mutual cordiality and frank conservation. The final session culminated spontaneously in a common silent prayer. At this point, when the participants were about to disperse, it seemed to us that a new starting point had been reached. There is very much need for this and similar groups to meet again and again and then to spread this attitude and way of proceeding on the local level.

The Seminar, in the final session, in fact proposed the setting up of a small permanent Muslim-Christian committee, acting (a) as a watchdog over inter-community relations and as possible court of appeal in case of conflicts; (b) promoting and planning further meetings of this kind and spreading relevant mutual information via the media; (c) fostering the teaching of Islam in Christian institutions of religious learning and vice versa, and to check, in a scholarly manner, any educational material as to its fairness in dealing with matters pertaining to either Christianity or Islam; (d) to initiate and foster theological thinking about central questions touching the faith and ethical teaching of both religions.

Unfortunately this committee was not set up. The Church-Mosque Seminar somehow did not have the determination to translate its insights into practical and effective terms. The proposals, however, are so obviously as expression of real needs that they are bound to find realization soon, in one way or another. This, at least, is our firm hope.

6. The Agra Consultation in March 1979 and the Task Ahead

The Consultation on Dialogue with Muslim in Agra of March 1979, which we mentioned in the Introduction, was the first representative Catholic meeting of its kind in India. Two years earlier, a group of Jesuits working among Muslims in India had constituted itself as JAMI group. In spring 1977, it started a cyclostyled quarterly bulletin, the *Jami Notes*, and has held several general meetings in order to clarify its vision of Christian-Muslim relations in India today and in order to foster unity and support among its members.

In Agra, the newly constituted group named itself C.M.R.I. (Christian Muslim Relations in India). It elected a committee of six which, in turn, elected as its Secretary, for the coming two years. Fr. Terence Farias, a research scholar in the sociology of religion at Aligarh University. The patron of C.M.R.I. in the Archbishop of Agra. Most Rev. D. Athaide for many years an active promoter of Christian-Muslim dialogue in his diocese and beyond.

For the future, the following main areas of concern emerged from the discussion at Agra:

(a) *Formation*: To this day corporate self-centeredness, ignorance and prejudice are effectively at work in the Catholic communities. The first task therefore is to form men and women who can help the Church leaders and the congregations to put into practice in everyday life the outlook at attitudes towards Muslims which are demand by the Vatican II Declaration *Nostra Aetate*. The C.M.R.I. Committee decided to give priority in the coming few years to the work of organizing, together with H.M.I. and with Muslim friends, formation programmes on Islam, mainly in three directions: training institutes on diocesan level, courses on Islam in seminaries and special programmes on Islam for women religious.

(b) *Information*: A quarterly publication in the line of *JAMI notes* will be published by C.M.R.I., under a name yet to be chosen. An effort will be made to introduce gradually more news and information regarding Christian-Muslim relations in the religious and secular Press, on Radio and TV and to produce audio-visual aids for the work of information.

(c) *Theological reflection*: Progress in this field depends first of all on persons being available in institutes of higher religious teaching and research who have a deep knowledge of both Islam and Christianity, based on a first-hand study of the ancient and recent sources and in living contact with leading representatives of both traditions[70]. Several young Catholic priests are engaged at the moment in advanced special studies of Islam, in India and abroad. Hopefully, young Muslim scholars will come forward to enter into a thorough study of Christianity. The orthodox Muslim religious leaders (ulama) have yet to be touched by the dialogue movement. One major practical difficulty is the language barrier. Who of the Christian partners is fluent in Urdu? Few, except some Protestant ministers. Very few *'ulamā* know English well enough to lead a theological conversation in it. In some of the southern regions the situation is, of course, different.

In the meantime, an ongoing religious dialogue on an academic level is gradually being initiated in places like Delhi where Christian and Muslim institutions concerned with religious training and research live in relative proximity. The dialogue promises to be especially fruitful in those areas of thought where the classical theologies meet with empirical research, in the fields, for instance, of psychology of religion, sociology of religion and so on[71].

The Catholic communities in India need the enrichment which a deep and prolonged encounter with Indian Islam will certainly effect in various areas of its life.

(d) Cooperation in social action: Here the field is wide open. Wherever initiatives in this line have been taken, as for instance joint work for the uplift of women in slum areas of Hyderabad or South Kannada, the results have been most encouraging, especially with regard to the establishment, there, of a hitherto unknown closeness in communal relationship.

(e) Multilateral and bilateral prayer meetings and live-togethers: It is to be hoped that the movement generated by various local Dialogue Centres and Ashrams and as promoted and coordinated by the Secretary of the C.B.C.I. Commission of Dialogue will grow in intensity. Once the Muslims and Christians, as well as the Hindus, Sikhs, Jains and others, are better formed and informed about one another, it will be easier to arrange multi-lateral meetings in a way that is fully acceptable to all participants. Perhaps, one day, creative Christians will come forward to establish Christian *khanqāhs* (i.e. Sufi centres) and to initiate Christian *khanqāh* life inspired by the witness of the great Sufi centres of deep spiritual life as well as of outstanding social concern, especially for the poor. Such groups, hopefully, may become agents of reconciliation and harmony amidst the various socio-religious communities that form the one composite national culture of India.

NOTES

1. The Muslims constituted around twenty-five per cent of the total population in undivided India.
2. Cf. N.A. Siddiqui, *Population Geography of Muslims of India,* New Delhi: S. Chand, 1976, *passim.*
3. Cf. The perceptive analysis of the specific predicament of Islam in post-Partition India by W.C. Smith in his *Islam in Modern History,* New York: The New American Library of World Literature, 1959, pp. 257-92, being *ch. VI: India: Islamic Involvement.*
4. *Ibid.,* p. 262.
5. *Ibid.,* p. 264.
6. *Ibid.,* p. 289.
7. *Ibid.,* p. 290.
8. The activities of the Jesuits were not confined to the court. Cf. Arnulf Camps, *Jerome Xavier SJ and the Muslims of the Mughul Empire. Controversial Works and Missionary Activity,* Schöneck-Beckenried: Nouvelle Revue de Science Missionaire, 1957, pp. 251-2.
9. Alfred d'Souza in *Islam and the Modern Age,* vol. III, no. 3, August 1972, p. 78.
10. *All-India Seminar: Church in India Today.* Bangalore 1969, New Delhi: C.B.C.I., 1969, p. 341.
11. Cf. Norman Daniel, *Islam and the West,* Edinburg: University Press, 1960, *passim.*
12. *The Jesuits and the Great Moghul,* London: Burns and Oates, 1932. A Camps, *op. cit.*
13. Akbar's favourite Secretary and Wazir, the celebrated author of *Akbarnāma and Ā'ýn-i Akbari and of the moral collection of leters Maktūbāt-i 'Allāmi.*
10. 14. In this and the previous paragraphs I either follow closely or quote from notes provided to me by Paul Jackson SJ on 'Christian-Muslim Dialogue in India'.
15. Cf. Samuel Lee, *Controversial Tracts on Christianity and Muhammadanism* (Cambridge: Deighton and Sons, 1824).
16. Cf. L.L. Van der Werff, *Christian Mission to Muslims* (South Pasadena: W. Carry Library, 1977), pp. 30-36.
17. A.A. Powell, 'Maulana Rahmat Allah Kairanawi and Christian-Muslim Controversy in India in the mid-19th century', *JRAS,* no. 1, 1976, pp. 42–63.
18. *The Bulletin of the Christian Institute of Islamic Studies,* vol. 1, no. 4, October–December 1978, pp. 39–40.
19. Quoted in L.L. Vander Werff, *op. cit.,* p. 59.
20. Quoted *ibid.,* p. 60.

21. For a detailed account of C.W. Troll, *Sayyid Ahmad Khan, A Reinterpretation of Muslim Theology*, New Delhi: Vikas, 1978, esp. pp. 58–99.
22. A dispassionate study of this short phase of Christian-Muslim relationship in Southern India, trying to separate fact from legend, has yet to be written.
23. *Notes on Islam*, December 1957, p. 129.
24. *Ibid.*, July-August 1948, p. 77.
25. *Ibid.*, November 1952, p. 125.
26. *Ibid.*, January 1952, p. 1.
27. *Ibid.*, June 1955, p. 49.
28. *Ibid.*, May-June, 1949, P. 60.
29. *Ibid.*, November 1957, p. 113.
30. *Ibid.*, June 1957, p. 55.
31. *Ibid.*
32. *Ibid.*, September 1946, p. 1.
33. *Ibid.*
34. *Ibid.*, March 1959, no. 1.
35. *Ibid.*, March 1951, p. 17.
36. Cf. L.L. Vander Weff, *op. cit.*, pp. 27ff.
37. The Henry Martyn School of Islamic Studies became the Henry Martyn Institute in 1959 and the Bulletin came to be known as *The Bulletin of the Henry Martyn Institute of Islamic Studies* from January 1960. Dr. S. Bhajjan, the present Director of H.M.I., suggested the name *AL-Basheer*. The first copy of the quarterly magazine appeared under the title of *Al-Basheer* in January 1972. *Al-Basheer* was discontinued from July 1976. The *Bulletin* was started again from January 1978. The headquarters of the Institute, which has regional offices in various parts of the country since 1971, are in Hyderabad (Deccan) 500 001, P.O.B. 153.
38. All through, the *Bulletin* mirfrors the constant self-critical reflection on missionary outlook and approach, cf. e.g. John W. Sadiq 'Plea for a fresh approach to Muslims' January-March 1947, pp. 3–11.
39. Cf. *The Bulletin H.M.I.*, October-December 1958, pp. 18–20.
40. He remained the editor until his retirement in October 1961.
41. *The Bulletin H.M.I.*, April-June 1959, p. 2.
42. *Ibid.*
43. *Ibid.*
44. *The Bulletin H.M.I.*, July-September 1959, p. 26.
45. *Ibid.*, p. 36. D.W. Bijlefeld is author of *De Islam als Na-Christelijke Religie* (Den Haag, 1959). Several contributions by John B. Taylor (Selly Oak Colleges, now WCC) also figured prominently in the pages of the *Bulletin H.M.I.*
46. E.g. S. Bhajjan, 'The Conception of Christ in Islam', October-December 1963/March 1964, pp. 42–53.

47. E.g. 'A Christian Approach to Islam'. Report on a talk by Fr. Parmananda SJ October 1964, pp. 2–5; R.A. Butler, SJ, 'The Image of Christ in Recent Muslim Literature', Octpber 1965, pp. 3–13. Also the 'Notes on Louis Massignon and his *Opera Minora*, on Charles de Foucauld and on Louis Gardet' by J.S. Moon in *The Bulletin H.M.I.*, April 1969, pp. 32 ff.
48. E.g. Syed Abdul Latif, 'Faith and Action', April 1966, pp. 3–12; Sa'Ìd A. Akbarābādi, 'Faith and Deeds', July 1966, pp. 2–7.
49. Most of the papers of this Seminar are published in *Religion and Society* (Bangalore), vol. XX, no. 3, September 1973.
50. *Bulletin H.M.I.*, vol. 1, no. 4, October-December 1978, pp. 49–50.
51. *Vidyajyoti, Journal of Theological Reflection*, vol. 39, 1975, p. 122.
52. Cf. *All-India Seminar: Church in India Today. Bangalore* 1969, New Delhi: C.B.C.I., 1969, pp. 342–3.
53. *Ibid.*, pp. 334–5.
54. *Light and Life We Seek to Share. All-India Consultation on Evangelization* (Bangalore 1973), p. 324. The General Meeting of the C.B.C.I. in January 1974 endorsed the Patna declaration and recommended exploring the possibility of establishing a Centre for Dialogue with Muslims. Cf. *Report of the General Meeting of the C.B.C.I.*, January 1974, p. 147.
55. D.S. Amaloparvadass (ed.), *Research Seminar on Non-Biblical Scriptures* (Bangalore: NBCLC, 1974), p. 620.
56. Neuner-Dupuis, *The Christian Faith* (Bangalore: T.P.I., 1973), no. 1032.
57. *Bulletin, Secretariatus*, 1975, X/2, no. 30, p. 257. Repr. of the article in *Journal of Dharma*, vol. 1, 1976, pp. 267–83.
58. *Ibid.*, pp. 255–6.
59. *Ibid.*, p. 256.
60. Dialogue in India. A Challenge to Redeem Hope, In: *Vidyajyoti, Journal of Theological Reflection*, vol. 49, 1971, pp. 112–13.
61. This passage is adapted from a report by Terence Farias SJ in the cyclostyled *JAMI Notes* (Delhi), vol. III, spring number.
62. (66, Varanasi Cantonment, U.P., India, 1977).
63. *Islam and the Modern Age*, vol. I, no. 1, May 1970, pp. 7–8.
64. *Ibid.*, p. 9.
65. *Ibid.*, vol. III, no. 1.
66. Cf. the report of the Seminar by C.W. Troll in *Vidyajyoti*, vol. 43, 1979, pp. 16–24.
67. *Christian meeting Muslims*, Geneva: WCC, 1977, p. 120.
68. *Ibid.*, p. 122.
69. Quotations here refer to the cyclostyled papers of the Seminar: They will be published in the forthcoming issue of *Studies of Islam*, New Delhi: I.I.I.S.
70. Obviously, in the Indian situation, any such specialization must go

hand in hand with a continuous deepening of one's knowledge of the classical and the living Hindu tradition and, according to the locale, of other traditions alive there (Sikh, Jain, Adivasi).

71. It is unfortunate that hitherto the secular character of the Indian Constitution has been interpreted generally in such a way as to exclude the study of religions and of theology from the State Universities of India. The Guru Gobind Singh Dpt. of Religions Studies at Patiala University as well as the Departments of Islamic Studies and of Islamic Theology (Sunni and Shi'a branch) of Aligarh University are exceptions. Since there is no teaching of religion at Secondary School level, the need to train teachers of religion at the Universities does not arise.

10

Mission and Dialogue: The Example of Islam*

1. A New Constellation

It would seem hardly necessary to mention at the beginning that during the past few decades there has developed a new situation in the relations between Christians and Muslims. This is first of all proven by statistical facts. The Muslims today count about one billion. Their overall number thus begins to equal that of the Christians. In eastern and Western Europe, taken together, their number comes close to 20 million, in Britain they count about one million, in Britain they count about one million.

Both religious communities today are present practically everywhere on the globe, are active on a world-wide level and live together in many if not most parts of the world. Both religions are essentially universal and missionary in character. They regard every human being as a potential member of their community and invite each and everyone to membership.

In the course of the first decades of our century a number of Western observers of the Muslim world doubted whether the religion of Islam would be able to cope with the challenges of modernity. But, what a remarkable shift! In our day, at the beginning of the last decade of the century and shortly before the end of the millennium, not a few begin to ask: Will Christianity be able to withstand the challenge of a newly awakened and strengthened Islamic faith? In the face of a rapidly growing, young

* This essay was first published in *SALAAM*, vol. 12, no. 3, July 1991, pp. 87–101.

and prophetically self-confident Islamic community the large churches come across as shaken by crisis and unsure of themselves. Obviously, this observation applies to the churches in North America, Australia and Western Europe rather than to those in Asia and Africa.

However, in stating this one must not overlook what cannot remain hidden to perceptive observers: Behind the self-assured façade and rhetoric of certain Muslim circles there seems to lurk the concern and fear, that the Muslims as believers may yet suffer greater damage from the breaking of in modern secularism and materialism than meets the eye. In fact, we see faith-conscious Muslims increasingly bemoaning the ever more frequent loss among Muslims of the genuinely religious, ethical and other-worldly content of Islam and at times total eclipse of the life of faith in the shadow of a political discourse couched in terms of an Islamic fundamentalist idiom.

Perhaps it is this hidden worry which explains some of the excesses in the Muslim reaction to the West, which, by the way, most Muslims mistakenly continue to equate with Christianity. The conviction that the Islamic faith and the Islamic way of life are constantly menaced and undermined by the 'Christian West' explain to a certain extent the extremely negative attitude of the Muslims to Christian Mission. No wonder that one of the most tense and difficult dialogue encounters between Christians and Muslims has been the Colloquium on 'Christian Mission and Dawa' organized in 1976 at Chambésy in Switzerland by the WCC (cf. *International Review of Missions*, Vol. LXV, No. 260, October 1976).

2. Common Ground in the Area of Faith and Mission

Christianity and Islam have much in common. Allah, the God of the Koranic revelation, is closely related to Yahweh, the God of the Jewish faith. The Koran frequently mentions and repeatedly alludes to events and personalities which are familiar to Christians through the Bible, e.g. Adam, Noah, Abraham, Jacob, Moses, Jesus and Mary. The God whom the Muslims adore is the Creator of heaven and of earth, a God who has made manifest His will and Law for humanity through the mouth of the prophets. He is a God, who will reward with paradise those among men who have believed in His Message and have obeyed his Will and Law, a God who, at the same time, will punish the ungrateful, the unrepentant unbelievers (*al-kāfirūn*) with condemnation to Hell.

Both, Christianity and Islam are essentially universal and missionary religions. To be a Christian means to participate in the mission of Jesus Christ by belonging to the Pilgrim People of God, the Church. The Church is sent to make effectively known everywhere the saving work which God has enacted and continues to enact in Christ. The whole Christian community therefore shares in one mission. This mission consists of various elements; e.g., prayer, liturgical cult, celebration of the sacraments; service of the poor, sick, repressed and exploited (*diakonía*); preaching, catechesis and theological reflection; contacts and conversation with the adherents of other religions, proclamation of the good news and invitation to men and women, to join the Christian community and thus to participate effectively in the Church's comprehensive witness for Jesus Christ.

Every aspect and all activities of the Church have to be imbued with the spirit of serving love—individually and corporatively. Otherwise they betray the true mission of Jesus. All members of the Church participate in its mission. However, not every Christian is called individually to translate into really each one of the elements of the mission of the Church as enumerated above. Rather, the special gifts (charisms) bestowed by the Spirit upon the individual or/and the group as well as the grace of the God-given, opportune 'moment' (*kairós*) determine the responsible 'choice of what has to be done here and now as well as the concrete manner of its execution.

In a comparable way the Muslim, too, has a 'missionary' vocation. To be a Muslim means membership in the Islamic community, the 'community of the Prophet' (*ummat un-nabi*). The *umma* knows itself constituted and entrusted by God through the last of the prophets, Muhammad with inviting men and women to be obedient to God's revealed will, in the footsteps of Muhammad. In other words, the Muslim as a member of the Islamic community, the *umma* is asked to invite others to Islam, i.e., to the continuing act of total submission to the One God and to membership in the *umma* (Q 3:19). This community of the believers 'is a community (of people), who guide with truth, and therewith they do justice.' (Q 7-159) It is 'the best community raised up for men', called to 'enjoin good and forbid evil' and to 'believe in Allah.' (Q 3: 110) The well-known Indian Muslim '*Êlim* (jurist-theologian) Muhammad Manzoor Nomani writes about the Missionary task of the Muslim today:

> The mission of the Apostles (*rural*—prophets, messengers) in this behalf comprises two parts: to receive knowledge of that way of life and that guidance from God (i.e. Islam by means of the revealed word, and then, to preach it to fellowmen, to instruct them in it, and to persuade them to put it into action in their daily life.
>
> The first part of the mission ended with the termination of the luminous line of the Apostles. The law and guidance brought by the Prophet. have permanently ruled out the necessity of another Messenger from Above. But the second part of the Apostolic work, the preaching of divine law and guidance and the persuading of men to enact them in their everyday existence, continues as ever, and it is the unique privilege of Muslims that, as successors of the Prophet, the sacred duty of discharging this responsibility and of carrying ahead the holy mission of the Prophet to fulfllment has now fnally fallen to their lot. (*Islamic Faith and Practice*, Lucknow (India), 1977, p. 117)

Any effort towards improving relations between the two religious communities will endeavour to respect these essential data of the perceived mission in faith on both sides.

3. Significant Differences and Their Roots

In spite of the fact that Christians and Muslims share basic convictions about God and His provision for the world of creation, there exist on the basis of the foundational Scripture and the foundational model of each of the two religious communities' essential differences. It is only in realizing and acknowledging the roots of these differences in doctrine and history that we can begin to understand why the missionary togetherness of the two religions is such a delicate affair, a minefield as it were, to be trodden warily. An important area of conflict between Muslims and Christians is the different view both sides have of Jesus and Muhammad. Muslims are correct in stating that the Christians have over centuries defamed Muhammad whilst they themselves on the very basis of the Koran hold Jesus and Mary in the highest regard. Only during the present century have Christian scholars begun to portray the prophet of Islam in more objective, and at times even sympathetic, terms and to do justice to his religious significance. The declaration of Vatican Council Ii about the relationship of the Church to the non-Christian religions speaks in very positive terms about the faith and practice of Islam. However, it does not mention the Prophet of Islam with any word whatsoever.

The Christians on their part have difficulties with the Jesus of the Koran. Jesus is presented by the Koran as a person of great sanctity, someone very close to God and a worker of miracles. However, the Koran regards Jesus unmistakably as a mere human being, as not more. but also nor less—than a great servant and prophet of God. The Koran strictly rejects the divinity of Christ and denies his death on the cross. In the same way the Koran has no place for the Christian doctrine of the Trinity. The fact that the Koran has its own full-fledged picture of Jesus - Jesus is mentioned 30 times in the Koran—means that Islam is in a sense less open to Jesus the Christ of Christian faith than other religions.

The two different foundational models shape the interpretation and the perception of the great principles that are common to Islam and Christianity. Furthermore, the ethico-social implications of these principles for everyday life are not interpreted and understood in the same way. This is so because both religions have different root-models: Jesus of Nazareth and Muhammad of Mecca. The same could be said for Judaism, in referring to Moses. As the whole of the spiritual reality of Christianity is imbued with the historical figure of Jesus and thus has to allow itself to be measured again and again by the mystery and the law of Jesus' passion, dying and rising to new life, in the same way the reality of Islamic doctrine and practice, however much it may vary from group to group and place to place, is governed by the foundational model of the life and doctrine of Muhammad. The Islamic foundational model is significantly shaped by the this-wordly success in Medina perceived in faith to have been granted by God and at the same time achieved by Muhammad in that he was able to translate effectively into political structures the message of surrender to God and of fraternity in justice.

The different foundational model impresses upon the main elements of each of the two religions its peculiar stamp, notwithstanding the varieties of interpretation to be found in both traditions. In Islam the absolute and utterly transcendental God and in Christianity the one, three-personal God of self communication. In Islam the Law as an all-comprehensive norm, in Christianity, the example of the radical love of Jesus determining the teaching of unconditional service of neighbour, fulfilling the old Law and inaugurating 'the new Law of the Spirit'. In Islam the human person as the servant of representative of God, called to obedience and responsibility to the Will of God as revealed finally and definitely in the Koran; on the Christian side the human person as the image of God, adopted in Christ as child of God, in the Spirit. In Islam human rights as dictated, determined and sealed by the divinely sanctioned Shari'a: in Christian teaching human rights as founded in the dignity of human nature as such, valid equally for every human being. In Islam the ideal of the utopia of a society united and guided by one strictly theocratic ally conceived Law and society; in the mainstream Christian tradition as authority interpreted today, the ready acceptance of political, cultural and religious plurality.

The ever new experience of such deeply-rooted differences regarding principles and attitudes of faith put the readiness to meet one another in dialogue and cooperation to a severe test.

4. The Burden of History

But the tensions that exist between Christians and Muslims are not only of the ideological-theological kind, they are also historical. At the beginning of his prophetical preaching Muhammad expected that Jews and Christians—in the Koran also called 'people of the Book', i.e. people, who had already received a written revelation— would regard his message and his claim as identical with the message and the law, that earlier had been proclaimed by Moses and Jesus. Instead the Jews of Medina rejected him, and later he met also with the rejection of the Christians. Consequently, the attitude of the Koran to the Christians has two sides: on the one he declares: 'You will find. that the nearest in affection to the believers are those who say: We are Christians. That is because there are priests and monks among them; and because they are free from pride'. (Q 5:85) Yet, on the other hand, at another instance, Jews and Christians are taken together and the Muslims are told:

'Fight against such of those to whom the Scriptures were given as believe neither in God nor the Last Day, who do not forbid what God and his apostle have forbidden, and do not embrace the true Faith, until they pay tribute out of hand and are utterly subdued.' (Q 9:29) This text was invoked later in order to justify the subordinate position of the Jews and Christians and the special tax, which was imposed upon them.

After the death of Muhammad the incipient Islamic empire expanded dramatically. The Arab Muslims pushed out of the Arab peninsula and within a hundred years erected an empire which comprised roughly the—probably more important—Near Eastern and African half of the Christian world. Centres of Christian civilization of such crucial importance as Jerusalem, Alexandria, Antiochia, Damascus, Carthage as well as Sicily and most of the Iberian Peninsula came under Muslim rule.

The common Christian explanation for the missionary success of Islam is that it was spread through fire and sword. The Muslim on the other hand are convinced, that the Christians adopted Islam willingly. They stress, that Islam does not tolerate forced conversions and quote in this connection Koran 2:256: 'No compulsion in religion'.

It is a historical fact, that apart from exceptions, Christians in general were not compelled to become Muslims. Islamic Law and Muslim practices granted the Christians (and Jews) a recognized status as a subordinate yet protected community (*ahl adh-dhimma*) under Muslim rule. The pressure upon Christians to convert to Islam resulted from the fact that Islamic society was highly successful, not only from the religious but also from the intellectual and political point of view. For centuries Islamic civilization was farf more highly developed than that of Western Christiandom. Many Christians strove to participate in this success in full equality. They were able to do this on a permanent basis only by joining the *umma*, thus relinquishing their shrinking and increasingly marginalized communities. However it can be safely stated that up to more or less the year 1000 the Christians constituted the majority in those areas of the empire that had been fully Christian before the Muslim conquest.

One may ask in this context whether the Muslim sufficiently understand and appreciate the resentment and the feeling of having been oppressed that generated in the oriental Christian communities and lives on to this day. Nobody cherishes to be reduced, in the country regarded historically as one's own, to the status of a, however much protected, second-class citizen. We say this in the full awareness of the fact that the institution of the *dhimma* as such contrasts impressively with the absence of any legally defined status for minorities in Christendom throughout medieval times.

It is furthermore important to recall that the expansion of Islam did not always take place within conquered empire or areas. In Africa, south of the Sahara, and in Southeast Asia the expansion of Islam normally took place outside the context of military expansion and militarily occupied territories. In other words, here the Islamic faith and way of life expanded entirely by peaceful, nonviolent means. Muslim 'lay' people, mainly traders and craftsmen, functioned as extremely effective propagation of Islam. Other significant contributing factors were conversions brought about by intermarriage and by accepting the offer to be freed from captivity and/or/slavery in exchange for choosing membership of the *umma*.

Then there occurred the phase of European colonial expansion. Between 1800 and 1950 there existed only very few rfegions in the Islamic world, that were not occupied or at least controlled by one or the other of the 'Christian' European powers (especially, Great Britain, France and the Netherlands). With the solders, the traders and the colonial administrators came the Christian missionaries, who in effect contributed to building up and maintaining the infrastructures of the colonies by their building of schools, hospitals and churches. This period constituted a traumatic and humiliating experience for the Muslims—to some extent comparable to the experience of the Christian Churches during the time of the Islamic conquests.

There were certainly Muslims who welcomed Western ideas and Christian values. However, the majority of Muslims considered it to be unacceptable to be ruled by non-Muslims, i.e. by *kāfir-s*. Today, after the Muslim recovery of political autonomy we witness the efforts of Islamically committed groups in many countries with Muslim majority, to bring about a comprehensive Islamic-political order and way of life, on the pattern of classical Islam as perceived by these groups. These strongly politically oriented Islamic groups are determined to oppose or thwart as far as possible non-Islamic influences and to reinstate the authority of Islamic Law, the *sharī'a,* in all spheres of life, as well as to recreate the traditional political order and supremacy of the *umma.* The present-day Islamic reassertion can to a good extent, if not totally, be explained as a religious, political and economic reaction to the experience of colonialism.

5. Mission as Christian Presence. Shared Commitment and Witness of Christians and Muslims

We have depicted aspects of the burden that continues to this day to weight on the encounter between Christians and Muslims in different parts of the world, including of course, here in Europe. On both sides there continue to exist hurt, fear and distrust. In the countries of Western and central Europe in our day the Muslims try to build up the structures, which in their view will help them to lead, in their minority situation a comprehensively Islamic life.

In Asia and Africa Christian communities resist Muslim efforts to introduce the Shari'a as an all-embracing order of individual and public life in areas where there live important non-Muslim sections of the overall population, as e.g. in Nigeria, Sudan and in parts of Southeast Asia. The Christians insist that minorities in preponderantly Muslim-populated countries, as for instance in Saudi Arabia, are granted the same rights (for instance, the celebration of Christian worship, the erection and use of Christian places of worship, the religious instruction of Christian children in their own religion) which in our day are as of law granted to minorities in countries traditionally shaped by Christianity.

The Muslims find it difficult to appreciate and to recognize it as justified that Christian communities living in Muslim majority countries should insist on the religious and ideological freedoms of the individual and of minorities—including the right to change one's religious allegiance and to propagate one's beliefs—which are enshrined in the UN Charter of Human rights, in other words, that they should plead for a legally sanctioned, positive tolerance of diverse convictions within the framework of a pluralistically constituted society. Muslims tend to perceive these demands of the Christians as undermining the religious cohesion and the religious rights of the Islamic societies.

Many Muslims are convinced that only an integrally Muslim society can resist the un-and antireligious attack of the modern, pluralistic world. In this connection it is an ever anew started accusation against the Christian missionaries that they continue to destroy, either deliberately or in effect, the unity and cohesion of the Islamic order of life and that, instead of helping Muslims to achieve a deeper experienced and perception of their own religion, they have in fact made them in the past to fall prey to atheistic secularism and in effect continue to do so.

In their assessment of the missionary activities of the other side Christian and Muslim believers insist, that followers of their religion are being literally bribed by members of the other religion with offers in education, health care and professional promotion, the objective being throughout to get the person in question to convert to either Christianity or Islam.

In this situation a truly Christian presence among the Muslims demands first of all accurate information, sensitivity, patience and courage. The principles of the correct, ideal attitude to be adopted by Christians have been unambiguously stated in a document published by the Pontifical Council for Dialogue with other Religions published in 1984. It deals with dialogue as an essential aspect of the overall mission of the Church. This document, it would seem, has not yet received the attention it merits. Mission here is understood as amulti-dimensional reality: it may be put into practice in one situation by a 'merely lived', but truly Christian, presence, whereas in another situation it may express itself as social and educational service (*diakonía*) or as the life of individuals or communities totally consecrated to liturgical and contemplative prayer. It may also be lived as formal dialogue or, wherever the opportunity (*kairós*) offers itself, the explicit proclamation of the Good News of Jesus Christ and his Church.

This document is named 'The Attitude of the Church towards the Followers of Other Religions. Reflections and Orientations on Dialogue and Mission'. Quoting the Vatican II Document 'Dignitatis Humanae' it resolutely rejects any kind of proselytism:

> In spreading religious faith and introducing religious practices, everyone ought at all times to refrain from any manner of action which would seem to carry a hunt of coercion or of a kind of persuasion that would be dishonourable or unworthly, especially when dealing with poor or uneducated people. Such a manner of action

> would have to be considered an abused of one's right and a violation of the rights of others. (DH 4)
>
> This respect for every person ought to characterize the missionary activity of the church today (cf. ES 77; AAS 1964, pp. 642-643; EN 79–80; RH 12). 'Man is the frst path which the church ought to traverse in carrying out its mission' (RH 14). These values, which the church continues to learn from Christ its teacher, should lead the Christian to love and respect all that is good in the culture and religious commitment of the other. 'It concerns respect for everything which the Spirit, who blows where he wills, has produced in man' (RH 12; cf. EN 79). The fact that Christian mission can never he separated from love and respect for others is proof for Christians of the place of dialogue within that mission. (p. 13–14)

In his introduction to the document the Pope underlines the Christian's duty to respect and loving esteem in any encounter with people of other faith communities.

> ... dialogue is not an easy thing. to engage in dialogue means to forgive, since all the religious communities can point to possible wrongs suffered through the centuries. It means trying to understand the heart of others, which is particularly diffcult when there is lack of agreement. It means, frst of all, putting oneself at the service of all humanity and of the one God. (*Ibid.*, p. 5)

Would it nor be appropriate, in the spirit of the convictions evoked here, to call into life a kind of world-wide Christian-Islamic control commission with the task, to observe the missionary together of both religions carefully and, as far as possible, to regulate it cooperatively?

If and whenever Christians wish to live among Muslims in a truly friendly fashion then this should be attempted first of all in the framework of personal encounters and relations. Christians should learn to esteem whatever is impressive and true in the world of Muslim faith and practice. Personal contact and related studies in the widest sense are crucial.

In the history of Christian-Muslim relations we have a model of peaceful presence 'among' Muslims in St. Francis of Assisi. Francis' encounter with the Sultan in Damietta in the year 1219, when Crusaders were engaged in bloody combat with the Muslim forces, and the experience there of mutual respect between him and the Sultan must have had a transforming effect on Francis. Not long after his return from Egypt, in chapter 16 of his *Rule of* 1231, he describes two ways of going 'among' the Muslims. One way is to avoid quarrels and disputes and be subject to every human creature for God's sake (1 Peter 2:13), so bearing witness to the fact that they are Christians. Another way is to proclaim the word of God openly, when they see that it is God's will.'

Unlike the Crusaders who were going against the Muslims to conquer them, Francis advised his followers to go among them and to be subject to them for the love of God and so bear witness that they are Christians. This quiet respectful witness of life is already part of the proclamation of the gospel and a legitimate form of evangelical presence. If and when they discern it to be 'God's will', then the second 'way' of going among Muslims—the more open proclaiming of God's Word—becomes appropriate. St. Francis' example and advice live on in our day—in countless places and ways.

Most impressive about the lived faith of Muslims is perhaps their deep consciousness of the divine majesty and pressure, nourished and expressed in the Islamic life of faith. The Muslims' sense for community, too, makes an impact on sensitive Christians, the deep earnestness of faith of countless lettered and unlettered Muslim men and women and the constant readiness, to share one's faith and its values with the other. Christians could learn from the Muslims in contemplating and reflecting upon the tremendously formative power of the publicly performed rituals as e.g. of the fast during the month of Ramadan, the pilgrimage to Mecca. In contrast the Christian practice of prayer and of other manifestations of the faith, especially in the West, has become so private and irregular or unpredictable that its impact in public and on the public has become minimal.

This aspect of Muslim practice was alluded to by the present Pope during his visit in Northern Africa in 1979. The public and corporative character of the witness to God, the Creator, which shapes the Muslim societies, is a challenge for us Christians. Today in many countries the expression of the faith is restricted to purely individual practice. However, the human person needs the public and corporative expression of his or her convictions, in order to live effectively in faith.

All these statements in no way intend to play down the fullness of the Mystery revealed in Jesus Christ or belittle the distinctive freedom of the Spirit which the Gospel effectively proclaims. The Christian believer out of love and in faith in the One God wishes to share the Gospel with his Muslim brothers and sisters. We can say: the Christian witness of faith is challenged to share with the Muslims precisely that which the Christians of the earliest days shared with the Jewish believers of their time. The message of the Gospel has to bring home—above all by means of a life that is thoroughly shaped and imbued by it—the fact that the immense majesty and dignity of God is not minimized when God in sovereign decision makes himself one with the need of sinful man, enacts the divine self-abasement (according to Philippians 2:5-11) and in this way transcends any idea of God's mercy that mere human thinking could devise.

In Jesus Christ God assumes solidarity with sinful man in orde3r to free him and to let him participate—as purified and transformed by divine glory. This faith, lived in and through genuine Christian practice, if accepted, instills deepest meaning into the frequently-repeated confession of the Koran that God is indeed the immensely good and merciful One. Furthermore, God refuses in Jesus to fulfill the extreme political and national ambitions of his people. Certain aspects of the contemporary self-realization of Islam, from a Christian perspective, will have to be questioned critically.

Just as Jesus demonstrated to the Jews of his time the insufficiency of a religion primarily shaped by the Law and its structures, in the same way will the message of the Gospel, if lived radically in our day, have a critically illuminating liberating and reconciling effect. Such a witness will of course again and again demand its price, as it did in the life of Jesus.

Muslim lives and the Muslim understanding of their own religion also could be shaped and enriched by the genuine example of serving and forgiving love of Christian communities who radically follow Jesus. Unfortunately these are not the qualities that come to the Muslims' mind when they think of Christians.

As Christians we believe, that in Jesus Christ we meet God and that we are called to receive in him the fullness of divine truth, goodness and beauty. Muslim believers on their part are convinced, that the definite and full divine message has been made available to them in the Koran. In the process of Christians and Muslims learning to witness to one another through lives shaped by the best in their respective beliefs and insights, it would seem to be critically important, that they recognize it as their shared mission to strive to translate into practice their faith in the power of God. A divine power expressed in mercy, forgiveness, reconciliation and guidance—in an environment that increasingly gives pride of place to merely this-worldly values and to immediate rewards.

This commitment has to become visible, first of all, in the effort to serve together those individuals and groups in our societies who are marginalized, forgotten, despised, exploited and persecuted.

'For each of you We have ordained a law and assigned a path. Had God pleased, He could have made of you one community (umma): but it is his wish to prove you by that which He has bestowed upon you. Vie with each other in good works, for to God you shall all return and He will resolve for you your differences.' (Sura 5:48)

You are light for the world. A city build on a hill-top cannot be hidden. No one lights a lamp to put it under a tub; they put it on the lamp-stand where it shines for everywhere in the house. In the same way your light must shine in people's sight, so that, seeing your good works, they may give praise to your Father in heaven. (Matthew 5:14-16)

Appendix

Interview with Prof. Troll

Professor Christian W. Troll SJ in this interview with Victor Edwin SJ, a Ph.D. candidate at the Department of Islamic Studies, Jamia Millia Islamia shares with the readers of *Islam and the Modern Age* his personal journey into the world of Islam, and his contribution to Christian-Muslim relations.

EDWIN : How did you come to study Islam?

TROLL : My commitment to pursue a deeper understanding of Muslims and Islam, their culture and religion, developed gradually during 1957 to 1961 when—as a seminarian of the archdiocese of Cologne/Germany in preparation for priestly ordination—I was studying Christian theology at the universities of Bonn and Tübingen. From 1959 I worked under the guidance of the church historian Hubert Jedin on an extended paper 'The China Missions in the Middle Ages'. One day by chance I came across the essay 'The Need for Islamic Studies' by the Dutch Jesuit J.J. Houben, then Professor of Islamology at Nijmegen (Holland) and Beirut (Lebanon). The following statement, made in the context of discussing the importance of a renewal of religious thought in contemporary Islam, impressed me:

> Not only the missionaries working in Muslim countries but every Catholic throughout the world must realize that the fate of hundreds of millions of Muslims hangs in the balance and that in order to help them to solve the diffculties along religious lines, a deeper knowledge of their mentality and of Islam in general as a religion and as a polity is certainly one of the most pressing needs for the Catholics of our times.

Soon after reading Houben's essay I managed to meet him in person. He stressed that a proper study of Arabic and of Islam was quite demanding. Hence I should think twice before embarking on this road. I persisted.

EDWIN : How did your higher authorities respond to your initiative?

TROLL : Father Houben entrusted me with a letter addressed to my archbishop, Josef Cardinal Frings of Cologne, in which he proposed that I should be allowed special studies in Arabic and Islam. I was to deliver this letter to the cardinal during my first official encounter with him in June 1961 on the occasion of the completion of my university studies in preparation for the priesthood. The cardinal, to my surprise, immediately expressed his agreement with Fr. Houben's proposal. For some time now, he said, I have been feeling the need for a priest of the archdiocese to get thoroughly acquainted with the Christians and Muslims of the Middle East. For this the solid knowledge of Arabic was needed, and since Arabic was a difficult language, I should learn it as soon as possible. So, the cardinal sent me, exactly as Father Houben had proposed in his letter, to the Centre Religieux d'Études Arabes (CREA), the language school attached to the Université Saint Joseph, Beirut, situated at Bikfaya, then a small, relatively remote township about nineteen miles northeast of Beirut, about 2,600 feet above sea level on the western slopes of Mount Lebanon.

EDWIN : What motivated you?

TROLL : My motivation for going beyond the boundaries of normal Catholic theological studies was missionary. From the time of my first Holy Communion at the age of ten, on the Sunday after Easter 1947, I had felt a calling to serve God in a special way. This calling persisted somehow throughout the following years; it moved me, after completing my *Abitur* (the final examination taken in Germany at the end of secondary school education at the age of 18 or 19. It entitles to pursue studies at university level) to ask to be admitted as a seminarian, which in the Archdiocese of Cologne meant living in a college with other candidates for the priesthood as a student of the Faculty of Catholic Theology of Bonn University.

However, the Church worldwide, 'the missions', had begun to interest me much earlier. My father was an internationally known geographer at Bonn University. We children, nine sisters and brothers, were regularly present when geographer colleagues, friends, and acquaintances of my parents, would share lunch or dinner with our family. The blessing and thanksgiving that my father recited at the beginning and end of each meal, was said equally in the presence of guests who obviously did not share our Christian faith. Over the years this made me think and ask questions.

The library at home spread over the corridors and along the staircases of the house. From the walls fascinating book titles as well as geographical maps carried my imagination to far-off continents. At the same time, almost daily, I served as an altar boy in the parish church and loved singing in the city's Bach Choir. One day, at the age of thirteen, I told my parents that I would like to train as a missionary. Thus I came to spend several years in two grammar schools. In the first, which was run by the Missionaries of the Divine Word, I lived as a boarder; the other, run by the Redemptorists, I attended as a day boy. My ideal was to serve somewhere in the world-wide Church. In both schools the regular practice of liturgical and personal prayer as well as meditation on Holy Scripture played a central role and we had countless opportunities to learn about far-off countries. To this day I vividly remember occasions when missionaries on furlough from Asia and Africa, with the help of slides and other visual aids, talked to us with fascination about the people and country they had adopted.

Not yet decided upon the concrete path towards realizing my ideals, I began with the study of Catholic theology at Bonn University. From the beginning of these studies I frequented additional lecture courses and seminars offered by Protestant theologians and by historians of religion. Two years into my university studies, during my three semesters at Tübingen University (1959–60), I took the initiative of founding at the Catholic chaplaincy, a circle of students from overseas. They were studying in various faculties of the university. Many of them were Muslims, Hindus, or Buddhists. We met every week during the semester in a private home. One of us would give a talk about a topic of interest usually related to her or his home country, culture or religion. These meetings and those I encountered made a lasting impression on me.

EDWIN : How did you prepare yourself to take up this new journey as a Christian into the world of Islam?

TROLL : With regard to the 'quest for the Muslims and their Islam'

I consider the two years of intensive study of Arabic (through the medium of French) in Mount Lebanon (1961–3) the most formative period in my life. We formed a group of about fifteen biennium students. Most of them were Jesuit scholastics from the Netherlands and France. I was the only German. Looking back, I consider the two years in Mount Lebanon, separated from home, secluded from city life, and fully concentrated on the intricacies of Arabic grammar and style, the novitiate as it were of my life in the service of Christian-Muslim understanding. The discipline this biennium demanded and the effort to give the best of ourselves to the study of Arabic, about ten hours every day, were accompanied by weekly excursions up into the mountains or down to the seashore, by frequent visits to families in the nearby villages and to monastic communities in the vicinity of Bikfaya. We also began to understand, through reading the local press, the complexities of Near Eastern politics, all this in a Lebanon that, although politically already in a somewhat precarious situation, was still considered then 'the Switzerland of the Near East'.

The founder and spirit of the Centre Religieux d'Études Arabes was Père André d'Alverny SJ (d.1965), professor of Arabic literature at the Institut Oriental de l'Université St Joseph. He was assisted by Père Louis Pouzet, SJ (d.2002), who later succeeded d'Alverny as professor of Arabic literature at the same university and who is the author of outstanding works on Yahya an-Nawawi's (d.1277) *Al-Arba'in* and on the religious life of thirteenth-century Damascus. Our language tutors were specially trained Lebanese schoolteachers.

This intensive and demanding effort to enter into the world of Arabic, together with the first encounter with central foundational texts of Islam in the Arabic original, left a lasting impression on me and has shaped my later encounter with Muslims and their culture and faith. The daily celebration of the Eucharist in the Melkite or in the Maronite rite helped to give these two years a religious and ascetic quality.

EDWIN : Did your formation as a Jesuit influence your approach to Muslims and to Islamic studies?

TROLL : In the summer of 1962, after my first year in Lebanon, while staying in a village of the Biqa plain to learn spoken Lebanese, I gained the certainty that I was to ask to be received into the Society of Jesus. But first I was told by the Jesuit provincial of the Near East that I should finish the course in Arabic for which the Archbishop of Cologne had sent me to Lebanon and complete it with the Diplôme de Langue Arabe of the Université St. Joseph, Beirut. When I returned from Lebanon to Germany, I entered the Jesuit novitiate in Westphalia and this was followed in Bavaria by two years of studying for the licentiate in Philosophy.

The thirty days' Ignatian retreat during the novitiate acquainted me with the method of discernment in spiritual matters. Ignatian discernment asks: What does God want of me in a concrete situation, in circumstances that are not clear and where reflection and conclusions do not result in a clear answer? The method of such discernment includes total openness (indifference) in the face of God and of all reality. It leads the person gradually into a real encounter with the Jesus of the Gospels who enables the seeker to assess the movements in his or her soul by the criterion of his life and spirit. I discovered in the course of time that the critical openness for God's Spirit at work in a given movement and its teachings—when applied *mutatis mutandis* to the world of living religions—definitely can help in trying to discern in the attitudes or teachings of such a movement the presence of 'good' or 'evil' spirits. Viewed in the perspective of Ignatian spiritual pedagogies for instance, the *a priori*, clear-cut dividing of the world of lived religions into natural and supernatural or into clearly evil/ erroneous and clearly good/ true realms, looked at from this perspective, turned out to be too simplistic. Such a view of things does not take sufficient account of the fact that in the perspective of Christian faith all reality, not least that of lived religions and cultures, is marked by signs of the Holy Spirit as well as by signs of the absence or opposition to this Holy Spirit. In addition, the study of philosophy made me convinced of the need, in the effort to understand religious traditions—one's own as well as others—to define concepts clearly and avoid tearing statements out of their context.

EDWIN : Did the Second Vatican Council, which took place during the time of your Arabic studies and your novitiate (two year period of spiritual initiation into Jesuit life) make an impact upon your approach to Muslims and to Islam?

TROLL : Spiritually and theologically the process of the Second Vatican Council (1962–5) and its final documents turned out to be crucial for the whole of my later engagement with Muslims and Islam. At the time of the announcement of the Council by Pope John XXIII, on 25 January 1959, I was still pursuing my theological studies at Bonn University. Hubert Jedin, the well-known historian of the Council of Trent and later a key advisor to Pope John XXIII in organizing Vatican II, was my main tutor at that time. Immediately after the announcement of the council, 'prophetically' he impressed upon us students the extraordinary impact this council would make on the future life of the Church. Lecture courses and personal contact with two other *periti* of the council, Joseph Ratzinger at Bonn and Hans Küng at Tübingen, brought the inner-Catholic wrestling with fundamental questions of *aggiornamento* close to my attention. This made me ask analogous questions regarding the development of contemporary Islam.

The importance of the documents of the council for any Catholic working in the post-Vatican II period in the field of Christian-Muslim relations is obvious. Texts like paragraph 16 of the Dogmatic Constitution on the Church (*Lumen Gentium*); the Declaration on the Relationship of the Church to Non-Christian Religions (*Nostra Aetate*), especially its paragraph 3, and, last but not least, the Declaration on Religious Freedom (*Dignitatis Humanae*) became for me firm points of reference and a constant source of motivation. I personally, however, was especially impressed by Pope Paul VI's encyclical letter *Ecclesiam Suam* of 6 August 1964. The key elements emerging for me from Paul VI's and the council's teaching on interreligious dialogue were these: reciprocal communication, mutual friendship, and respect, as well as a joint effort for the sake of shared goals, all in the service of a common search for the fuller realization of the truth.

EDWIN : What was the Muslim contribution in your preparation for the Muslim apostolate?

TROLL : During the first half of 1966, towards the end of my licentiate course in philosophy, I asked to be sent to work as a member of the Jesuit community in Lahore, Pakistan in order to engage in the study of

Muslim culture and in interreligious dialogue in the spirit of Vatican II. In preparation, in the autumn of 1966, I went to the School of Oriental and African Studies in London and began with a B.A. (Honours) course in Urdu Language and Literature. The honours course included the study of classical Persian and of medieval and modern Indian history. These years culminated in my Ph.D. thesis and subsequent book: *Sayyid Ahmad Khan (1817–98): A Reinterpretation of Muslim Theology* (New Delhi: Vikas, 1978; Karachi: Oxford University Press, 1979).

The decade in London from 1966–76 was a period of intensive study and encounter with Muslims, most of them from South Asia. The first two years were dedicated almost entirely to acquiring basic language skills in Urdu and Persian. The Urdu course was designed to enable the student, practically from the beginning, to converse with Urdu speakers. I spent many weekends in Urdu-speaking homes practicing the language, talking about South Asian Muslim tradition, reading Urdu poetry or listening to its recitation, and watching Urdu videos and films. It was exciting thus to enter into the world of Indian and Pakistani Muslims. As far as Persian is concerned I remained on the level of reading texts of classical works of historiography and literature and of Sufism in the original. For four years my main tutor in Urdu was Ralph Russell, an outstanding teacher, together with Khaled Hasan Qadiri and Dr. Timur Gandjei. During those years I also had the opportunity of spending several extended summer holidays reading selected classical Sufi texts in Arabic and Persian under the personal guidance of the outstanding scholar of classical Sufism, Richard Gramlich, SJ.

Surely, there were times during this long period of preparatory immersion into the world of South-Asian Muslims in London and South Asia—at a relatively advanced student age—when I felt stretched and became impatient. But my curiosity and fascination with the languages of Urdu and Persian and with the whole South-Asian Muslim universe that these languages and literatures opened up to me, carried me on. The British academic system allowed me to spend a whole year of my course traveling on my own in Iran, Afghanistan, and South Asia, visiting Muslim scholars and institutions, and finally taking tutorials with Urdu scholars in

Lahore, whom I had met at the University of London earlier. During my years of doctoral research under the intensive guidance of the historian of South Asia, Dr. Peter Hardy, again I was able to travel to Pakistan and India, meeting scholars knowledgeable in the field of my research and frequenting the relevant libraries in Aligarh, Rampur, and Patna.

EDWIN : Has the fact that you are an ordained priest of the catholic Church have an impact on your approach to Muslims and to Islam?

TROLL : Reflecting on this period now I notice that my priestly ordination in July 1971 did not alter my desire to spend all my energy in the study of Islam and in frequent personal encounters with Muslims. However, being sent to give myself to this task as an ordained priest of the Church not only strengthened my sense of commitment but also gave me the knowledge of doing this work in the name of the local and universal Church. The Church, by assigning me as an ordained priest to this work, had committed herself to the task of intensive Christian-Muslim dialogue. So, for example, studying a Muslim text possibly for weeks or spending whole weekends discussing with educated Muslims trends in contemporary Islamic thought, I considered to be an expression of my priestly apostolate. These activities—including, for example, the learning of a language like Turkish relatively late in life—constituted for me one and the same process of being drawn ever more deeply into a presence, an encounter to which I had been empowered and sent officially by my religious order and thus by the Church. I have never lost this sense over the years. Meeting Muslims and thus Islam at a deep level, I consider to be my way of participating as a priest in the larger and centuries-old encounter between Church and Mosque. In and from the regular encounter with the Lord in the daily celebration of the Eucharist, I receive the motivation and strength needed to follow on his way.

EDWIN : How did Muslims respond to your work?

TROLL : The greatest gift of the years that I spent teaching and researching in London and then in Delhi and many other parts of India, I consider to be the lasting friendships with a number of Muslims who represent to me some of the finest qualities of Indo-Muslim culture and religion. I can mention here only a few of them: Syed Vahiduddin (1909–98) who over the years conveyed to me a unique synthesis of Hindu and Muslim philosophy, modern Western thought, Sufi wisdom and contemporary Christian theology. Syed Vahiduddin made me understand and appreciate essential aspects of the Koran idea of God and of the meanings of Islamic prayer. Then Khwaja Ahmad Faruqi, the accomplished scholar of English and Urdu literature, Muhammad Ishaq Khan, the outstanding historian of Sufism, past and present, in the Kashmiri environment, Maulana Wahiduddin Khan, the remarkable leader of the Al-Risala movement, these and many others—among whom especially those who collaborated with me for the book series *Islam in India: Studies and Commentaries*—became dear and esteemed colleagues, and some even admired friends.

EDWIN : Coming to India, was that your choice?

TROLL : Early in 1976 I moved from London not to Lahore but to New

Delhi. The Jesuit superior general wanted me to teach Islam and Christian-Muslim relations at the Vidyajyoti Institute of Religious Studies, the Jesuit Faculty of Theology in Delhi. In this way I was to be of help to the Indian Church in the effort of entering into dialogical relations not only with the Hindus but also with the Muslims of India and their Islam.

EDWIN : You were a professor of Islam and Christian-Muslim Dialogue at Vidyajyoti. You were able to build up within Vidyajyoti a Library which has a very rich collection on Islam and Christian-Muslim Dialogue. You also started the Vidyajyoti Institute of Islamic Studies (VIDIS) and, together with Fr. Paul Jackson, founded JAMI and ISA. Together with Fr. Jackson and others you founded the quarterly *SALAAM*. What was the purpose of these initiatives?

TROLL : In Delhi my main assignment was to introduce the Catholic students of theology to Islam, to Indian Muslim culture and to the encounter and dialogue of Muslims and Christians. Already at my priestly ordination in 1971, I had chosen the motto from the Second Letter to the Corinthians: 'Servant of Reconciliation' (2 Cor 5:18f). Now in India I saw myself being called in some small way to help the Church in her task of promoting reconciliation between the worlds of Hinduism and of Islam.

Soon after arriving in India in 1976, I met Fr. Paul Jackson, SJ, in Patna/Bihar who, inspired by the late Fr. Vincent Courtois, SJ, of Calcutta, was engaged already in the study of Islam, especially of mediaeval history and Sufism of South Asia, and the dialogue with Muslims. We began in 1977 to meet regularly and eventually formed JAMI, a group of Jesuits Among Muslims in India, which in 1983 became ISA (Islamic Studies Association). During the same year we founded the quarterly publication *SALAAM*, which is now in its thirty-second year of publication. The small group of Indian Catholics organized in ISA, made it possible to maintain the vision, and to pursue the work, of initiating dialogue at various levels—contacts as neighbours in everyday life, teaching and publishing, discussing questions of common social, cultural and religious interest and so on—within an environment that was and remains largely uninterested, if not at times hostile to it, because reaching out deliberately to the Muslims was seen then (not only by Hindus and Sikhs but also by many Indian Christians) as weakening enculturation of Christian life in Hindu culture and religion.

EDWIN : You have also been active for the Church in dialogue with Muslims on the international level?

TROLL : On the international level, from 1975 onwards I participated in almost all the meetings of the *Journées Romaines*. These meetings, from 1956 onwards for nearly half a century, were held every two years in Rome (or, as often later, in its vicinity). They allowed hundreds of Christians to reflect on the theological, spiritual, sociological and cultural dimensions of their dialogue with Muslim friends. It was a meeting of Catholics (and an increasing number of Christians from other traditions) who in different parts of the world practiced and promoted Christian-Muslim encounter in the spirit of Vatican II. Maurice Borrmans, who for decades has been one of the outstanding figures of Christian-Muslim dialogue, in a recent article describes the *Journées Romaines* as 'a school of formation and a place of information' in this field ('Les 'Journées Romaines' et le Dialogue Islamo-Chretien.' *Islamochristiana* 30 (2004): 111–22, esp. Conclusion on p. 121). At the *Journées Romaines* I developed personal contacts with such key figures in Christian-Muslim relations as Jacques Jomier, Georges Anawati, Robert Caspar, and Louis Gardet, and I was able to feel the pulse of Christian-Muslim dialogue worldwide.

EDWIN : You are also one of the founder members of ISA. How is it different from Islamic Studies in the Universities?

TROLL : The founding of the ISA is due to the vision of the Second Vatican Council. It aims to help the Catholic Church in India to reach out through the various well-known forms of dialogue to the Muslims just as the Church reaches out to Hindus, Jains, Sikhs and others. ISA wants to encourage the Christians to get to know and to relate to Muslims better on all levels and in the various constellations of national life: neighbourhoods, villages, towns and cities, states and national institutions. It hopes that in this way Muslims, too, will gradually acquire a more adequate and better informed knowledge of Catholics and their Church so that mutual relations may become more and more characterized by respect, mutual knowledge and the determination to join hands wherever possible for the promotion common national goals in the spirit of the service of God and neighbour.

EDWIN : Tell us something about how Indian Muslims recognized and cooperated with your work?

TROLL : From the day I arrived in India to be member of the staff of Vidyajyoti I experienced through the 12 years there a great openness and eagerness, not least among Muslims, to meet, to get to know one another and to exchange on matters of shared cultural and religious concern. This hospitality was offered to me mostly by Muslim individuals whom I met as a scholar of religion and of Islam, as a Christian theologian and as a Catholic priest. It constitutes one of the most precious gifts I have received during my life. In Delhi I used to visit regularly a small number of respected Muslim scholars. Between us developed bonds of trust and friendship that facilitated an open conversation on basic questions of religion, the history of Islamic thought and spirituality, and not least on issues common to Christians and

Muslims. After his retirement from Delhi University Professor Syed Vahiduddin (1909–98) had moved to Hamdardnager in Tughluqabad, where, with Syed Ausaf Ali and others, he worked on the translation of Avicenna's monumental works on medicine and philosophy, esp. *al-shifā'* and *al-qāanūun*. I used to visit Professor Vahiduddin at least once a month; we exchanged new publications and became trusted friends. I owe him, above all, an understanding of Islam as unconditional surrender to the God of creation and the Koran, the Transcendent and yet Near one who remains the Hidden (al-ghaib), inspiring us with reverential fear and attracting us by His mercy and love (*jalāl-o-jamāl*). Syed Vahiduddin's name brings to mind the name and personality of another, quite different but equally respected scholar, Maulana Wahiduddin Khan, the founder of the *al-Risālah* movement. Only a few days after my arrival at Vidyajyoti Institute in Old Delhi in summer 1976 he knocked at my door. From that afternoon onward we have been continuously in friendly contact. The conversations with, and study of, the development and thought of this remarkable *'alim* has not ceased to fascinate me.

From summer 1976 onwards I also met Dr. Syed Abid Husain (1896–1987), one of the three intellectual pillars of The Jamia Millia Islamia. With his initiative had started in 1970 the 'Islam and the Modern Age Society' for which he edited the periodical *Islam and the Modern Age*, now edited by Prof. Akhtarul Wasey, the director of the Zakir Husain Institute of Islamic Studies. Dr. Abid Husain introduced me to the basic ideas underlying his Institute and its publications. Thus I also met Professor Mushirul Haq (d.1990) and Prof. Ziya ul Hasan Faruqi. Both had studied in renowned Indian institutions of Muslim learning and, later, under Wilfred Cantwell Smith at McGill University in Montreal/Canada. Here again very friendly relations developed. I was introduced into a deeper understanding of the South Asian Muslim tradition, past and present and regularly was invited by the scholars named and by others for instance to Aligarh, Patna's Khuda Bakhsh Library, Osmania University in Hyderabad and to Asghar Ali Engineer's Institute in Bombay/Mumbai in order to participate in seminars and meetings discussing various aspects of past and present Indian Muslim culture. At Delhi University the renowned scholar of Urdu literature, Professor Khwaja Ahmad Faruqui (1917–86) invited me regularly to his home. Over breakfast we exchanged and thus he helped me to keep alive and deepen my love for Urdu prose and poetry. The Ghalib Academy sponsored by Hakeem Abdul Hameed (1908–99) of the Hamdard group and inaugurated by President Dr. Zakir Hussain in 1969 and the Dargah of Hazrat Nizamuddin Auliya offered regularly opportunities to attend *mushāira*-s as well as *qawwāli* sessions. The Thursday evenings spent at Nizamuddin remain unforgotten.

Being professor at Vidyajyoti, Institute of Religious Studies, and editor of the series *Studies of Islam in India*, and between different Muslim institutions, helped me greatly to develop cordial and fruitful collegial relations with a good number of Muslim colleagues belonging to various academic institutions all over India, from Srinagar to Hyderabad (Deccan), from Ajmer to Kolkata.

EDWIN : Moving from India you worked in Birmingham, Rome, Berlin and now in Frankfurt. how do these places and people there helped you to deepen your commitment to Christian-Muslim Dialogue?

TROLL : In 1988 the Centre for the Study of Islam and Christian-Muslim Relations at the Selly Oak Colleges, Birmingham, officially invited me to join its staff. David Kerr, the founder of the Centre, had left England to take up the directorship of the Duncan Black Macdonald Centre for the Study of Islam and Christian-Muslim Relations at Hartford Seminary in Connecticut as well as the editorship of the renowned quarterly *The Muslim World*. In the study centre at the Selly Oak Colleges, Muslims and Christians together engaged in studying, teaching, and researching in the field of Islam and Christian-Muslim relations. Its academic courses and exams formed part of the programme of the Faculty of Theology of Birmingham University and included undergraduate and postgraduate courses, up to the level of Ph.D. At the same time the centre offered in the Midlands and beyond training courses and study sessions to Muslims and Christians who in their pastoral and social activities were in need of knowledge about Islam and Christian-Muslim relations. The Centre's activity and concern thus had both a worldwide and a local dimension.

In India, at Vidyajyoti Institute, as well as at various other faculties and seminaries throughout the country, I had been teaching students of Christian theology, introducing them to Islamic faith and practice, South Asian Islam and Christian-Muslim relations past and present. For all of these students the courses on Islam and on Christian-Muslim relations were of relatively marginal importance. Regrettably, they had neither the time nor the languages nor the sufficiently strong motivation, to go deeper into the study of Muslim culture and Islam. Now, at Selly Oak, I was working as part of a team of Christian and Muslim colleagues, teaching students graduate and postgraduate courses as well as directing Ph.D. theses. This new challenge attracted and motivated me considerably. At Selly Oak I entered naturally into regular conversation with religiously educated young Muslim women and men hailing from different parts of the world, where Christians and Muslims together were trying to enter into meaningful dialogical relations with one another. Staff and students at Selly Oak were united in the effort to deepen their own and one another's understanding of Islam and of Christian-Muslim relations, in the framework of a common academic undertaking. So, for example, I was able to teach a one-year course called 'The development of Islamic religious thought from the Qur'an to our time' in close collaboration with the Pakistani scholar Dr. Khalid Alawi (d.2008). This turned out to be a refreshing and satisfying experience for me in both human and academic terms. Also, initiating together with my Muslim and Christian colleagues on the staff at Selly Oak a new international biannual (later to become quarterly), *Islam and Christian-Muslim Relations*, brought me into regular contact and intellectual exchange with Muslim and Christian scholars of Islam and Christian-Muslim relations the world over. And last but not least, in and from Birmingham, one of the important centres of Muslim immigration in Britain, I began to learn rapidly and in concrete ways about the problems Muslim immigration to Great Britain posed for local and national politics, for the Muslim communities themselves as well as for the Christian churches.

EDWIN : First from England, and later from Rome, you went nine times to teach a guest professor in Turkey. In which way did this experience enrich your life and work of dialogue?

TROLL : In 1993, I was asked by my superiors to take up a professorship at the Pontifical Oriental Institute in Rome, an academic institution mainly dedicated to teaching and research about the Oriental Churches. The main reason for asking me to move to Rome was to enable me to go regularly—in the name of the Pontifical Gregorian University Consortium—as exchange guest professor to the University of Ankara's Ilahiyat Fakültesi. A Turkish professor from the Ankara Faculty would teach on aspects of Islamic culture and faith at the Pontifical Gregorian University in Rome, and in return I would give lectures and seminars on Christian and Christian-Muslim themes at the Ankara faculty, and from there, as it turned out, sporadically in a number of other Muslim theological faculties. I taught at the Ankara faculty over a period of nine years, on each occasion for one to two months. After having been engaged in India and in England in explaining aspects of Islam and Christian-Muslim relations to Christians, especially students of Christian theology, I was asked now to do the opposite, namely to explain aspects of Christian faith and practice, such as the biblical scriptures and the history of the Christian Churches and of their relationship with Islam, to Muslims. Frequently I was also asked to discuss more recent Christian developments such as the Protestant Reformation and the Catholic Counter Reformation, the Christian responses to the

Enlightenment and to modern, critical scholarship, the ecumenical movement and the First (1869–70) as well as the Second Vatican Councils.

Eagerly I took advantage of the opportunity to learn Turkish. At the well-known *TÖMER Institute for Turkish Language at the University of Ankara* I found myself learning Turkish from scratch, in the company of students—most of them some thirty-five or even forty years younger than myself—hailing mainly from Central Asia and from the Caucasus region. In these and countless other fascinating ways I was able to approach yet another great geographical and cultural region of the Islamic world, different from, and yet also in many ways related to, the world of Arab and of South Asian Islam that had hosted me earlier.

EDWIN : How do you serve the cause of dialogue between Christians and Muslims in Germany and in other countries in Europe?

TROLL : Right from the beginning of my guest lecturing in Ankara for the Pontifical Gregorian University I had an idea at the back of my mind that one day, upon my eventual return to Germany, my acquaintance with Turkey and its language might be of significant help in mediating between the majority population and Turkish immigrants. From 1993 onwards this thought provided me with additional motivation to enter the world of Turkish language and culture. And in fact, in 1999 I did return to Germany, first to the Catholic Academy of Berlin, where I established the Forum for Christian-Muslim Dialogue. There I became acquainted with a city that not only was still reeling from the effects of the rather sudden event of reunification of East and West Germany but which also, at least in its Western half, in the course of two or three decades, had turned into a major centre of Turkish and Muslim immigration and permanent presence. However, after two-and-a-half years, in 2001, I left Berlin to become once more part of an academic setting, the Jesuit Faculty of Philosophy and Theology of Sankt Georgen, in Frankfurt. There I started a certificate course called Introduction to Islam and Christian-Muslim Relations for students and professionals and found the time and space to enable me to accompany Christian-Muslim developments in critical study and debate.

So after encountering Muslims and studying Islam in many settings and facets for more or less four decades, I find myself back in my home country. However, Germany's society—its social, political, and ideological preoccupations and debates—when compared with the mid-sixties, have changed beyond recognition. I feel privileged now to have the opportunity to try to understand my country and continent anew. I notice that the massive immigration into Germany not only poses problems but also, and above all, has brought about a vitality and plurality that turns out to be enriching as well as stimulating. Having lived over the past decades in countries with various majority-minority constellations, I look at the present-day German and European discussions about identity, integration, and assimilation with a sense of calm and confidence.

EDWIN : Over the past years you spent much of your time answering Muslim questions on Christian faith and practice on a multilingual website. Why?

TROLL : On many occasions over the past decade but especially during my repeated periods off teaching Christian themes in Turkish faculties of theology impressed upon me that not a few young Muslims, especially those engaged at the numerous faculties of theology (Ilahiyat Fakültesiler) at various Turkish state universities in the study of Islamic theology and of religions in general increasingly desire to be better informed about the Christians' faith and practice as explained by Christians. The electronic media, especially the internet, enables me in to answer questions about Christian faith and practice put to me regularly by Muslims and Christians from around the world in various languages (English, German, French, Indonesian, Italian, Russian, Spanish and Turkish, Arabic, Persian and Urdu; see: www.answers-to-muslims.com). I now offer this worldwide and discrete service in response to a felt need. In this I am inspired by the exhortation of the first letter of Peter: 'Always have your answer ready for people who ask you for the reason of the hope you have. But give it with courtesy and respect and with a clear conscience' (1 Petr 3, 15f).

EDWIN : What has, succinctly put, inspired and sustained you in your life of study of Islam and encounter with Muslims?

TROLL : Three elements above all else have inspired and sustained me as a student of Islam in my lifelong engagement:

The daily celebration of the Eucharist;

The daily contact with Muslims, in immediate, personal encounter as well as through study of texts and other media; and

The awareness that grows daily of global interdependence and of the responsibility this puts on Muslim and Christian believers everywhere.

Index